Getting Into Graduate School

Getting Into Graduate School

A Comprehensive Guide for Psychology and the Behavioral Sciences

Gregory J. Privitera

St. Bonaventure University

Los Angeles | London | New Delhi
Singapore | Washington DC

Los Angeles | London | New Delhi
Singapore | Washington DC

FOR INFORMATION:

SAGE Publications, Inc.
2455 Teller Road
Thousand Oaks, California 91320
E-mail: order@sagepub.com

SAGE Publications Ltd.
1 Oliver's Yard
55 City Road
London EC1Y 1SP
United Kingdom

SAGE Publications India Pvt. Ltd.
B 1/I 1 Mohan Cooperative Industrial Area
Mathura Road, New Delhi 110 044
India

SAGE Publications Asia-Pacific Pte. Ltd.
3 Church Street
#10-04 Samsung Hub
Singapore 049483

Acquisitions Editor: Reid Hester
Editorial Assistant: Lucy Berbeo
Production Editor: Olivia Weber-Stenis
Copy Editor: Melinda Masson
Typesetter: C&M Digitals (P) Ltd.
Proofreader: Caryne Brown
Indexer: Terri Corry
Cover Designer: Candice Harman
Marketing Manager: Shari Countryman

Printed in the United States of America

Library of Congress Cataloging-in-Publication Data

Privitera, Gregory J.

Getting into graduate school : a comprehensive guide
for psychology and the behavioral sciences / Gregory J.
Privitera, St. Bonaventure University.

pages cm
Includes bibliographical references and index.

ISBN 978-1-4833-5672-3 (pbk. : alk. paper)

1. Universities and colleges—United States—Graduate
work. 2. Universities and colleges—United States—
Admission. 3. Social sciences—Study and teaching
(Higher)—United States. I. Title.

LB2371.4.P75 2015
378.1′55—dc23   2014007567

This book is printed on acid-free paper.

MIX
Paper from
responsible sources
FSC® C014174

14 15 16 17 18 10 9 8 7 6 5 4 3 2 1

Brief Contents

SECTION IV: THE DECISION LETTERS AND NEXT STEPS

Detailed Contents

SECTION II: WHAT SHOULD YOU BE DOING FROM FRESHMAN TO SENIOR YEAR?

SECTION III: COMPLETING PARTS OF THE GRADUATE SCHOOL APPLICATION AND MORE

SECTION IV: THE DECISION LETTERS AND NEXT STEPS

About the Author

 **Gregory J. Privitera** is an associate professor of psychology at St. Bonaventure University and a member of the Board of Trustees at an International Baccalaureate (IB) World school in Olean, New York. Dr. Privitera received his PhD in behavioral neuroscience in the field of psychology at the State University of New York at Buffalo. He went on to complete postdoctoral research at Arizona State University before beginning his tenure at St. Bonaventure University in 2009. He is an author of multiple books on statistics, research methods, and the psychology of eating, in addition to authoring over two-dozen peer-reviewed articles aimed at advancing our understanding of health and promoting the intake of healthier diets. He oversees a variety of undergraduate research projects at St. Bonaventure University, where over 20 undergraduate students, many of whom are now earning a PhD or other graduate degrees at various institutions, have coauthored research in his laboratories. For his work with students and fruitful record of teaching and advisement, Dr. Privitera was recognized in 2014 with the highest teaching honor at St. Bonaventure University, The Award for Professional Excellence in Teaching. He was also honored as the Advisor of the Year at St. Bonaventure University for his work as the advisor of the Class of 2013. The above photo shows Dr. Privitera accepting this award from one of the students who nominated him, Danielle Antonelli. In addition to his teaching, research, and advisement, Dr. Privitera is a veteran of the U.S. Marine Corps, and is married with two children: a daughter, Grace, and a son, Aiden.

Acknowledgments

To my son, Aiden Andrew, and daughter, Grace Ann—may you always value the gift of an education throughout life. Never stop learning.

Thank you to the following select group of students who have graciously agreed to share their experiences and application materials in this book so that I can demonstrate how this plan has worked for them, and how it can work for you (note the diversity of the types of degree programs to which these students were accepted, since 2011):

Jaela Agnello, accepted for doctor of chiropractic (DC)

Danielle Antonelli, accepted for MA, mental health counseling

Jessie Briggs, accepted for PhD, social psychology

Alexis Cosco, accepted for PhD, industrial-organizational psychology

Heather Creary, accepted for MS, educational psychology and methodology

Michael Gargano, accepted for PhD, clinical psychology

Hannah Lapp, accepted for PhD, behavioral neuroscience

Nicole Marinaccio, accepted for PsyD, counseling and school psychology

Taylor Phillips, accepted for PsyD, school psychology

Kristin Sotak, accepted for PhD, organizational behavior

Maxwell Wallace, accepted for PsyD, clinical psychology

Faris Zuraikat, accepted for PhD, nutritional sciences

And to the entire psychology Class of 2013 at St. Bonaventure University—know that I am grateful for the experiences we shared, which have indubitably contributed to the development of this plan. Thank you.

To the Student

The Story of *Your* Time in College, and How This Plan Can Help Make It Extraordinary

College really is an extraordinary time for any student. You sit in a classroom among other students, who for all you know will be the millionaires or billionaires of the future. Indeed, about 4 in every 5 billionaires and about 4 in every 5 millionaires hold a college degree, which means that at one point in time, these wealthy people were just classmates. They studied the same as you, took notes, attended classes, ate at the dining halls, lived in the dorms, and had all the other bells and whistles that come with being a college student. College is exciting because students are surrounded by people who are largely just starting, restarting, or continuing their paths toward success. Importantly, one of these students in college is you.

Whether you are a college student in psychology or another field that falls within the behavioral sciences, or if you plan to attend college, this book should appeal to your interests in that it is written for a full range of college students. You do not need to have set all your future plans in order to be ready to read this book. In fact, this book will actually help you identify your plans and goals; it will help you to realize every way in which you can find and create opportunities to achieve your goals; it will provide a road map to show you how to be competitive for and gain acceptance to graduate schools—even doctorate-level programs. All students deserve an opportunity to reach their goals, regardless of what college they attend or what aspirations they have; this book will reveal how this can be achieved. It will show any student what makes the "best" students so competitive for graduate schools, and then it will show you how you can attain all of those opportunities so that you can be among, and even stand out among, the "best."

What brought me to write this book is that I wanted to make accessible the "how" in a graduate school preparation book. It is one thing to explain *what* you need to achieve to be competitive for graduate schools; it is quite another to explain *how* you can achieve those opportunities needed to be competitive. Most books tell you "what" you need to do, but rarely do they sufficiently explain *how* to do it.

My frustration as a student was that I had to figure everything out myself. Many advisors were helpful in telling me *what* I needed to do: have a high GPA, apply for internships, do well on my GREs, find teaching and research opportunities, apply to colleges, write my curriculum vitae, and much more. But *how*? These things do not just happen; it would be helpful to have some really good advice on *how* to get all of that done—and just for good measure, why not also throw in some good examples from students who have succeeded at getting into graduate schools?

In truth, I was your typical undergraduate student, who happened to earn a PhD in behavioral neuroscience (a field of psychology). I was frustrated then, and am still frustrated now, by the lack of answers to such a simple question: *How* do students find and create the opportunities they need to be competitive for graduate schools? To answer this question, I spent four years advising a single undergraduate class from freshman to senior year, with the goal in mind of finding as many possible answers to "how" students can achieve their goals for graduate school. I wanted to be satisfied that the ideas in this book would be not just opinions, but instead real solutions to finding and creating opportunities that could specifically lead to admission into graduate schools. The results were impressive.

My advisement class graduated in May 2013, and many other students also sought my advisement during this time. In total, I advised 34 students during this four-year span from 2009 to 2013. Of those students, 28 (about 82%) received acceptance letters to graduate schools, and 10 (about 30%) went on to doctorate-level programs to include top research programs in the country. Keep in mind that the national averages for acceptance rates to graduate schools are typically below 50%, and acceptance rates to doctoral programs are much lower, at only about 10%—well below the acceptance rates of the students I advised. These students deserve all the credit for their success. Still, many will tell you that the plan I shared with them as their advisor, which is the same plan I share with *you* in this book, was a catalyst in helping them to achieve the opportunities they needed to be competitive for graduate schools. So much so that many of the most successful among them have agreed to allow me to share their graduate school application materials and experiences in this book so that I can reveal further how to find and create opportunities as they did to obtain acceptance into graduate schools.

In April 2013, I was honored as the Advisor of the Year at my university—my author photo for this book is of my acceptance of that award. It was my students who nominated me for the award, making it the most meaningful award I have ever accepted. It was quite an honor, and it was the work that went into that moment that has produced the book that is written here. In truth, it is largely my experiences with that advisement class that have allowed me to write such an insightful book, with so many great examples to show you *how* to achieve your goals. Few people will achieve great success in isolation, and the writing of this book is no exception. My experiences as an advisor of the Class of 2013 at St. Bonaventure University (and as an advisor of others over the years) have contributed to my perspective and ideas in a way that is indubitably recognized and appreciated.

In truth, you can take one step to find a person who will tell you what you can't do in life; you can walk miles before you find one person who will tell you what you can do. It's a sad reality, but it tends to be true. We all need someone to show faith in us; I need this as much as anyone else. It feels good to see that other people believe in our hopes and dreams to achieve great things, and it can be difficult when people we respect, or people we think are in a good position to judge us, express disbelief. The best advice for countering such criticism is to empower yourself with the know-how to achieve your goals, and with the confidence to realize your goals. This book can help you accomplish just that by showing you not only *what* to do to achieve your goals, but also *how* to do those things necessary to achieve your goals. And this graduate school plan takes it one step further to show you *what* to do and *how* to do it in a way that can help you to stand out among your peers.

One theme certainly arose during my four-year path toward writing this book: Being successful is not about becoming qualified; it's about standing out among all those who are qualified. This theme brings to light two important perspectives. First, the world is filled with qualified applicants—many job fields and most graduate schools have no problem finding qualified applicants; their problem is in choosing among those who are qualified. For this reason, my plan is not to show you how to be a qualified applicant; it is to show you how to stand out as an applicant. Second, whatever you believe for yourself now, know that you are capable of so much more. "Becoming extraordinary" is a mission that is served at the university where I advise and teach. In my advisement, I explain to my students that becoming extraordinary is not about achieving those things they thought possible; it is about achieving those things they *never* thought possible. My hope is that by reading this book, you will realize a world of opportunity you never thought possible, and you will challenge yourself to believe in even greater things for yourself. It is a valuable lesson of life: Always strive to be greater; always believe that no matter how strong you are today, you can be even stronger tomorrow.

I thank you for choosing to read this book and to use this plan to help guide you through your enduring experience in college. I hope the ideas in this book build you up, strengthen your resolve, and bring you ever closer to your ultimate goals; after all, it is *your* goals and aspirations that have inspired the writing of this plan.

Sincerest regards,

Gregory J. Privitera, PhD
St. Bonaventure, New York
March 2014

SECTION I

What Are Graduate Schools Looking For?

CHAPTER 1

Making the "Grade" in College

Is College Worth It? Of Course It Is!

"Education is the best provision for life's journey."

Aristotle

So much is made of the question "Is college worth it?" It is a silly question with a simple answer: *Yes*, absolutely it is. What you need to realize is that college is more than just an investment; it is an experience—and experiences are what you make of them. For the purposes of being transparent here, consider the following:

- Is college expensive? Yes, it can be very expensive.
- Will you go into debt after you graduate college? Likely; about two-thirds of students graduate with student loan debt.
- Are textbooks included in tuition costs? No, they typically are not.
- Are textbooks expensive? Yes, they are.
- Do college graduates earn more money on average than those who do not attend college? Yes, they do—they earn about two to three times more on average than a high school graduate.
- Will graduating college lead to a high-paying job? It can.
- Will graduating college lead to the job you want? It can.

The idea here is that yes, college is expensive, and yes, there is a risk that you will still find few job opportunities after earning your college degree. But the rule is that your degree can and will pay off. It is not a matter of whether college is worth it; it is a matter of whether you are prepared for such a big investment. After all, why spend so much time and money on an education if you do not have a plan? The reality is a college degree has the potential for a huge payoff. The ability to realize the potential of your education will depend largely on how prepared you are for college in the first place.

For most degrees across all majors, the biggest payoffs can be realized if you pursue graduate school. While being in college is a great accomplishment, preparing for your next steps upon graduation may be even more important. Finding a path to graduate school requires a plan and the preparation needed to be competitive for applying to and being accepted into graduate programs for the field of study you choose. This book is largely your *plan* aimed at showing you how to create and realize opportunities available to you as an undergraduate—opportunities that can in turn help you stand out among your peers and be highly competitive for graduate programs. To begin, let's think about what it means to plan and prepare.

Getting on the Path to Graduate School: Planning and Preparing

"By failing to prepare, you are preparing to fail."

Benjamin Franklin

Going to college is a great idea—if you have a plan. Being prepared substantially increases the likelihood that you will find great success after college. Certainly, college is an investment; a college education is a *big* investment. Having a plan for college can be difficult because, in truth, the preparer (that would be you) has likely never experienced college and therefore is not entirely sure what to prepare for. You are not alone—many students struggle with how to prepare for college.

While you can have elaborate plans to prepare for college, we can start simply. There are three core questions you should answer right now. The first big question that you need to answer is:

> ➤ What do you want to be when you grow up?

If you have already answered this question, then you are honestly ahead of the game—many college students have difficulty answering this question. However, you do not necessarily need to have the answer to this question before you go to college. If you do not know "what you want to be when you grow up," then you will want to make it a priority in your first year of college to find the answer. The reason it is important to narrow your interests to specifically what you want to do after you graduate pertains, in part, to how the graduate school selection process works.

It is interesting that for most undergraduate schools, the selection process looks specifically at how diverse your skills are. For example, suppose a student applies to a college for a major in psychology. If the student has high grades in psychology but rather low grades in an unrelated subject like language, you may think that his or her high grades in psychology will carry a lot of weight. However, undergraduate selection committees will often prefer a student who can demonstrate high grades in all academic areas beyond just the major for which he or she is applying. To get into competitive undergraduate schools, then, an applicant needs to be a "generalist"—he or she needs to show competency across multiple (often unrelated) academic subjects.

In contrast, to get into competitive graduate schools you need to be *focused*. If you want to pursue psychology, for example, then your strengths, activities, research, internships, academics, and more should be largely focused on that subject: psychology. Hence, you arrive to college as a "generalist"—you have general competencies across various academic subjects. However, as you progress through undergraduate school you will need to narrow or focus your competencies. In other words, the other end of college is to have an "expertise," as it will be called once you have a degree to back it up! I will share a full plan in this book for accomplishing this. Figure 1.1 summarizes the basic aims of narrowing one's focus.

Figure 1.1 Develop expertise to demonstrate interest in a particular topic or academic subject.

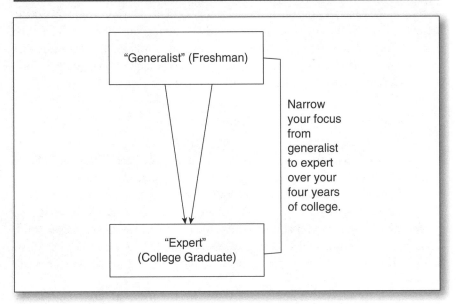

In my view, the first question is the most important. If you do not know and/or have no plan to find the answer to this question in your first year of college, then college may not be worth the investment. Graduate schools, even employers, want to know that you have answered this basic question. Obvious evidence that you answered this question is to show a narrowed focus to demonstrate that you are interested in the particular area or discipline to which you are applying (for a job or for graduate school). Seeking an answer to the first question is essential if you want to be prepared to realize the potential of your education. However, there are two more basic questions you need to answer. The second question you need to answer now is:

➢ What are your priorities?

While teaching an introductory psychology course on the topic of motivation, I asked my students, "Why did you decide to go to college?" I was expecting answers like "To get a degree" or "To learn." However, the first response I received was not at all what I expected. Instead, one student in the front row was eager to give her response, and when I called upon her, she exclaimed, "To make friends!"

I understand that college should be fun. Certainly, have fun! That being said, you need to prioritize your time. "Making friends" is great, but paying tuition for the purpose of "making friends" is nonsense. Of course you know this, but it is also important to put this into practice. Have fun—responsible fun—after you take care of your work. In other words, get your work done first. If you have to sacrifice time out with friends, then that is what you will do. Make your schoolwork your priority. Don't lose sight of the fact that you are attending college for the opportunities you gain by earning an education and eventually a degree. Honestly, it is in your best interest to keep your priorities straight; *you* gain the most by putting your work first.

Part of having a plan is realizing that how you perform in college will bear heavily on the opportunities available to you upon graduation. As you are fully aware, putting in the necessary time to learn and study is essential if you want to realize the potential of your education—it will be worth reminding yourself of this from time to time. There is no reason why you cannot have fun in college; just make sure that you keep your priorities straight along the way. The third question logically follows from the second question. The third question you need to answer now is:

➢ What grades will you aim to achieve?

Every once in a while I hear the phrase "Cs get the degrees." While this phrase is generally true—a C average will earn you a degree—it is also true that a C average will almost certainly eliminate you from being accepted to a respected graduate school, or possibly to any graduate school. As a general rule: In a worst-case scenario, you should obtain at least a 2.8 grade point average (GPA) to even think about applying to (low-ranked) graduate schools. Such a GPA is a little higher than a B– average. Hence, Cs may "get the degrees," but Cs do not get you into graduate school.

Using the GPA scale, your GPA ranges from 0.0 (F) to 4.0 (A). Some universities extend the GPA scale to 4.33 (A+), but most colleges conform to the standard 4.0 scale. This GPA scale is important because it is one key criterion used by all graduate schools to select candidates for a graduate program. For this reason, you should keep track of your GPA, which is fairly simple to do nowadays. Most colleges have a GPA calculator on their website. You can use the calculator to plan for ways to improve your GPA. As a general rule for getting into graduate schools, you should strive for A and B grades only, if possible. Also keep in mind that once you complete your degree, your GPA for that degree is basically set in stone—it cannot be changed once you accept your degree. So yes, grades must be important to you.

In college, it is also important to recognize that often "you take the professor, not the class." In other words, one professor may teach a course at a very difficult level, whereas another professor may teach that same course at a much easier level. The result for two students in the same course who have the same level of mastery: The student in the more difficult course may have a lower grade. Therefore, sometimes your GPA can reflect how much you learned, and other times it can reflect how "difficult" a professor was. In this way, realize that your GPA is an *estimate* of how well you have preformed in your classes. Many faculty members, particularly those at graduate schools, recognize that a 3.8 GPA, for example, may not mean the same thing at all colleges. Some students may have worked much harder to obtain their 3.8 GPA than others. For this reason, your GPA does not need to be perfect; but it should be high if you want to be competitive—how high it needs to be will depend on your goals for graduate school.

Throughout this book I will describe ways to help you improve your grades and create opportunities to help you achieve your goals. I will outline a plan for making your work and studying easier and also give you ideas to help you figure out what you want to pursue upon graduation. This book will help you find certainty in an otherwise uncertain endeavor. You will know how to answer these questions, and in the process devise a plan that can make you competitive for graduate schools, even at the doctorate level—right out of an undergraduate degree.

Graduate School: A Career Path

"Nothing is really work unless you would rather be doing something else."

J. M. Barrie

Now, of course, with all of this talk of graduate school, a fair question is "Why go to graduate school in the first place?" There are two ways to answer this question. The traditional answer is to throw out some statistics. Why not?

Based on reports from the U.S. Census Bureau (2012), Figure 1.2 shows the expected earnings by degree across academic disciplines. Using data in the table, if you earn a bachelor's degree, then you can expect to earn over a 40-year work life about $1.1 million more than a person with a high school diploma—that is almost doubling your expected work-life salary. Earning a doctoral degree will pay out about $2.2 million more than a high school diploma and about $700,000 more than a bachelor's degree. The highest total is for a professional degree (e.g., MD, JD), which will pay out over a 40-year work life about $2.8 million more than a high school diploma, about $1.7 million more than a bachelor's degree, and about $600,000 more than a doctoral degree. The full 2012 U.S. Census Bureau report for data on educational attainment and commensurate salaries can be found at www.census.gov/hhes/socdemo/education.

The take-home message here is that a college degree has value in terms of money earned. The reason for higher earnings over your work life is that having a college degree creates job opportunities that would not otherwise be attainable. While being hired for one of these higher-paying jobs is likely competitive, you nonetheless can compete for these jobs because of your college degree. Keep in mind also that the earnings reported in the figure are *average* work-life earnings; so your college degree could potentially have even larger payoffs. Being prepared and having a clear plan can go a long way in helping you to achieve that larger payoff.

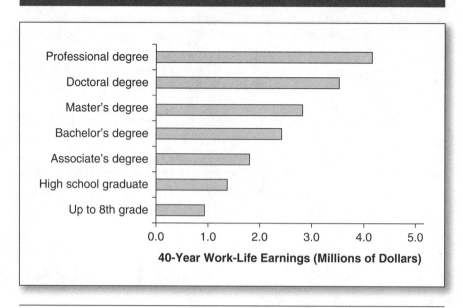

Figure 1.2 Lifetime earnings increase with education level.

Source: U.S. Census Bureau, Current Population Surveys, 2012.

While going to graduate school can substantially augment your income, there is yet another important reason why graduate school is a great option: to pursue a *career*. A career can be distinguished from a *job*. A job is a position of regular employment—that controls you. You go to work; you "clock in" and "clock out"; you are told what hours to work, what shifts to fill, what pay to receive. There is limited freedom in a job. The less education you have, the more likely it is that you will find a job. Jobs can certainly come with high-end salaries, but also often with frustration. Time off can be hard to get when you need it, schedules are often not flexible, and job security is often perceived as job insecurity. A job tends to provide little freedom to the worker.

A career, however, is a position of regular employment—that *you* control. That is not to say that a career cannot in some ways still "control you." Yet, unlike a job, a career enables you to "build your résumé" and sell yourself to others. When you apply for career opportunities, it can be more exciting. You can have some control over the careers you pursue and opportunities you seek. You often have greater negotiating power in terms of salary. You often have greater flexibility in your work schedule, and have greater opportunity for growth and professional development. If they had to choose between a job and a career, I believe most people would choose to pursue a career. Going to college with a plan is the most viable way to take advantage of that opportunity.

There are certainly those who have found great success without a college degree. Some notable names include Bill Gates (Microsoft), Mark Zuckerberg (Facebook, Inc.), Michael Dell (Dell, Inc.), Larry Ellison (Oracle Corporation), and Ralph Lauren (fashion designer). All of these accomplished men established careers that allowed them to amass billion-dollar fortunes without obtaining a college degree. However, these men are the exception to the rule—I'm confident that even they would agree. Some billionaires who do not have a college education inherited their billions. And the majority of billionaires in the world—about 4 in every 5—have a college education. This statistic also holds true for millionaires: About 4 in every 5 millionaires are college graduates. Moreover, about 40% of college-educated millionaires have graduate-level degrees. Therefore, the undeniable truth is that if you want to find a path to success, then an education should be one of your stops along that path.

A career can be more rewarding because it is something you want to do, something you can master, something you can market, something that can give you more flexibility to work around other aspects of your life, such as family. As J. M. Barrie stated, "Nothing is really work unless you would rather be doing something else." If a career is that "something" that you wish to pursue, then obtaining an education will likely be a necessary step in your pursuits.

The Path to Graduate School

"You have brains in your head. You have feet in your shoes. You can steer yourself in any direction you choose. . . . You are the guy who'll decide where to go."

Dr. Seuss

The "path" you choose in life should include a college education when you are ready to plan and prepare for it. And if you really want to bolster your opportunities for success, then that path will likely include graduate school. What is important to recognize up front is that you choose your path. As Dr. Seuss put it: "You are the guy [or girl] who'll decide where to go." You need to take responsibility for your own choices, which begins with the choices you make to pursue an education, and ultimately a career. Again, this is something you already know, but it can be worth reminding yourself from time to time. In many ways, it is knowing that your path is your responsibility that makes your time in college exciting—inasmuch as you play a substantial role in treading the ultimate path toward your own success.

As you tread your path, keep in mind that your path is set only after you have lived it. It can be easy to get discouraged from time to time as you continue your journey through college. You may earn bad grades in a class, be turned down for an internship or other opportunity, lose friends or family, or get nervous about whether the major you are in is "right for you." These experiences may teach you something about yourself or lead to an epiphany that causes you to change your goals, switch direction—reroute your path. You need to realize that plans can change . . . and changing your plans can mean changing the direction of the path you take to reach your goals.

This book will provide a guide for how to reach the goal of being competitive for graduate schools by providing a full plan that is laid out to allow you to "map out" your own path to success. The lesson here is to map out your path in pencil, but be prepared to use your eraser. You must be willing to "adapt to and overcome" the challenges ahead, be prepared to make changes as needed, and be able to recognize that many paths can lead to your success. For example, note that in Chapter 9 I describe opportunities that can arise from acceptance and from rejection from graduate schools. Rejection is not the end of the road; it is where you can create alternative routes to the same success. In this spirit, keep your head up and look forward. No matter how often you "use the eraser," there is almost always a route you can tread to find your path to success.

Clearing the "Fog of War"

"It is best to learn wisdom by the experience of others."

Latin Proverb

In truth, by preparing for graduate school, you are preparing for something you have never experienced. To help you prepare for graduate school, it would be useful to know what graduate schools are looking for and to identify how you can be competitive for admittance into these graduate schools. What may be most insightful is to sit in on a graduate school selection committee meeting, to listen to the questions being asked, to take note of the criteria for selection, and to identify with the interests of the members of the committee. There is always some uncertainty stemming from not knowing exactly what is being considered among those selecting candidates for graduate programs. Conditions of uncertainty are referred to as the "fog of war."

Fog of war is a term used in the military to describe the experience of soldiers and Marines in war. A battle or firefight is unpredictable, and it is often thought that it is the unpredictability that is most stressful to those who fight these battles. In a similar but much safer way, it is the "not knowing" that can be most stressful for college students: not knowing what graduate schools want, not knowing how to prepare for graduate school, not knowing what you need to be competitive. This book will help to reduce the uncertainty or "clear the fog" by providing a detailed step-by-step guide for following a path to make you competitive for graduate schools. In this way, this book will reveal the process so that you can focus on reaching your goals and not worry so much about *how* to reach your goals.

A Look Inside a Graduate School Selection Committee Meeting: Imparting a New Perspective

"No two persons ever read the same book."

Edmund Wilson

One way to "clear the fog" is to take a look inside a graduate school selection committee meeting to get a perspective from the selection point of view. In this section, I will describe a graduate school selection committee meeting, based on my own experiences in such meetings. The meeting described here is meant to give you insights into what is actually being discussed in these meetings—however, of course, know that many factors can and will be different from one school to another and from one meeting to another.

Very early in my career I got my first glimpse into how decisions are made by graduate schools. What I saw in that process was not entirely expected. It forced me to reconsider the kind of advice I give to students. It was a truly revealing experience that imparted to me one important lesson among many: Getting into graduate school is not about your interests; it's about how *your* interests (the applicant) match *their* interests (the graduate school). Not every point made in the meeting I describe will come up with all graduate school selection committees, but these points can, do, and are likely to come up. Being able to anticipate what topics may be discussed in a selection committee meeting and how you can preemptively address possible concerns can give you a competitive advantage over those who do not realize they should even address certain issues. The following is my experience on one such committee for the selection of candidates to a PhD program in psychology.

The "Cutoff" Criteria

As the submission deadline passed to apply to our graduate program, I anticipated reviewing many applications. What I soon realized was that a lot of my work would be done for me. When the secretary received all the applications, her first job was to eliminate all applicants whose GPA and standardized exam scores did not meet the minimum requirements. Thus, applicants who did not meet our minimum requirements were not even considered.

The more interesting part is that for the rest of the selection process, "grades" were rarely brought up. In other words, students' "grades" were an all-or-nothing criterion—either the applicants had the grades required by the school, or they did not. The selection committee did not spend much time quibbling over the difference between a 3.7 and a 3.8 GPA, for example. Once the school agreed that an applicant's grades were good enough, that was the end of the discussion. The main focus shifted to everything else in the application. I couldn't help but think about all those students who worked so hard to get high GPAs—if only they knew how little time we spent talking about their grades. Their grades got them considered, but it was largely the rest of their application upon which decisions to select or reject them were ultimately made.

The Letters of Intent

As we gathered to review the applications, I was interested to see how the other committee members prioritized the application materials. I recalled thinking as a student that nobody actually reads the full graduate school application, but I quickly learned that I was wrong. In truth, one part of the application—a part that I thought nobody read—quickly arose as being among the most important application materials: the letter of intent. The letter of intent is sometimes called a cover letter or a statement of interest, or can be given other names as well. Ultimately, these are letters in which you describe who you are and your intentions for graduate school. Some have word limits of 300 to 500 words; others can be up to five pages or more. These letters can be critically important in the final decisions made by graduate schools. For this reason, I devote an entire chapter to showing you how to write these letters in Chapter 6.

Of course, we reviewed the quality of the applicants' writing. However, our review of the letters was much more detailed than that, as will be addressed in greater depth in Chapter 6. Among the additional criteria evaluated in the letters of intent were the two criteria listed next: scholarly matching and geographic matching.

Scholarly Matching

Our selection committee considered the extent to which the applicants' interests fit with (1) the goals or aims of the graduate program and (2) the interests of the faculty members, particularly their research interests. Faculty members who oversee graduate programs usually have a program of research or an applied program of study, and thus prefer to accept graduate students who share their interests. In the selection committee meeting, many strong candidates expressed interest in an area of research that did not specifically fit with the interests of our faculty or the graduate program; these applicants were eliminated. On the other side, many less qualified applicants expressed an interest in research that was specifically being done at our school; these applicants rose to the top. Hence, students who expressed their interests, without concern for the interests of those at the school, were largely eliminated. However, applicants who expressed interests that matched the interests of the faculty or school rose to the top—even if their grades were good, but "middle-of-the-pack."

Geographic Matching

A surprising criterion was to identify if the committee "thought" an applicant wanted to actually live in the area. We asked, "Do we think an applicant will like it here?" Keep in mind that graduate schools want to select candidates who will not only be a good fit, but also want to stay. Often, schools are located in unique parts of the country or are surrounded with unique culture. If an applicant did not express his or her interest in or intent for living in the area, then that applicant was likely to be eliminated, particularly if the applicant was not already a top candidate.

The "Will They Come Here?" Criteria

As the selections were narrowed, we placed the top names on a board. The impression in the room was that any of the top picks were good to choose. Now the question was whether or not the applicant, if accepted, would actually come to our school, even if another school accepted him or her. This was a particular concern for the best-qualified applicants—those likely to receive multiple acceptance letters. If applicants did not directly identify our school as one of their top choices, then they left themselves open to allow the selection committee to "figure out" where they stood on this. Many applicants did not receive acceptance letters, in part, because the committee felt that they would not come, if accepted.

The "Did They Show Excitement?" Criteria

The selection committee then followed up in phone interviews with top applicants whom they liked. Such impromptu phone calls, or quasi-interviews, are difficult to prepare for because the reason for the call is really almost impossible to know for sure. The protocol for making phone calls was to call a candidate to see if he or she expressed excitement about being called. The key feedback from our meetings was that the more excited the applicant was or the more interest he or she expressed during the phone call, the more excited the committee member was to select the applicant. Yes, the biggest criterion of the phone interviews was less the content of the call, and more the impression the applicant left regarding his or her excitement or interest in our school.

The "Did They Get Along?" Criteria

As a final phase, many graduate schools will bring students in for group or individual interviews—we brought students in as a group. Of course, only the top candidates were invited for an interview, and the interviews were set up so that much of the applicants' time was spent with the graduate students in the program. Part of the criteria in these interviews was how well the applicants got along with the graduate students and faculty. After all, the applicants selected to the program will work for the faculty and be fellow graduate students, so they need to be able to work together. Hence, these interviews were, in part, an elaborate social-personality test. In our final discussions, we specifically addressed if we felt that any of the applicants *may* be difficult to work with. Feedback from graduate students was a key criterion for determining this answer.

The committee met on a few occasions during that spring semester, and decision letters were sent out around March. What struck me, and should strike you, is how so much of the selection process is qualitative. It is based, in part, on how your interests match those of researchers or programs at the graduate school, how willing you are to live in the area, how excited you are to join the graduate program, and how well you get along with others in an interview. Getting accepted to graduate schools can take a lot more than just grades. As a general rule, the key to gaining acceptance into graduate schools is to tell the story you want graduate schools to read—and this book will share the detailed steps you can take to tell that story to be competitive at any graduate level.

Please revisit this section after you finish each subsequent section in this book to try to connect what you have learned to what is described here. Test your new knowledge to see how you can apply the lessons and steps in this book to address the concerns of a graduate school selection committee. Of course, the criteria shared here will not be the same for all schools, but it is a safe bet that addressing these criteria can go a long way in ensuring that you are most competitive when it comes time to apply. In the final chapter of this book, I will revisit this graduate school selection committee meeting to identify how this book addressed the criteria described here.

Making the Graduate School Plan Work for Traditional and Nontraditional Students

"The greatest accomplishment began as a decision once made and often a difficult one."

Michael Rawls

To help guide your journey in college and to help you prepare to compete for graduate schools, the freshman- to senior-year plan given in Section II is organized into 16 comprehensive goals, collectively referred to here as the "Sweet Sixteen." Each goal that is listed is spread across your four academic years: freshman (5), sophomore and junior (7), and senior (4) years. For reference, each goal that is described in Section II is listed here in Table 1.1. Keep a copy of these goals on you and use it as a checklist to track your progress and success in college.

While the goals are listed by academic year, keep in mind that these same goals can be achieved much more quickly. For example, maybe you are a junior transfer student or a nontraditional student who is finishing up college or starting college for the first time. If you are picking up this book for the first time, then rest assured that the goals and how to achieve them have no absolute timeline. The goals for Year 1 mostly include tips and steps you can take to find a career path—to answer the all-important question, "What do you want to be when you grow up?" You can research this in weeks, or take your entire freshman year if you are a traditional student. The goals for Years 2 and 3 provide many ways to find and gain opportunities that will impress most graduate schools. You can start taking advantage of these opportunities immediately, or you can follow the timeline organized in this book.

The truth is that many students are not certain of their career path. Therefore, this plan for getting into graduate school is written so that traditional students at four-year colleges can lay out this plan over four years to achieve their ultimate goal of getting into graduate school. The layout of the plan is meant to give a realistic timeline for any student—whether it is a student who confidently knows his or her career path or a student who needs some help finding his or her career path. But that is not to say that the plan must be spread across a four-year span. You can lay out this plan along any timeline you choose—you can take advantage of the tips and suggestions in this book at any time.

Table 1.1	The "Sweet Sixteen": 16 Key Goals for the Freshman-to-Senior-Year Plan Given in Section II of This Book

Freshman Year: Find a Direction
1   Get acquainted (with the college and resources available).
2   Know your major requirements (so that you can *plan* to graduate).
3   Find good study habits (that you can use throughout college).
4   Meet friends; choose carefully (surround yourself with supporters).
5   Choose your career path (and stay committed to it).
Sophomore and Junior Years: Pursue Opportunities
6   Get connected (to establish professional contacts).
7   Pursue scholarship (and apply for scholarships).
8   Find opportunities to present and publish (if possible).
9   Pursue activities and international studies (to show an interest in your field).
10   Write a résumé or curriculum vitae (and revise it as you go).
11   Keep track of your GPA.
12   Prepare to take the GRE or other standardized exams.
Senior Year: Select Schools and Complete Applications
13   Search for graduate schools and be realistic.
14   Request letters of recommendation and follow up.
15   Complete all parts of each graduate school application.
16   Apply on time and communicate effectively with schools.

Moreover, the goals for Year 4 will be useful for any student in the process of applying to graduate school. These goals identify the steps for applying to graduate school. To support the goals for Year 4, Section III is entirely dedicated to showing you exactly how to complete key parts of the graduate school application, with templates and samples provided based on those written by students recently accepted to graduate- and doctorate-level programs across the country. The takeaway message is that no matter what year of undergraduate school you are in, this book will provide invaluable insights into how to be competitive for graduate school, and how to effectively apply to graduate schools. Whether you choose to lay out this plan over four years, as described in this book, or to move more quickly is your choice—either way you can take advantage of the insights in this book to achieve your goals.

Making the Plan Work for You

"To change one's life: Start immediately."

William James

Regardless of the timeline you follow to pursue the "Sweet Sixteen" goals in this plan, it should be apparent that competing to get into graduate school is less about being qualified and more about how much you stand out among the applicants who are just as qualified as you are. This plan was therefore written to show you how to stand out among all those qualified applicants, not simply fit in among them. Being more than qualified is more attainable than you may recognize. Realize that most students do not even know what they need to do to be competitive. Having this book, and following this plan, can therefore help you gain a competitive advantage. The plan in this book will do more than just tell you what you need to do—it will show you *how* to do it with templates and examples given throughout the book.

Of course, you need to be cautious in deciding whether college is right for you. Having fun is certainly part of college, but you need to be ready to work hard as well. You need to be prepared to put in the time to prepare, study, and pursue opportunities beyond just coursework. Certainly you will find many useful tips and resources to help you achieve your goals for becoming competitive for graduate school. However, it is you who need to take action; you need to realize your own success. Take responsibility for what you can control, and trust in those who can help you along the way.

The title of this chapter refers to making the "grade." Making the grade refers to many aspects of college beyond your GPA or test scores. To make the grade you need to find a direction (Chapter 3), pursue opportunities (Chapter 4), apply to graduate schools (Chapter 5), know how to complete the application process (Section III), and know how to plan for next steps (Section IV). Thus, making the grade in college is about doing the right things to be competitive. Whether you plan to pursue a master's or a doctoral degree program upon graduation, this book will help you be competitive in your pursuits. Be confident in yourself and know that with this book and these resources as a guide, you can find your own success; you can make the grade.

CHAPTER 2

The Big Three: Academics, Scholarship, and Activities

The Big Three: Identifying the Core Areas of Interest to Graduate Schools

"Action is the foundational key to all success."

Pablo Picasso

It should not be surprising that graduate schools want certain types of students from diverse backgrounds, with an appropriate level of preparation prior to coming to the graduate program. For you, the initial step is to identify the type of graduate degree you wish to pursue. There are literally dozens of different types of degree programs you can pursue. Table 2.1 shows the more common master's degree programs, and Table 2.2 shows the more common doctoral degree programs pursued by students who have earned their undergraduate degree in the behavioral sciences. Choosing among these types of degree options can be tricky, which is why this plan helps show you how to decide.

Different schools will have slightly different requirements. Some programs weigh grades heavier than others; some have a specific list of prerequisite courses to take (this is rather common for medical schools); some will expect that you have sought internships, whereas others will focus more on your research experience. You need not only to navigate the many degree options available to you but also to identify a field of study for each degree. For example, at the master's and doctorate levels you can study a range of fields, including clinical psychology, medicine, neuroscience, counseling, social psychology, behavioral health, law, and education. The only way to choose which field of study is right for you is to do your research. For this reason, the full first-year plan is to show you how to identify a field of interest to you.

Table 2.1   Common Master's Degrees Pursued
Following a Bachelor of Arts or Bachelor of Science

Degree (abbreviation)	Degree (meaning)	Description	Common Job Titles
MA	Master of Arts	Graduate degree primarily for behavioral sciences.	Varies
MS	Master of Science	Graduate degree for biobehavioral and neurosciences.	Varies
MEd	Master of Education	Graduate degree in education, often aimed at K–12 levels.	Teacher, Principal
MBA	Master of Business Administration	Graduate degree in business, usually earned with a specialization in a subfield of business.	Varies

No matter what field you choose to study in graduate school, know that you can pursue just about any field with a behavioral sciences undergraduate degree—and this plan will help you decide on a field of study that most interests you. Graduate schools rarely require you to earn a specific type of bachelor's degree. For example, if they have special course requirements, then they will list them as prerequisite courses. You simply need to check that you have taken those courses, and thus meet program requirements for the degree program to which you apply. Hence, you do not need to earn a degree in biology to go to medical school, or in prelaw to go to law school—just take the prerequisite courses listed for a given school.

For all graduate schools, you can find the details of what they want on their webpage. Students often ask, "What do I need to do to appeal to graduate schools?" Often the answer from an advisor is "It depends on where you apply." Translated, this response actually means "Go find schools that interest you, visit their webpage, and see what those schools say they want." This is great advice because all graduate schools are a little different and may ask for different things that most appeal to them. Yet this advice is hardly helpful to many students, mostly because they are still left with no concrete answer, and are therefore "back to square one" in many cases.

It would therefore be helpful to conceptualize the requirements of a broad range of graduate schools in the behavioral sciences. In other words, it would be helpful to review the wide range of requirements of graduate schools and to summarize or categorize those requirements so that students can conceptualize what they need to do to appeal to the interests of graduate schools. This is exactly what I have done here. In this chapter, I share with you the "Big Three" core areas of interest to just about any graduate school in the behavioral sciences. These categories have been developed

Table 2.2	Common Doctoral Degrees Pursued Following a Bachelor of Arts or Bachelor of Science		

Degree (abbreviation)	Degree (meaning)	Description	Common Job Titles
Medicine			
MD	Doctor of Medicine	Professional doctoral degree required to practice medicine.	Doctor, Physician, Surgeon
DDS	Doctor of Dental Surgery	Professional doctoral degree required to practice dental surgery.	Dentist
DPT	Doctor of Physical Therapy	Professional doctoral degree required to practice as a physical therapist.	Physical therapist
DC	Doctor of Chiropractic	Professional doctoral degree required to practice chiropractic.	Chiropractor
Law			
JD	Juris Doctorate	Professional doctoral degree required to take bar exam to practice law.	Lawyer
Behavioral Sciences			
PhD	Doctor of Philosophy	Research doctoral degree in various disciplines to include psychology and the sciences.	Researcher, Professor
PsyD, DPsy, DP	Doctor of Psychology	Professional doctoral degree in psychology, often for clinical practice.	Clinician, Consultant, Professor
EdD	Doctor of Education	Professional doctoral degree in education.	School administrator

from an extensive review of over 100 graduate programs across the United States and Canada. The "Big Three" are a central part of the graduate school plan in this book because they help conceptualize how to understand what graduate schools are looking for. The "Big Three," which are identified and explained in this chapter, are:

- Academics
- Scholarship
- Activities

Academics tend to be desired by all graduate schools. Across most graduate programs, there will be minimum requirements for GPA and standardized exams, and often schools will include a list of prerequisite courses that they prefer you have taken prior to applying. Hence, academics will be important to achieve no matter where you apply to graduate school.

Scholarship includes what I call the TRIfecta: Teaching, Research, and Internship. These core areas tend to be heavily reviewed by graduate programs, particularly for doctorate-level programs in the behavioral sciences. Teaching, as described in this chapter, is positively reviewed across most, if not all, graduate schools. The emphasis you place on research and internships, however, will depend on what types of programs you apply to. In general, there are applied programs, and there are research programs. An applied program is often found in medical, clinical, or counseling settings where you tend to apply your skills in a practice or workplace setting. As a general rule, if you aim to apply to applied programs, then lean more toward internships. A research program can be found across all disciplines and involves a desire to conduct or engage in research in a certain discipline. If you go this route, you are interested in working in research settings, which includes universities and medical centers. As a general rule, if you aim to apply to research programs, then lean more toward research.

Activities include clubs, sports, service, and more. Having no activities can hurt you, but rarely, if ever, will activities be the key reason for being accepted to a graduate school. In other words, you will want to add activities to your résumé to show that your achievements in academics and scholarship were balanced with engagement in activities. It is not necessary, however, to prioritize activities in most cases. Sports can often be an exception because this experience can include scholarships and can demonstrate the maturity and leadership skills of a student.

The takeaway message here is that you can develop a concrete plan for getting into graduate school. Academics and activities tend to be positively reviewed across all graduate schools (that is two of the Big Three). The one place that varies drastically from one school to the next is scholarship (the third of the Big Three). It should not be surprising, then, that this also tends to be the area in which graduate schools tend to place the greatest emphasis for deciding to accept or reject an applicant—particularly for doctorate-level graduate programs. With this in mind, our conceptualization in terms of the "Big Three" allows us to develop a plan for getting into graduate school that can be applied by all students.

In this chapter, I introduce the Big Three. In the plan for getting into graduate school, I show you how to achieve the Big Three, with details for every way in which these can be achieved, beyond the typical tips and suggestions you would get elsewhere. The goal of this plan is to help you to achieve your goals. It is with your goals and aspirations in mind that these Big Three were identified and this plan was devised. Yes, not all schools emphasize the same thing—it depends on the school or program. But one fact is certain: All schools evidently want the Big Three to some extent.

Appealing to the Big Three

"If you always do what interests you, at least one person is pleased."

Katharine Hepburn

If we return for a moment to appealing to the interests of graduate schools, consider the following analogy. Suppose you are about to go on a date with someone you really like. You are really excited, and you want to make a good first impression. You ask a friend how you can make a good first impression on your date. Your friend responds, "Find something that your date is really interested in, and talk about that." That's actually really good advice. One way to get people really interested in you is to first show an interest in things that interest them. It is a basic rule of *making your interests appeal to the interests of others*. People tend to like it when they feel that other people are interested in the same things that interest them.

The advice your friend gave you to impress your date is the same advice you should follow to impress members of a graduate school. Admittedly it is not as romantic, but it works all the same. Thus, before you begin preparing for and applying to graduate schools, you must be considerate of what interests the schools you apply to. For example, here are just a few questions you should ask yourself before you begin the application process to a master's- or doctorate-level program:

✓ What are the areas of research or scholarship for the faculty employed?
✓ What is the size of the university or college?
✓ What is the mission of the university or college?
✓ What is the mission of the academic program to which you are applying?
✓ When is the deadline for submitting an application?
✓ What are the minimum requirements for applying to a program?

The list given here is only a fraction of the questions you will want to ask. What is most important is that the last two questions listed above are only two of the many more questions you should try to answer in the graduate school application process. If you know only the deadlines for applying and the minimum requirements for applying to a graduate program, then you are not being sufficiently considerate of the other important questions that are relevant to getting to know the faculty and the college or graduate program to which you apply. The more you know about the interests of those schools, the more effectively you can make your interests appeal to the interests of those at the school or program to which you apply.

In this chapter, I will take a closer look at each of the "Big Three," which are the core areas of interest to graduate schools. Throughout this book, I will identify ways to make your application appeal to these interests and ways to find and create opportunities that fit within the "Big Three." First, however, it is important to understand "What are the Big Three?" Answering this question up front is essential for gaining the perspective you will need to recognize how to appeal to the interests of the graduate programs you apply to. I therefore begin here by evaluating each of the Big Three: academics, scholarship, and activities.

Academics: GPA, Standardized Exams, and Course Enrollments

"An investment in knowledge always pays the best interest."

Benjamin Franklin

In many ways *academics* tend to be the most salient criteria for getting into graduate school. Many students realize the importance of getting good grades and have quivered at the thought of a "stain" on their "permanent record." The generations entering college now have been fully exposed to the standardization of education with standardized testing being administered as early as kindergarten or elementary school. In addition, not all courses are created equal. Some courses can be more important than others, and the grades you receive in those courses can come under greater scrutiny by graduate school selection committees. These committees will review these and many more factors related to testing and course grades, so you should recognize the importance of them. Therefore, in this section I briefly introduce each factor that falls under the *academics* category:

- Grade point average
- Standardized exams
- Course enrollments

Grade Point Average

"The GPA is not the be-all and end-all."

Patricia Rose

Obtaining a high grade point average, or GPA, is one of the most revered endeavors in academia. Students who want to be competitive for graduate schools or jobs will work hard to manage their GPA and to improve their GPA whenever possible. A GPA is typically measured on a 4.0 scale. Each letter grade you receive corresponds to a numeric value on this scale. Table 2.3 shows the conversion of a letter grade to a numeric value on a 4.0 scale. If you are at one of the few institutions that allow for an A+ grade, then an A+ is beyond the standard 4.0 scale and corresponds to a 4.33 GPA score.

Your GPA is really a weighted mean in that your grade is "weighted" by the number of credits of a given course. Each course you take is associated with a number of credit hours, which reflects the number of classroom hours per week. Most courses in college are 3–credit hour courses. Special topics or independent study courses can be less than 3 credit hours, and laboratory courses are often more than

Table 2.3 Letter Grade and GPA Conversion	
Grade	**GPA**
A	4.00
A–	3.67
B+	3.33
B	3.00
B–	2.67
C+	2.33
C	2.00
C–	1.67
D+	1.33
D	1.00
D–	0.67
F	0.00

3 credit hours. The larger the number of credit hours for a course, the heavier the weight placed on that grade. To get a sense of the consequences of a weighted grade, consider the following example of two students who receive an A and a B in a given semester:

Student 1:	Statistics	6–credit hour course	A (4.0)
	Health Psychology	3–credit hour course	B (3.0)
Student 2:	Statistics	6–credit hour course	B (3.0)
	Health Psychology	3–credit hour course	A (4.0)

In this example, these two students do not have the same GPA. A weighted mean is calculated by summing the products of each grade × weight, then dividing that total by the sum of the weights.

To calculate the GPA for Student 1, first sum the products:

$$4.0 \text{ GPA} \times 6 \text{ credits} = 24$$

$$3.0 \text{ GPA} \times 3 \text{ credits} = 9$$

$$\text{Sum of products: } 24 + 9 = 33$$

The weights are the credit hours for each course. Sum those weights and divide 33 by that total:

$$6 \text{ credits} + 3 \text{ credits} = 9 \text{ total credit hours}$$

$$\text{GPA for Student 1} = \frac{33}{9} = 3.67 \text{ (A– average)}$$

To calculate the GPA for Student 2, first sum the products:

$$3.0 \text{ GPA} \times 6 \text{ credits} = 18$$

$$4.0 \text{ GPA} \times 3 \text{ credits} = 12$$

$$\text{Sum of products: } 18 + 12 = 30$$

The weights are the credit hours for each course. Sum those weights and divide 30 by that total:

$$6 \text{ credits} + 3 \text{ credits} = 9 \text{ total credit hours}$$

$$\text{GPA for Student 2} = \frac{30}{9} = 3.33 \text{ (B+ average)}$$

Notice that even though both students earned the same grades, earning higher grades in courses with a greater number of credit hours heavily impacted the final GPA. In the example here, Student 1 has an A– average because his or her A was earned in the 6–credit hour course; Student 2 has a B+ average because his or her A was earned in the 3–credit hour course, which carried less weight in the final GPA calculation.

Keep in mind, however, that your GPA is an estimate of how much you learned. Many tips and strategies for improving your GPA will be given in Sections II and III of this book. You will notice that many of the strategies given have nothing to do with studying harder or learning more. For this reason, many graduate schools recognize that a GPA is not an absolute value. For example, one person with a 3.6 GPA is not necessarily ranked above a student with a 3.7 GPA—not among many graduate school selection committees anyway. Maintaining a high GPA in undergraduate school is certainly important, but your GPA does not need to be perfect. Your GPA is only one of many factors that will be given strong consideration in the review process. Your GPA is important, but it is "not the be-all and end-all."

Standardized Exams

"Not everything that can be counted counts, and not everything that counts can be counted."

Albert Einstein

Whether you agree with their use or not, standardized tests are used as primary selection criteria into all levels of college, from undergraduate to doctorate. Even before college you took standardized state tests, or maybe earned an International Baccalaureate degree or a Regents Diploma, both of which also required passing standardized tests. All of these tests have one thing in common: They follow the assumption that a standard level of competency should be reached and that such a competency can be measured with a single standardized testing instrument. Regardless of whether or not you agree with this assumption, standardized tests are nonetheless a key factor used in the selection process to colleges and graduate schools, so you need to be prepared.

To apply to most undergraduate schools, you take the SAT. The type of stand-ardized exam you take to apply to graduate school depends on the type of program or school you apply to. Table 2.4 lists various degree programs you may be likely to pursue following a behavioral sciences degree in undergraduate school. The GRE revised General Test is most common, but note that you may have to take subject-specific tests, depending on your graduate school choice. Each standardized test meas-ures different skill sets that reflect competencies required in a specific field of study.

For the GRE, most schools require only the revised General Test; however, some schools require the subject tests, which include the subject-specific tests listed under

Table 2.4 Graduate Programs, Standardized Tests, and Links for More Information

Field of Program to Which You Apply	Standardized Test Typically Required	Link for More Information
Most master's and PhD programs; some business schools	GRE revised General Test	www.ets.org/gre/revised_general/about
Psychology	GRE: Psychology Test	www.ets.org/gre/subject/about/content/psychology
Physics	GRE: Physics Test	www.ets.org/gre/subject/about/content/physics
Mathematics	GRE: Mathematics Test	www.ets.org/gre/subject/about/content/mathematics
English, Literature	GRE: Literature in English Test	www.ets.org/gre/subject/about/content/literature_english
Computer science	ETS Major Field Test for Computer Science	www.ets.org/mft/about/content/computer_science
Chemistry	GRE: Chemistry Test	www.ets.org/gre/subject/about/content/chemistry
Biology	GRE: Biology Test	www.ets.org/gre/subject/about/content/biology
Biochemistry, Cell and molecular biology	GRE: Biochemistry, Cell and Molecular Biology Test	www.ets.org/gre/subject/about/content/biochemistry
Medical school; other health professions	Medical College Admission Test (MCAT)	www.aamc.org/students/applying/mcat/about/
Law school	Law School Admission Test (LSAT)	www.lsac.org/jd/lsat/about-the-lsat.asp
Most MBA programs; business	Graduate Management Admission Test (GMAT)	www.unhmba.org/the-graduate-management-admission-test-gmat.html

the GRE revised General Test in Table 2.4. Some business schools also require the GRE revised General Test, but most require the GMAT, particularly if you are applying to an MBA program. Law schools and medical schools are also viable options for students with a behavioral sciences undergraduate degree (depending on prerequisite courses completed in many cases). Law schools have their own entrance exam: the LSAT. Medical schools likewise have their own entrance exam: the MCAT. Links for learning more about the format and process for each test are given in Table 2.4.

Many international students will be required to take an additional standardized test. International students will likely have to report scores for a test that measures their ability to communicate and write in English. Two common tests are the TOEFL and the International English Language Testing System (IELTS). At some schools, your TOEFL or other international test score will be accepted in lieu of the SAT or other required exam, although few institutions use this practice. If you are an international student, then you can get more information about the TOEFL at www.ets.org/toefl. For more information about the IELTS, you can visit www.ielts.org. Check with each school for the international test it requires, as each school can have different requirements.

Keep in mind that standardized tests are high-stakes tests, meaning that they are a one-time, often one-day, brief assessment of learning. In this way, a standardized exam is a one-shot case study, meaning that it only can take a snapshot of your preparedness for college. In the words of Einstein, "Not everything that can be counted counts, and not everything that counts can be counted." It is not always clear what exactly these tests are measuring. However, because they can predict with some accuracy how well a student will do in graduate school, these tests are used all the same. You will need to prepare for them, and you will need to do well—and you can!

In Section III, I work through the process of getting these tests completed. Many tips and strategies will be included to help you prepare and study for these tests. If you have a plan, you can substantially improve your grade on these tests by preparing, using the many resources and exam preparation guides provided by the makers of these tests. For each test, it is hard to say what a "good score" is because it really depends on which school you are applying to. Sections II and III will help you to develop a plan to prepare for these tests and do well.

Course Enrollments

"I decided on science when I was in college."

Sally Ride

A course enrollment is the specific course you enroll in. For an undergraduate degree, you must enroll in at least 120 credit hours of courses. Hence, if you enter college with zero college credits, then you will need to complete 15 credit hours per semester (30 credit hours per year) to finish your bachelor's degree in the expected four years. The rule of 120 credits is true for most schools and majors, although a few programs may require a little more than the 120. Make sure you check the degree requirements for the school that you are enrolled in.

Graduate schools will look at the types of course you have taken. Enrollments that are important include:

- Honors courses
- Upper-level courses
- Independent study courses
- Major-specific courses

Course enrollments are important inasmuch as they can tell a story about you. For example, honors courses are generally looked at as more difficult than nonhonors courses; upper-level classes (listed as 300 or 400 level) are regarded as more difficult than lower-level classes (listed as 100 or 200 level). Hence, if you have a high GPA and have taken many upper-level and honors courses, then you are often ranked higher than another student with the same GPA, but with fewer "difficult" courses listed on his or her transcript. An independent study course is a course that is taken one-on-one or in a small group setting between a student and an advisor/faculty member. A student who took an independent study course, and therefore studied a specific topic under the advisement of a specific professor, is often viewed as being more determined or driven than a student with no independent study courses—because by taking the independent study course, the student (1) was accepted in the course by the faculty member and (2) took initiative to take such a class in the first place. Likewise, students who take many classes in their major field of study are viewed as being more certain of "what they want to be when they grow up." All of these factors are telling a story about you—whether or not you intended to tell a story.

Sally Ride, the first American woman to fly in space, commented that she had "decided on science when [she] was in college." This is exactly how many students decide on their career—in college. The first-year plan is entirely for helping you decide on a career path. Then, when you do decide, focus your coursework toward those classes that relate most to your interests or career path. In many ways, that story of deciding your career path will be told in your course enrollments. Tips and strategies for enrolling in courses and how to tell the story you want to tell will be given throughout Sections II and III. Section II includes a full plan for how to "shape your story" by enrolling in courses from freshman to senior year. Also, in Section III, you will be given tips and strategies for identifying the best courses to take and which courses you should prioritize—in terms of how important those courses are to graduate schools.

Scholarship: Teaching, Research, and Internships

"True scholarship consists in knowing not what things exist, but what they mean; it is not memory but judgment."

James Russell Lowell

Scholarship is the second major category of interest to graduate schools. Scholarship can include teaching in that teaching assistant opportunities can exist for undergraduates. It can include research in that faculty at most institutions are actively seeking students to work with them in laboratory or applied research projects. It can also include internships, some of which can be rather competitive. These types of opportunities exist for undergraduate students, and such opportunities are equivalent to the "work experience" that is so valued outside academia. Graduate school selection committees will review these factors, so you should recognize the importance of scholarship. Therefore, in this section I will briefly introduce each factor that falls under the *scholarship* category, or the "TRIfecta":

- Teaching
- Research
- Internships

Teaching

"In learning you will teach, and in teaching you will learn."

Phil Collins

Teaching, of "course," is something that your instructors and professors do. However, there are opportunities for you to gain experiences in undergraduate school that you can list as teaching experience. The most widely recognized teaching opportunity is via the teaching assistant (TA) opportunity. Many universities and colleges in the United States offer this option. The typical structure of this option is to offer it as a 400-level 3–credit hour course. The name of the course for a TA opportunity can vary substantially. A review of listings by universities and colleges shows that such a course can be listed in a university course catalog under the following common names: fieldwork, special topics, or independent study.

The setup for this course can also vary. Typically, a TA does not teach. Instead, as a TA you learn about grading, academic honesty, and fairness. You hold office hours each week, which gives you the unique opportunity to teach what you know to students who come to you for help. After all, it is "in teaching [that] you will learn" inasmuch as you gain insights into the ways in which students learn and how to frame your answers to make sense of material that is confusing to them. Graduate schools value this level of experience because it is achieved when you (the student) seek out such opportunities—a TA course is not mandatory at the undergraduate level.

Typically the only way to enroll in a TA course is to speak to a professor one-on-one or e-mail him or her to request to be considered. You should seek out TA opportunities in your junior or senior year and typically for courses that you have already completed and in which you received an A or B+ grade. In Sections II and III, I will therefore revisit possible TA opportunities to discuss ways to make requests that will appeal to professors and the types of courses that would be best to TA—in terms of appealing to the interests of the graduate schools to which you will apply.

Research

> *"If we knew what we were doing it wouldn't be research."*
>
> Albert Einstein

Engaging in research is a very important experience to be competitive for many master's degree programs, and particularly for PhD programs. Actively seek out these opportunities because research is likely what you will be doing in graduate school, if you pursue a master's or a PhD. This is also why many graduate schools heavily weigh research experience—because it demonstrates your interest in conducting research and is a strong predictor of success in graduate school.

Getting an opportunity to conduct research is often a matter of asking a professor or researcher if you can join his or her labs, so be proactive. At many universities, the main way to gain research experience is to find an independent study opportunity on campus. Such opportunities typically require an interview, and a certain GPA (at least 3.0 in most cases). You will also want to be cognizant of the types of research you engage in. It is important that the research experience you get as an undergraduate relate to the field of research or discipline you will apply to in graduate school.

Because selection committees can heavily weigh research experience for master's and PhD programs, this book adds a substantial focus on showing you how to compete for research opportunities and how to create these opportunities. You will want to seek out opportunities for being a research assistant as early as your sophomore year, but typically in your junior or senior year. For this reason, tips and strategies for engaging in research are discussed in greater detail beginning in Section II to help you make the most of the research opportunities available to you—specifically in terms of tailoring your research experiences to the interests of the graduate schools to which you will apply.

Internships

> *"Internships have always been important to college students,*
> *but never more than now."*
>
> Katie Riley

Internships are applied academic or job-related experiences that relate to the discipline to which you will apply in graduate school. Academic internships may include jobs on campus in the library or in a counseling clinic where patients are observed. Job-related internships can be any type of work in the community, such as at a hospital, a law firm, or an elementary school. The key is that the work you do in your internship must in some way relate to the field of study you are pursuing in graduate school. A job as a cashier at a fast-food restaurant, for example, may not be highly regarded, but an internship at the company headquarters of a fast-food restaurant may be highly regarded—if you can show that your experiences related to the field of study to which you applied.

Internships demonstrate more applied skills that translate well to applied programs, such as medical schools, law schools, business schools, some doctoral programs, and many fields in science. It shows skills and experiences that are typically "outside of the classroom" and therefore demonstrate that you have the initiative to do more than just the minimum requirements to earn your degree. It demonstrates your passion or desire to develop or grow in a particular field, and to work toward mastery of a particular skill or ability beyond satisfactory achievement. Thus, an internship can go a long way toward getting graduate schools interested in your application.

As a general rule, having research or internship experience will be great; both would be extraordinary. But of course you have only so much time in a day, so you may need to pick one and not both. This is fine—just make sure the choice you make fits best with the type of program you are applying to. Many other important factors should be considered in terms of how to compete for internships and to choose internships that will benefit you the most. For this reason, Section II will describe ways in which you can obtain and create internships, with particular emphasis placed on helping you stand out as an applicant for the many internship opportunities available to you.

Activities: Clubs, Sports, Service, and More

"To live well is to work well, to show a good activity."

Thomas Aquinas

The third category of the Big Three is activities. This category tends to be a "miscellaneous" category in that it is everything other than academics and scholarship. With some common exceptions that will be identified throughout this book, this last category tends to be the least weighed in the graduate school selection process. This does not mean that having activities is not helpful. In fact, it can substantially improve your ranking among other candidates if you have high marks in academics and scholarship. In many cases, activities can be used as a "tiebreaker" when two or more applicants have similar academic and scholarship credentials. Regardless, you will still want to have some activities to show for your four years in college. These activities can take up a lot of your time or very little, depending on the types of activities you seek. Therefore, in this section, I will briefly introduce each factor that falls under the *activities* category:

- Clubs
- Sports
- Service and more

Clubs

"How could youths better learn to live than by at once trying the experiment of living?"

Henry David Thoreau, *Walden*

Club activities usually involve opportunities to apply your education—to try "the experiment of living." Getting involved in club activities is important, particularly for clubs that are related to the area of study for which you will apply to graduate school. In psychology, for example, your department may have a psych club—join the club as early as possible and participate in club activities and events. Clubs may put together an event to help students learn more about graduate schools, or may volunteer to refurbish a run-down room to improve study areas on campus for psychology students. This type of club will also likely have offices, such as president, vice president, and secretary. Students are typically selected to these positions by a vote from their peers in the club. You can run for one of these offices to gain leadership experience in a club related to psychology, which in this example would be your major.

Club activities also involve activities off campus. On a national level, you can join Psi Chi, which is the International Honor Society in Psychology. Join this society in your sophomore year and, as with the psych club, make a run for an office to demonstrate your leadership skills in psychology. Even if you do not get elected to an office, being an active member of the society will look good to graduate schools because it is experience that is related to your intended field of study. Whatever your major, there will be clubs and societies to join; join them, and be actively involved in them. How to join these clubs and get involved without overextending your time will be discussed in Section II. A list of some of the most common clubs and organizations in the field of psychology are also listed and described in Chapter 4 (see Table 4.1).

Sports

"Champions are made from something they have deep inside them— a desire, a dream, a vision."

Muhammad Ali

Athletics may not apply to everyone, but if you do join a sports team, either club or scholarship, then make it known. Scholarship athletes, particularly those who maintain a high GPA, can be held in high regard for having strong leadership skills, being highly collaborative (being part of a team), and being driven, or committed to something challenging. In other words, being an athlete is a great way to demonstrate the intangibles of your character that may otherwise be difficult to demonstrate. Frame the discussion of your experiences in athletics around the three strengths most commonly recognized from an athlete: leadership, collaboration, and commitment. Use your experiences as an athlete to demonstrate strengths in each area.

Club sports are typically not viewed as prestigiously as scholarship sports or other sports in which players are selected for a team. Regardless of the level of sports that you play, the same argument can be made in terms of connecting that experience to the three strengths of leadership, collaboration, and commitment. How to connect these three strengths to your experiences in sports and to the interests of a graduate school will be described in Sections II and III, with many examples given for how other student athletes have related their experiences in sports to each strength.

Service and More

"The best way to find yourself is to lose yourself in the service of others."

Mahatma Gandhi

Service is also important in that it demonstrates strong character. There are many different ways in which you can show evidence of service, including:

- Volunteer work (at a soup kitchen or as a youth coach, for example)
- Involvement in prosocial activities (such as participating in an Earth Day rally to promote a cleaner environment)
- Educational awareness (to promote literacy among children at schools in a poor community, for example)
- Fund-raisers (for local schools, charities, or not-for-profit organizations)
- Emergency readiness (such as being a volunteer firefighter or participating in efforts aimed at improving campus safety)
- "Feel-good" projects (such as organizing a team of students to fix up a home that has been neglected)

A little bit of service in four years of college can go a long way toward demonstrating strong character. Service learning shows that you are willing to give back to others who are less fortunate. This type of behavior is typically attributed to "good people," and who doesn't like a "good person"? It is basic psychology that people (including faculty on graduate school selection committees) like other people who do "good" things. Your service alone is probably not going to get you into graduate school, but it will certainly help if you also have strong academics and scholarship to support it.

The "and more" part is everything else you could have done that may also be relevant or of interest to graduate schools. The most obvious among the remaining factors is your work experience, although you should list only your work experience that is relevant to the type of program to which you are applying. Other accolades that you may want to consider adding include the following:

- Resident assistant (RA). An RA is a student who lives in a university residence and acts as a primary mentor, role model, and community leader in his or her hall. RAs are typically regarded as strong leaders with strong interpersonal skills.

- Special academic skills sets (such as having high proficiency using statistical software or Microsoft® Office).
- Special miscellaneous skill sets (such as being a talented singer, a hip-hop dancer, or a first-degree black belt).
- Specialized trainings (such as completion of the National Institutes of Health web-based course "Protecting Human Research Participants" or being CPR certified).

As with service learning, these experiences alone are not likely going to win over a graduate school selection committee. However, the "and more" does demonstrate that you are a well-rounded student with a diverse set of skills and experiences. Combined with a strong record of academics and scholarship, the "and more" can go a long way toward impressing members of a graduate school selection committee. How to make your service and added experiences and skills appeal to the interests of a graduate school will be described in Sections II and III. In addition, many examples will be given to show how students have used these experiences to help them get accepted to graduate school, even at the doctorate level.

Making Time for the Big Three

"Sleep, good grades, and a social life. Pick two. Welcome to college!"

Unknown

To be fair, the Big Three sound like a lot of work, and to be fair—they are. But let's put this into perspective. Thousands of students will be rejected from graduate schools and doctoral programs each year, not because they aren't qualified, but because they aren't organized. *How* you present yourself is as important as *what* you present. There are so many subtle factors that play into whether or not you will be accepted to a graduate school.

Preparing for graduate school is a difficult task that will require a lot of work. The advantage for you is that you can use this book to organize your academics, scholarship, and activities into one cohesive story—one that specifically appeals to the interests of the graduate schools you are applying to. That being said, it is also important to manage your time. Working too much can be as detrimental as working too little. So let's take the time to list some useful tips to help you manage your time.

Tips for managing time in college in general:

1. <u>Use a calendar.</u> You will have a lot of planning, courses, and opportunities. You will want to record all your commitments. A calendar, particularly an electronic calendar, can be especially useful to help you stay on track.

2. <u>Be sensible when scheduling classes,</u> if possible. Try to leave breaks between classes such that you never take more than two or three classes in sequence.

In other words, try to think of "studying, eating, and time for yourself" as a course in and of itself; then schedule your classes around those times.

3. Prioritize and reprioritize, as needed. Ultimately you need to prioritize your time if you want to manage it. Certainly have fun—responsible fun. But *responsible* fun involves taking care of your work first, then taking some time off. The exception to this rule is next on this list.

4. Be realistic; schedule breaks. Yes, you need to finish your work, but sometimes it is simply overwhelming. You are exhausted; you just read four pages and have no clue what you just read; you spent the past 10 minutes staring at your computer screen or searching random websites without even realizing it. The fact is that sometimes, no matter what your priorities are, you just need a break. If you reach this point, or even a bit before you reach this point, schedule some time off to hang out with friends, go out for dinner, or enjoy a movie—and relax knowing that you had planned this time off.

5. Work backward when planning ahead. You will likely know the due dates for many of your assignments once you get the syllabus for the course on the first day of classes. Write down the due dates in your calendar for each assignment that is due. Then work backward to plan for completing each assignment or studying for each test—to give yourself enough time to get your work done. And please do not procrastinate—it may seem OK at first, but it will likely lead to more stress in the long run.

6. Sleep, exercise, and be healthy. Exercise and sleep have positive effects on mood. Find a sleep pattern. It's not necessarily "sleeping in" that is good for you; it's finding a consistent time period for sleep. Try to find some consistency; typically you will want to make time for at least 6 to 8 hours of sleep per day. And make time for the gym. If you get tired in the evening, then work out in the morning. If you are more of an "evening person," then work out in the evenings after all of your classes. Working out can help you feel good, improve your mood, and even energize and motivate you to get studying.

Tips for specifically managing classroom time:

1. Take notes. Duh.

2. Use the supplemental materials for the course. Many courses have textbooks, and the publishers of those textbooks likely have student study sites. Go to those sites; take the practice tests; print out the note cards and chapter summaries; use the study materials already created by the author of the book or by your professor to organize your notes and study for exams. It's simply practical.

3. Note how long a professor speaks on each topic (in the margins of your notes). It is likely that the topics that a professor spends the most time on will be the most heavily tested topics.

4. <u>Always be respectful.</u> Ultimately, your professor is the person who grades you. Do not forget that. Whatever the topic—and no matter your actual opinion of that topic—you always refer to it as "interesting" or refer to how well your professor "makes the material interesting." Please do not feel like you have to lie. Yet at the same time, there is no reason for you to be overly critical of your professor—it does not at all stand to reason that criticizing your professor is in your best interests. Be sensible; be kind; be respectful.

5. <u>Study as you go; have questions prepared.</u> If you study material as it is taught, then you will have less to study around exam time, and you will find that you have better long-term retention of the material taught. In addition, this will allow you to realize what you don't understand as you go, which will give you the chance in class to ask questions to get clarification. Asking relevant questions in class is a good thing: It demonstrates that you are prepared for classes.

6. <u>Do not miss class; sit toward the front.</u> Professors can tell who the "regulars" are, particularly if students sit in the front row and are seen each day. Professors can hold a bias that those who attended regularly care about their grade more. With this in mind and as you will see beginning in Section II, being in the good graces of your professor can not only improve your learning environment but can improve your grade as well.

7. <u>Visit office hours.</u> A professor holds office hours each week. Even if you don't have questions, try to visit his or her office hours at least a few times during the semester. Efforts like this distinguish you from the majority of students who will never go to an office hour. Professors often view students who take time to make an office hour visit as being more studious and hardworking—this is how you want to be seen by your professor. And who knows? It may help you answer questions you didn't even know you had.

8. <u>Form study groups with the "smart" students.</u> If you want to do well, then find classmates who are doing very well and study with them; after all, they must be doing something right if they are doing well in class.

Keep Focused; Stand Out!

"Some people think they are concentrating when they're merely worrying."

Bobby Jones

There are two key takeaway messages from these opening two chapters:

1. <u>Keep focused</u> (on a specific area of interest to you), then make your interests appeal to the interests of others. Keep in mind that graduate schools have specific (or narrow) interests, so you also need to narrow your interests. Then and only then can you *make your interests appeal to the interests of others* (i.e., the members of graduate school selection committees).

2. <u>Stand out</u> (among all qualified applicants). To stand out, you not only need to have strong academics, scholarship, and activities; you also need to be able to communicate your accolades in an organized fashion. *How* you present yourself is as important as *what* you present.

Keeping focused actually makes graduate schools more confident that you will stay in the graduate program, if selected. Graduate school is associated with high dropout rates, and members of graduate school selection committees recognize this as they decide whom to accept and whom to reject. Graduate schools not only want to select the best applicants; they want to select the best applicants who they believe will actually accept the offer and stay until they earn the degree. This brings some truth to the axiom that it is more difficult to get into a graduate program than it is to get out of one!

Also, standing out is important because, especially today, there are plenty of qualified applicants to graduate schools. The challenge of selecting students for graduate schools is not about finding enough who are qualified; it is about selecting among the large stack of applications for applicants who are qualified. The reality of graduate school is that there are typically more qualified applicants than there are "seats" available each academic year. Therefore, becoming qualified isn't enough, and sadly, most books ignore this reality. You must stand out among all qualified applicants, and this book will help you get there—to stand out among your peers.

So where to begin? Well, let's start with freshman year. Even if you have finished your freshman year, it will still be helpful to review the freshman year plan, and to review the full four-year plan for that matter. The plan includes more than just a plan for getting into graduate school; it reinforces life skills that can be applied in any endeavor you wish to pursue. In Section II, you will be shown steps that you can take to build your résumé and create opportunities in your freshman year (Chapter 3), in your sophomore and junior years (Chapter 4), and in your senior year (Chapter 5). No matter what year of college you are currently in, you will find that many tips and strategies for each year of the plan can be useful and applied in any year of college. So please read the full plan, and apply it as it best suits your situation. While the plan is written for freshman to senior year, it is also written so that it can be adapted and applied by any student, no matter when he or she first reads the plan. In all, the comprehensive plan given in Section II can take away your "worrying" about what you need to do so that you can "concentrate" on mastering what you are doing. With that in mind, let's get planning.

SECTION II

What Should You Be Doing From Freshman To Senior Year?

CHAPTER 3

Freshman Year— Find a Direction

Welcome to College

"There isn't a child who hasn't gone out into the brave new world who eventually doesn't return to the old homestead carrying a bundle of dirty clothes."

Art Buchwald

For many of you, college will be your first experience away from home; for others, it is just another experience. Regardless, college is a unique experience that comes with unique expectations and challenges. College is like a job in that you should plan on putting in "full-time hours" of studying and class time. College is not like a job, however, in that you have full control over your time. Whether or not you attend classes or study is entirely up to you. You need to own responsibility for your actions.

Because college can be so informal, students often behave as they would around friends when they are around their professors. This approach is not a good idea. There are some basic rules of engagement that should be clarified before you begin even thinking about how to navigate your freshman year. For this reason, let's first look at some useful tips for how to effectively communicate with your professors and other faculty, staff, and administrators during your time in college.

Communicating Effectively

"Constantly talking isn't necessarily communicating."

Charlie Kaufman

A lot of success in college comes from simply doing the little things. Among these "little things" is to be appropriate. You need to recognize that your professors are good people to know. They can add you to their class, even when enrollment is full; they can help you create opportunities for research and internships; they assign grades in class; and eventually, you will need some of them to write a letter of recommendation for you. Many of these things—class enrollments, research, internships, and grades—fall within the Big Three identified in Chapter 2 and should therefore be important to you. You will only make it more difficult for yourself if you do not take advantage of the opportunity to get to know your professors.

The more your professors like you or think of you as studious and hardworking, the more they will want to help you achieve your goals. I understand that we like to think that we can do everything on our own, but in truth, you should take advantage of getting to know people who can help you achieve your goals and create opportunities that would otherwise not be possible. The human condition is a social one; it is one of collaboration, not isolation. Why not start collaborating in college?

Of course, to collaborate with your professors, you must effectively communicate with them. Effective communication with professors, staff, and school administrators can be key to successfully managing your time in college. Therefore, let's look at some basic rules for two common methods of communication between students and faculty: in e-mail and in conversation.

To communicate in e-mail, apply the following rules:

1. <u>When in doubt, write "Doctor" to a faculty member.</u> Not all professors have a doctoral degree, but if you are not sure, then call him or her a doctor until he or she corrects you. A doctor may be offended if you do not call him or her a doctor, but someone without a PhD is rarely going to be offended by being accidentally called a doctor. If anything, he or she will probably be flattered.

2. <u>Do not use texting language.</u> Your professor is not your friend. Treat him or her professionally. In your e-mails, use proper English, write complete sentences, and do not use inappropriate or offensive language.

3. <u>Be concise.</u> Professors receive many e-mails from many students. And for most professors, their teaching is only one aspect of their job. So be respectful of their time. Get to the point in your e-mail, but still be thorough enough to clarify the purpose or intent for your e-mail.

4. <u>Do not overuse e-mail.</u> Yes, you should keep it brief, but you also need to ask all of your questions in one e-mail. It can be frustrating for a professor to see multiple e-mails sent from the same student when the content in each e-mail could have been sent in a single e-mail. For example, if you have questions about an exam review, then send all your questions in one e-mail.

5. <u>Always include a subject line.</u> All too often students write hasty e-mails. Include a subject line to indicate the topic or purpose of your e-mail. Professors may not notice the subject line when you include one; but they will usually notice when it is left blank. To make a good impression, fill in the subject line.

6. <u>Always open an e-mail with a greeting.</u> Do not begin an e-mail to a professor with the actual content of your message. Start all e-mails with a greeting line,

such as "Dear Dr. Smith" or just "Dr. Smith." You then follow it with a comma or colon, press enter, and begin your message on a separate line. Adding a greeting line is a respectful gesture.

7. <u>Include a closing and/or an e-mail "signature."</u> When you have finished your message, press enter and add a closing, such as "Sincerely," "Regards," or "Thank you." You then follow it with a comma, press enter again, and write your name; or you can use your "signature" in place of your name. You can create an automatic "signature" for your e-mail usually found in an options tab in your e-mail account.

8. <u>Do not use e-mail to make a complaint or to dispute a grade.</u> E-mail is too informal and all too often exacerbates conflict rather than resolving it. Conflicts should never play out over e-mail. If you have a complaint or want to dispute a grade, pick up the phone or schedule a time to talk to your professor.

9. <u>Be aware of the "reply all" option.</u> If your professor sends an e-mail to multiple students, then be cognizant of whether you need to "reply all" (your message is sent to all those listed in the e-mail, including the sender) or hit "reply" (your message is only sent to the sender). Your professor will usually imply or state directly in his or her e-mail the type of response that is desired. It is typically important that the intended recipient or recipients receive your message.

10. <u>Be prompt in your response.</u> In some cases a response may be needed the same day, but as a general rule you should try to respond to all e-mails with 24 hours. If you cannot, then send a reply indicating that you have received the message and will reply in full as soon as possible. Doing so demonstrates professionalism and implies that you consider the e-mail important.

To communicate in conversation, apply the following rules:

1. <u>When in doubt, say "Doctor" to a faculty member.</u> Again, this makes it least likely that you will offend a professor.

2. <u>Listen.</u> Many studies show that a person will listen to less than a quarter of what is said before he or she formulates a response. Do not respond hastily; listen to everything your professor says before you respond. It is considerate to do so and shows that you respect what the professor is saying.

3. <u>Make eye contact.</u> One way to really show that you are listening is to make eye contact during conversation—when you are talking and when you are listening. Eye contact conveys that you are interested in the conversation—who wouldn't like that? It can sometimes feel awkward to hold eye contact continuously, so use the technique of alternating eye contact from one eye to the other. Another trick is to scan the area between the other person's eyebrows and nose. Alternating between eyes or scanning around the eyes can be more comfortable and achieves the same goal: to make eye contact.

4. <u>Do not interrupt.</u> It is all too common for a student to talk over a professor, interrupt a professor while he or she talks, or to talk about the same points over and over again, even when his or her professor has already addressed them. This goes back to simply listening. Wait for your professor to finish speaking or answer a question before you formulate a response. Doing so is viewed as considerate and respectful.

5. <u>Do not ask questions with answers that can be easily found in a syllabus or other readily available resource.</u> Find the answer yourself. For example, if the syllabus says that a book is assigned for the course, then do not ask your professor if you need a book for the course—yes, you do. Also, as another common example, do not ask your professor where his or her office is the first time you meet. The answer is in the syllabus, and the answer will be somewhere on the school website too. Do not waste your professor's time asking questions that you can find the answer to yourself.

6. <u>Be courteous.</u> Say "Please" and "Thank you." Use common courtesies. If a professor calls on you or asks if you agree with something, do not be rude in your response. Do not appear as if you do not care, do not make snarky comments, and do not act as if you are annoyed that you are being called upon. If you act as if you do not care about your professor's interests, then why would your professor care about your interests? Do not be rude; be courteous.

7. <u>Watch your body language.</u> Do not slouch in a chair when in class or when in your professor's office. Do not roll your eyes during class—even if you think the moment calls for it. Orient yourself toward the front of the class. Do not talk during class. If you bring your computer, then use it for class-related purposes only. Do not laugh or snicker with friends. Basically, do not give your professor the impression that you are not paying attention or that you are not on task. Appropriate body language is respectful, and if you want your professor to care about your interests, then be respectful to your professor.

8. <u>Use your words; watch your tone.</u> Speak clearly. Do not talk under your breath or mumble. Speak loudly so that others can hear you. Use a dynamic (not monotone) voice to be more engaging. Pronounce and use words correctly to avoid being perceived as less competent. If you are not sure how to say a word or if you are not sure of the definition of a word, then the best strategy is to simply not say it. Use a synonym or rephrase what it is that you want to say.

9. <u>Get to the point.</u> If you want to make a simple point, then make it simply. Be respectful of a professor's time by staying on topic and making points clearly that can be specifically related to the content being taught. Avoid backstories and off-topic discussions, unless these somehow illustrate a relevant point. Using a map analogy: Don't bring your professor through Miami, if you want to get from New York to Los Angeles.

10. <u>Share the conversation.</u> If your response is long, then add pauses throughout to see if anyone else will chime in. Let your professor talk. Do not do all the

talking. This is especially true in an interview. In an interview, the less you talk, the better the interview is probably going. People like to talk a lot when they get excited, so if the interviewer is doing most of the talking, then that probably means that he or she is excited about you. Don't get caught up in talking about yourself; when you are really great, you won't need to tell people; they will tell you.

Present Yourself Professionally

"And remember, no matter where you go, there you are."

Confucius

Part of communication is presentation. Again, college can be such an informal setting. Classes in the early morning are littered with students in their pajamas, and in the afternoon, many students come to class right out of the gym, or surprisingly right out of bed because of a "long night" they had the night before.

You need to get out of the mind-set that college classes are "just classes." When you are dressed in your pajamas or in workout clothes straight out of the gym, how do you think your professors see you? Again, get out of the trap of seeing the world from your own perspective. If you really want to create opportunity for yourself, then take the perspective of those who can create those opportunities for you—present yourself to them in the light in which you want to be seen.

To present yourself professionally, apply the following rules:

1. Dress as if you are going to work. Do not wear pajamas to class. Take the time to shower before class if you just worked out. Dress professionally or even casually, but look sharp. Some professors may even find it offensive if you wear a hat. Maybe your professors do not care what you wear, and that is very possible. But there is a good chance they will view you as lazy if you come wearing pajamas, for example; it is hard to imagine that such a negative stereotype will be created if you come to class wearing jeans or dress pants and a shirt tucked in.

2. Eat something before class. Even with the best of intentions, it can be difficult to stay awake in class. Eating before class or bringing a small snack (if you are allowed to eat in class) can help you stay awake. If you notice that you are dozing off, then ask to be excused for a moment, gather yourself, stretch, get a drink of water, and come back to class refreshed. You want to always give the impression that you are attentive during class.

3. Turn your cell phone off or on silent mode. Whether you are in class or in your professor's office, it is unprofessional to interrupt your professor's time with the ringing of your cell phone. This problem is easily avoidable; turn your phone off or put it on silent mode.

4. <u>Do not fidget toward the end of class.</u> With one or two minutes left in class, students, almost on cue, begin to pack up, even when the professor is still talking. Do not join the masses. Be disciplined. Stay in your seat, look forward, and write notes—until your professor is finished. Fidgeting around toward the end of class has no benefit to you. The professor is not going to dismiss everyone simply because some students decided to be rude and disrupt the end of his or her lecture. Being that student who is still attentive to his or her lecture can go a long way in connecting with your professor.

5. <u>Give a firm handshake.</u> When meeting your professor, offer a firm handshake, greet him or her, introduce yourself, and pay a compliment if possible. For example, offer a firm handshake and say, "How do you do, Dr. Smith? My name is Sam, and I am excited to be in this course; it really interests me." Adding a firm handshake to this formal introduction indicates that you are confident and that your dialogue is genuine.

6. <u>Do not eat while speaking.</u> Whether in person or over the phone, do not eat while speaking. Even if you do end up being able to speak clearly (not likely), it is still considered disrespectful, so do not get into the practice of doing it. Also, when making a phone call, try to find a quiet place to call, if possible, to avoid background noise and distractions.

7. <u>Use appropriate examples in conversation.</u> Discussing your exploits over the weekend is not an appropriate topic in class, even if such an experience actually applies to the topic being taught. I'm not saying you can never share this. But ask yourself first, "Do I want my professor to know this about me?" If the answer is no, then do not share it with your professor.

8. <u>To dispute a grade, take responsibility first.</u> You need to take responsibility for your own grade. You would be amazed at how willing a professor is to review and/or change your grade, if you first take responsibility for that grade. Blaming your professor only increases the chances that he or she will become defensive, shut down, and no longer be willing to help you.

Keep in mind that the rules given in this book are not exhaustive of all rules you could follow. If you see other ways in which you can present yourself in a better light, then do it. The takeaway message is simple: Present yourself as you would want to be perceived by taking the perspective of those who can create opportunities for you. You want to get your professor to *want* to help you—taking his or her perspective can go a long way in achieving this goal.

Also, consider that the results from employer surveys across the country show that communication is the most desirable skill set among employers. The following is a summary of the most desired communication skills, adapted from a list provided by the career development center at Binghamton University:

✓ <u>Verbal:</u> Develop your vocabulary and do not use slang. Take turns when speaking, and do not dominate the conversation.

- ✓ <u>Nonverbal:</u> Keep good posture, make eye contact, be respectful of facial expressions and personal space or distance, smile, and give full attention to the speaker to convey that he or she is important.
- ✓ <u>Written:</u> Be polite, concise, and error-free (proofread!).
- ✓ <u>Listening:</u> Limit talking, show an interest, ask to-the-point questions, and do not interrupt.

Notice that the rules shared in this book fit nicely with what employers will look for anyway in your communication skill set. Hence, you will need to apply these skills eventually. Therefore, start applying these basic rules of communication now—to create opportunity in college by presenting yourself in the light in which you want to be seen.

Effective communication is very important. You never know what opportunities can arise each day, so be considerate of what you can control: your actions. The rules shared in this book are aimed at a communication style that will allow you to seize opportunity as you navigate your years in college by building relationships with many professors who can work with you to help you achieve your goals. You should always take advantage of getting to know people who can help you achieve your goals and create opportunities that would otherwise not be possible.

Carpe Diem: A True Story of How Communication Led to a PhD

"Confidence in the absence of humility is arrogance."

Gregory J. Privitera

As evidence of the importance of the rules of communication, allow me to share with you the true story of an undergraduate student who was accepted into a PhD program without applying most of the lessons in this book, except to embrace the communication rules stated already in this chapter.

Not too long ago there was an undergraduate student (we will call him Greg) who worked hard and did well, but was having difficulty finding a path—something he should have found in his freshman year. Greg was majoring in psychology and had a 4.00 GPA in his major and a 3.98 GPA overall. He was a very good student. By now, though, it was the second semester of his senior year. He had yet to apply to a single graduate school, or even a job. He had not taken the GRE, although he did have some ambitions to attend law school and had taken the LSAT a few months earlier. But alas, he simply wasn't sure. So, he decided to take the next year off before going back to school. That is, until something extraordinary happened.

You see, Greg also was very respectful. In one course in particular in the second semester of his senior year, he was doing quite well. Even though he rarely had questions about the material taught in class, he still made occasional visits to his instructor's office hours to ask questions and let the instructor know just how much he enjoyed the class. Greg always completed his assignments on time and aced every exam in class. He read the textbook from cover to cover and studied to do well. He asked questions and actively participated in class. As you can imagine, his professor also enjoyed having him in class. Greg did very well, as one would expect; he scored an A.

In the final exam week in May of the year he would graduate, he went to his scheduled exam time to take the final exam for this class he enjoyed so much. He took his time on the exam, as he usually did, and double-checked his answers before turning it in. After completing the final exam, he handed it in to his instructor, and let him know (one last time) that he really enjoyed his class. Greg went out of his way, as he usually did, to respect his instructor. And as he walked away, he heard someone from behind him call out, "Greg, hold on; wait one minute!"

The voice from behind him was the voice of his instructor. It turns out that his instructor was very impressed by him, and—as should be obvious—really enjoyed having a student in class who expressed such an interest in the topic taught. He knew that Greg worked hard and was always prepared for class. He was quite impressed with the young student and enjoyed the fact that Greg always expressed an interest in the material taught. Now he had something quite extraordinary to offer Greg:

"How would you like to earn a PhD in this field? We have an opening in our labs, and you seem like just the kind of student we are looking for. I really enjoyed having you in class this semester," he explained.

In that moment, in May of his graduating year, Greg realized that he was being offered an opportunity to earn a PhD starting in the fall, which was only a few months away. He had no plans for this; he didn't even believe he was "PhD material" to be quite honest. He hadn't taken the GRE; he hadn't applied to any other graduate schools; he had no intention of going to graduate school for that matter. But none of this mattered any more; Greg now had an opportunity to earn a PhD.

The instructor of his course happened to be the top graduate assistant in the labs of a major researcher at the university. When he shared Greg's name with his advisor, Greg was immediately interviewed and told to take the GRE and sub-mit an application for the program. Greg was allowed to submit his application and was accepted within about a month of applying. That fall, he was offered and accepted a full tuition scholarship and stipend at that major research university to earn his PhD in psychology—and all because an instructor "really enjoyed having him in class."

It's not a matter of why; it's a matter of why not? How much added time to your day does it really take to apply these communication rules? And yet the payoff if you do could be huge. In Greg's case, which is a true story, the payoff was an offer and acceptance to a PhD program in psychology. Greg would go on to earn his PhD four years later and is now a tenured professor, and the author of many research articles and books—including this book. The takeaway message is to always recognize the real possibility that how you act can substantially impact what you can achieve.

Five Goals for Your First Year in College

"Man is a goal seeking animal. His life only has meaning if he is reaching out and striving for his goals."

Aristotle

There are key goals you will want to pursue in your freshman year. This is your year to find a direction and to build a strong foundation for pursing opportunity in your sophomore and junior years. This chapter is organized by using each goal stated here as a heading. A full range of ideas, plans, and templates will be shared to help you meet and exceed each goal. In all, there are five key goals you should have listed and be actively working toward in your freshman year:

1. Get acquainted (with the college and resources available). Visit buildings on campus, find your classes, and introduce yourself to people you will want to know, such as your advisor.

2. Know your major requirements (so that you can *plan* to graduate). If you are going to have a plan in college, then you need to at least know what you need to do to graduate—so that you can *plan* to graduate.

3. Find good study habits (that you can use throughout college). It is easy to fall into the trap of poor study habits. The best way to avoid this is to make a concerted effort to establish good study habits early in college.

4. Make friends; choose carefully (surround yourself with supporters). Do not follow crowds simply because they are "popular." Popularity is a form of success that is seldom worth the things you have to do to obtain it.

5. Choose your career path (and stay committed to it). Think of college as a road map. You have the map—now plot a course. First, you need to identify "what you want to be when you grow up" so that you can plot your path or course to achieve what it is you want to be.

Get Acquainted

"[A person] must go without his familiars in order to be open to influences, to change."

Katharine Butler Hathaway

When you decide on a college, make sure you research it. You want to know what the college has to offer in terms of supporting your overall experiences at college. So often I hear students say, "Oh, I didn't even realize we had that." Well, you should know. All you basically need is a campus map and your student records—you can take it from there. To help you, the following is a list of things that you should and can do even before your first week of classes:

- Get to know the campus. Find a campus map and do a walk-through. The campus map is likely going to be available on the college website. Pick a day to walk (or drive) to all the buildings. Eliminate the worry of "not knowing" where classes are by getting familiar with the setting where you will spend years of your life in college. If you don't have time, then as a shortcut make sure you try to visit the following buildings:

  o Gym. Find hours of operation and scope out the equipment and layout of the gym. There may even be more than one gym on your campus.
  o Libraries. Libraries can be general, or contain content only from specific disciplines (e.g., law library). Visit each library to see which library will be most helpful to you.
  o Department offices. Whatever your major is, your professors will likely all have faculty offices together in the same building. You will likely visit a lot of these offices, so find them.
  o Teaching and learning center. This is a key area for finding tutoring and help. You will want to know where to find this building on campus.
  o Health and counseling center. Many colleges offer health and counseling services free to their students. Why not take advantage of this? If you have a headache or need someone to talk to, these services are likely available on campus. Find them.
  o Campus security. It can't hurt to know where the security services are on campus. An emergency can be serious or small, like locking your keys in your car. But if you do have an emergency, it will be good to know where campus security services are, and have their number in your speed dial.

- Do a walk-through of your classes. Grab your class enrollment information, and find all of your classrooms. All too often, students arrive late to class on the first day because they had trouble finding the classroom. There is no need to be late. Just do a run-through of your class schedule before the first day of classes.

- Do not throw away your syllabus. For each course, it is required that a professor provide you with a syllabus. At a minimum all syllabi should include the name and purpose of the course, the faculty member's contact information, office hours, required textbooks, an outline of the topics that will be covered, and attendance, testing, and grading policies. It is a contract for the course. You will need to refer to it from time to time, so always have one available.

- Buy your textbooks *before* you get to class. Purchase your books before classes begin, if possible. Your classes have specific course and section numbers that distinguish them. Go to the campus library and show a clerk the course numbers for your courses. The clerk can often lead you to the books you will need, even if you haven't seen the syllabus.

- Seek advisement. Visit your advisor's office. In smaller colleges, this person will likely be a faculty member in the department; in larger colleges, he or she will likely be someone hired to just do advisement. Regardless, find that person and say hello. Your advisor will appreciate the rarity of a student's taking the initiative to meet him or her!

The key to your first week of classes is to make a smooth transition to college. Following the tips listed here will make your experience more fun and less stressful. You will begin to plant seeds of good habits and meet many of the people you will want to get to know anyway while at college.

Know Your Major Requirements

"Education is what survives when what has been learned has been forgotten."

B. F. Skinner

Many freshman college students will have already chosen a major; others will be undecided. Many freshman students who have chosen a major will likely change their major while in college. Choosing a major, and committing to it, can be one of the greatest challenges for many college students. However, regardless of whether you have chosen your major, you need to have a plan for what courses to take in your freshman year. First, let's look at the reality of registering for courses as a freshman.

Almost all schools have enrollment procedures that give preference to seniors, juniors, sophomores, and then freshmen. Preference is given by allowing seniors to register before any other student, then juniors, then sophomores, and then freshmen. This means that you will most likely register after all other students have finished registering, if you are a freshman. The obvious result is the frustrating reality that many courses you will want to enroll in will be closed—because the upperclassmen have already filled those courses. You are not likely to get the exact schedule you want as a freshman student, and this is true for just about any college or university you could attend.

One way to get around the problem of enrolling in a "closed" course is to contact the professor of that course and request to be added. Two ways you can go about this are (1) e-mail the professor your request and (2) request in person. The first option can work, but it is a lot easier for a professor to say no in an e-mail than in person. Also, to be added to a class that is closed often requires that you complete a course enrollment or "drop/add" form to be signed by the professor of the class that is closed. For this reason, the second option can be better because you can come prepared to have that form signed. To apply this option, get the required form and fill it in. Then, on the first day of classes, attend the class you want to enroll in. At the end of the class, introduce yourself to the professor, and make the following request with that completed form in hand (anywhere there is a bracket, you can change the wording to fit your name, or the name of your professor):

"Hello Dr. [Smith]. My name is [Greg]. I have heard great things about your course and teaching. I would like very much to take this class, but it is unfortunately full. I'm a hard worker, and I would be very grateful if I could add into your class and learn from you. I have the required form completed here; all I would need is your signature to add in. Would this be OK?"

It is always effective to compliment the professor. To be truthful here, just make sure during class you ask a few students about the professor. If you hear a lot of good things, then you are being honest when you pay the professor the compliment. If you hear a lot of bad things—then maybe it is a sign that you should avoid that class and not request to be added! Either way, making the request in person is most effective because it is hard for a professor to say no in person to a student who says, "I really like your teaching and your course." Many professors will sign the form or at least consider it.

No matter what course you want to enroll in, have contingency plans. Plan on not getting into at least one course you want, and have a contingency plan for other courses you can take. In all, the types of courses you can take to graduate can be classified into three broad categories:

1. Major requirements. The major requirements for your major will be listed on the department website for the school and in the handbook for your university. You can also visit your advisor or the registrar's office at any time to get a copy of the requirements for your major. Requirements can vary substantially from one school to the next, although you will likely be required to complete about 30 to 36 credit hours of coursework in your major.

2. General education requirements. General education ("Gen Ed") requirements are required to graduate in general, and can include courses in art, biology, physics, chemistry, language, literature, English, social sciences, history, and more. For a list of specific courses you need to take at your institution, visit the registrar's office or your advisor. These requirements will also be listed on your school's website. When you add the "Gen Ed" requirements with your major requirements, these usually total around 60 credits, or a little more. To graduate, however, you will need to complete 120 credit hours of total coursework.

3. Electives. The remaining requirements are electives, which are any courses you want to take—so that you can reach the "120 requirement." Some schools or majors require a little more than 120 credit hours to graduate, so make sure to check this requirement. Regardless, if you have only one major, then you will have upwards of 50 to 60 or more credit hours of electives.

If you are committed to your major, then take major requirements if you can. In fact, take many more major requirements than are required. If you are still undecided, then take general education requirements or electives first because those courses will count toward graduation for any major you decide on.

Also, most schools offer an option to enroll in an honors program in which you take honors courses each year and are also typically required to complete an honors thesis in your senior year. It is extra work to complete the honors requirements to graduate with honors, but it can be worth it. Graduating with honors helps you stand out among your peers because few students graduate with honors. Details for how to meet the honors criteria and apply for the program at your school should be provided on your school website. Once you have committed to a major or enrolled in an honors program, you can narrow your coursework to major-related courses so that you can *prepare* for graduate school and *plan* to graduate on time.

Find Good Study Habits

"Don't ever let anyone tell you that college is for smart people. College eats smart people alive."

Hannah Moskowitz, *Invincible Summer*

Whether you are going to college straight out of high school or returning after years away from school, you need to find good study habits. And, yes, it is very possible that what worked in high school will not work in college. Even if you think your study habits are good—college is different.

High school is required (at least up to 16 years of age). Unless you received a private school education, students did not compete to get into your high school. Instead, they got in based on where they lived. For this reason, you competed against students who were very good and very poor. Being among the best in your high school was likely easier than it will be to be among the best in college because colleges have a selection process. Many colleges accept only a certain group of students based on test scores. The better the college or university you were accepted to, the higher the standards—and the better the students. In many cases, you are competing against the top 15% of high school students. From this perspective, to be the best, you need to be near the top of the top 15% in many cases. Hence, as illustrated in Figure 3.1, keep in mind that you are competing only against the students who were accepted to your college, and these students were typically among the best as high school students.

Very good high school students fail out of college each year. Why? Often, because they could "get away with" limited studying in high school, and so they thought the same would be true in college. No. College is more fun in many ways because you have so much greater freedom to choose classes and pursue your goals. However, it is also more challenging because the students you compete against are likely a "smarter" group than the group you competed against in high school. One important way to adapt to this change is to improve your study habits. To help you get started, here are 12 useful and effective strategies for improving your study habits:

1. Study as you go. Attend classes assuming that what is taught will be tested. Study the material as you learn it to reduce time spent studying later and to avoid "cramming" for tests.

2. Schedule "study times" each day. Add studying to your schedule same as you add your classes. Making studying a part of your schedule can help ensure that you get it done. As a rule, schedule at least two hours of studying each week for each course, depending on your schedule and workload.

Figure 3.1   The approximate normal distribution of students by academic achievement in high school and the relatively small portion at the top who are selected to many colleges

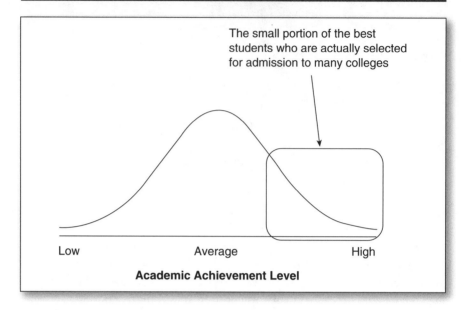

The small portion of the best students who are actually selected for admission to many colleges

Low   Average   High

Academic Achievement Level

3. Rank or prioritize your classes to help you organize your study time. You have only so many hours in a day to study. You need to have a plan for how much study time to devote to each class. Prioritize your classes by importance and difficulty level. Take these factors into account when deciding how much time to devote to studying for each course.

4. Preplan short breaks during studying, perhaps every 20 to 30 minutes, if needed. You can even make this fun. For example, if you have many pages to read, then reward yourself every few pages, such as by eating a jelly bean or some other treat you enjoy—to help motivate you to finish the reading. Breaking readings or other assignments into smaller chunks can make studying more manageable and fun.

5. Find *your* "study place." If you want to make studying a natural part of what you do, then having a place to study can help make studying routine—in the same way having a place for classes makes attending class routine. Your study place can be anywhere you choose. If you prefer a little background noise, then you can play music while you study; if not, then find a quiet place to study so that you do not lose focus, such as in a library.

6. Wake up early each day and spend that time reading or doing work. If your goal is to wake up by 9 a.m., then wake up an hour earlier instead to get some reading or coursework done. In all, try to gain about five or more hours of studying each week during times you would have just slept anyway.

7. Drink water and have a healthy snack during studying to keep yourself from dozing off. Studying can be fun, and it can also be long and tedious. Bringing a snack can energize you; after all, studying burns calories!

8. Study with a purpose. Make an effort to really *know* the material you study. Do not cram; what you recall quickly diminishes within an hour. Read (the content), write (it out), and recite (to yourself) as you study to enhance long-term recall. Use tabs or highlighters to mark key content to make it easier to find and review the content later.

9. "Date" your notes. A professor often spends more time talking about topics that will be tested more. Jot down in the margins of your notes the start and end times of each topic. The more time your professor spends on a topic, the more important it generally is—and the more likely it will be tested.

10. Don't stop studying until you get 100% twice. Test yourself until you are at 100%; then stop. The next day, or at least one hour later, test yourself again. When you get 100% both times, you know the material very well. This level of studying can help you master the material and thus reduce unnecessary mistakes on an exam or assessment.

11. Study with a friend or in a group. Preferably work with a friend or group of students who are doing well in the class, particularly if you are struggling in that class. In this setting, you gain the advantage of learning with others who likewise know the material.

12. Communicate with your professor for important questions. Your professor wrote the test; go to him or her for help. Write your professor an e-mail to get your answers, or visit him or her during office hours. Your professor knows what *you* need to know—ask your professor to get the most credible and reliable answers to your questions.

A final important suggestion to get you started is to know your learning style. The concept of "learning styles" comes from the meticulous work on multiple intelligences by Harvard University professor Howard Gardner. At a basic level, you can prefer a visual (seeing), an auditory (hearing), a kinesthetic (moving, animated), or a tactile (touch) way of learning. One predominant view identifies seven learning styles in total. Each learning style comes with recommendations for how you can set up your learning environment to study more effectively. For more information on these and more recommendations, you can visit the Institute for Learning Styles Research at www.learningstyles.org. You can also visit the British Council at www.teachingenglish.org.uk/print/413 for more information and useful recommendations.

If you want to be competitive for graduate schools, odds are that you will have to improve your study habits in college. Studying is likely to be a daily routine. Indeed, if you want to avoid overwhelming yourself every time there is an exam or assignment due (which can be often), then making studying a *daily* routine can help you manage your time and help you keep pace with coursework so that you do not get overwhelmed. Using the strategies and resources given here can help you get started to find good study habits and improve your grades in college.

Make Friends; Choose Carefully

"It is better to be alone than in bad company."

George Washington

Whether you live in a dormitory or at home, you are very likely to meet new people in college. It is good to make friends and have fun. But remember, you are not paying tuition to make friends; you are paying tuition to create opportunities for success after college. Do not make friends or follow crowds simply because they are "popular." Popularity is a form of success that is seldom worth the things you have to do to obtain it.

Have fun, but also be responsible—get your work done first; then go out, relax, and have some fun. Often, college can turn into so much fun that students allow their fun to overtake their hard work. You cannot allow this to happen. The people you hang out with can have a significant impact on your behavior and your priorities. For this reason, consider the following four vital tips for choosing your friends wisely:

■ Socialize in places other than bars and clubs. You need to make friends and be productive while at college. Good people hang out at bars and clubs, but how many A students do you really think make bars and clubs a routine part of their life in college? Play the odds, and go out of your way to meet people elsewhere. Find a student in class who is doing very well, and introduce yourself. Go to a library or a coffee shop to meet people. Find other places that students are known to study in, and meet people there. The goal is to make friends with people who can help you achieve your goals—not get in the way. Having the wrong friends can be counterproductive to your goals.

■ Find friends who "pick you up." A common phrase is that you can take one step to find the next person who will tell you what you can't do in life; you can walk miles before you find the next person who will tell you what you can do. It can be discouraging to make friends with people who are negative or critical of your goals and aspirations. Friends can make negative comments or be discouraging in your time of need. They can try to get you to "go out" even when it is in your best interest to stay in. Be selective when choosing friends. Find friends who support you; it will make college a lot more enjoyable.

■ Be an observer of people's behavior. Your friends are a reflection of who you are. So often you are judged as much by the behavior of your friends as by your own behavior. You are ultimately responsible for the friends you choose. Choosing the wrong friends can even cost you opportunities. For example, suppose you and a friend meet with your professor. If, in that meeting, your "friend" is disrespectful, your professor may also view you as disrespectful, making it more difficult to now connect with that professor. Watch how your friends behave and treat others. Avoid making "friends" with people who can sabotage your success, and choose those friends who can set you up for success.

- Choose friends who "fit" into your schedule. Friends should be supportive of your goals and interests. Make time for your friends, and make sure they support your need to make time for them. For example, find friends who have the same classes as you or do the same extracurricular activities as you. Find friends whom you can go to lunch with, or even study with at times that are convenient for you. If you do not share many interests or activities with your friends, then it can cause many conflicts that you simply will want to avoid. It will be easier for you in the long run to choose friends who "fit" your schedule.

Friendships can certainly be spontaneous, and so can relationships. You will experience many spontaneous moments in life, and often those moments can result in long-lasting friendships. If you meet friends who are important to you but who do not "fit" with the criteria of choosing wisely, then try to find a compromise. Regardless, you cannot just sacrifice your own goals and time for your friends. That is not fair to you, and your friends should understand. Find a balance between your friends and your education. You can have the best of both worlds if you make friends and choose carefully.

Choose Your Career Path

"What we see depends mainly on what we look for."

John Lubbock

Ultimately, it is in your best interest to find a definite career path or direction in your freshman year. You can, of course, change your mind later, but you will likely find greater opportunity in your sophomore and junior years if you find your path now. It can admittedly be difficult to commit to a career path, particularly for students enrolling in college right out of high school. But also ask yourself—and be honest—how much time and effort do you really spend researching different career paths?

In your freshman year, you need to set aside a few hours each week to research career paths—and continue researching a few hours each week until you find a direction or career path. Indeed, you should do this in any academic year until you find a definite career path. Once you know your career path, you can pursue opportunities to help you compete for graduate schools in that field, and this book will show you how to realize those opportunities. In your search, the following suggestions can prove helpful as you do your research:

1. Choose a career for the happiness, not the money. Finding meaningful work is a lot more rewarding than finding work to make you rich. Of course, the job you love may also pay a high salary—great, but make sure it is a job

you love. Your career is presumably a lifetime commitment, and it is not worth the pursuit to be miserable for a lifetime. Money makes you rich, not happy.

2. Examine your interests; narrow your search; explore career options. Begin your search with an open mind. There are many more careers out there than you are probably aware of, so search for any career to start. In psychology alone, there are many fields to choose from—any job that involves "people behaving" is a field of psychology. Once you have identified your interests, you can narrow them before deciding on a career or researching it further.

3. Interview people who do the work you find interesting. You can call or e-mail a person in the field and meet with him or her. Have questions prepared to gain insights into whether or not the field is right for you. Or you can take this option one step further and actually volunteer to work or find an internship to "try out" the job yourself. Too often, students change a major because they decided on the major before they "tried it." Try the job and see if you like it. This simple step can help you choose a major and a career that is right for you.

4. Take your time; be patient. Keep in mind that to keep pace with the freshman-to senior-year plan in this book, you are given a full year to find your direction. Take your time and be patient. If you follow this plan starting in your freshman year, then devoting just three hours a week (less than 30 minutes a day) to researching a career path means that you will spend over 160 hours doing research. If you start this plan a little later, then you can put more hours in per week to get caught up. Regardless, you can certainly research a career path in that kind of time—and if you cannot, then so be it. Continue doing your research each week until you find a career path that most interests *you*.

Much of your searching can be simple Google searches: Just enter key words that relate to possible careers of interest to you. That is a great way to begin a search. As you find more resources, you can zero in on specific materials that may provide greater detail about a direction that interests you. Regardless, know that you have time to complete this search and find a path or direction. There is a good reason that a full year is given to achieve this—it can be harder than it looks to decide on what you want to be when you grow up. Now is the time to answer this important question. Make an effort to find your answer, and to begin your pursuit of your career path.

Transitioning to Sophomore Year

"A map with no legend—they'd have one now."

Eric Beeny, *Snowing Fireflies*

Many tips and strategies have been shared in this chapter to help you find a direction in your freshman year. Overall, the goals provided here are aimed at helping you present yourself to professors in the most positive light. Communicating effectively with professors, getting into good habits, finding the right friends, and finding a direction will go a long way in helping you to realize opportunities that can help you reach your goals. Once you have achieved your freshman goals, you are ready to pursue opportunities. If you achieve your freshman goals early, then read ahead and start applying your skills to create opportunities now.

Think of your freshman year as a time when you choose your desired destination (i.e., your major or career path). Once you have chosen your destination, this book shows you the routes you can take to get there, and goes even further to show you how to travel each route. Essentially, think of this book as a map legend. A map legend is a key that identifies the meaning of symbols and routes in a map. In the same way, this book shows you how to pursue opportunities to reach your destination (the routes) and also how to recognize and realize those opportunities (the meaning). For many of you, it is in your sophomore and junior years when you will pursue, recognize, and realize opportunities. In the next chapter, you will find that opportunity is everywhere—find a direction, and the opportunities you seek can be realized.

CHAPTER 4

Sophomore and Junior Years: Pursue Opportunities

Recognize Opportunity

"A wise man will make more opportunities than he finds."

Francis Bacon, *The Essays*

By following through with the goals for your freshman year in Chapter 3, you became acquainted with your college, realized your major requirements, found good study habits, chose supportive friends, and found your path or direction for a career. These may not seem like big feats, but by meeting these goals, you will likely have realized more opportunities in your sophomore and junior years, which is exactly what you need to do in these years: pursue opportunities.

While we tend to think of "opportunity" as something concrete, it is not. There are many ways in which opportunity "knocks," so to speak. To break this down, let's look at two basic types of opportunity you can pursue:

1. <u>You can seek opportunity that is made available to you.</u> For example, you can enroll in a course that still has seats open, or you can apply for an internship that is posted on a university notice board. The majority of students will wait around for opportunities like these; they will think they have exhausted their search for opportunities by looking only for those that are made available to them, but they are wrong.

2. <u>You can also seek out opportunity you create yourself.</u> For example, if the class you want is full, then you can contact the professor and ask if he or she will add you anyway; if no internships are available, you can find people for whom you'd like to work and propose an internship. These strategies work just as well and can be just as prestigious, but are pursued less often.

Opportunity is any occasion in which one can advance his or her goals, even if the person who stands to advance his or her goals is the one who created such an occasion. While we tend to think of opportunity as something to be found waiting, it is more than this; it is any occasion in which one can advance his or her goals—to include occasions of opportunity that we create ourselves.

Whether you are competing for academics, scholarship, or activities (i.e., the Big Three; see Chapter 2), there are many ways to "compete" for these opportunities, and not all of them involve waiting around for opportunities to "come knocking." In this chapter, you will be shown how to compete for opportunities that are made available to you, and also how to create opportunities when none are otherwise available. Opportunity is treated as dynamic, with many possible ways shown to find it and to create it.

Believe in Your Pursuits

"Whether you think you can or think you can't—you are right."

Henry Ford

As you pursue opportunity, not only is it important to realize that opportunity is something you can literally create, but you also need to believe in your pursuits. You need to believe that the opportunities you seek are possible—that they are something you can achieve. To achieve great things, you must believe that you can achieve them. I don't care where you think you stand in comparison to your peers; you can compete for graduate schools—believe that!

Whether or not you appreciate it, your belief in yourself largely guides your actions. As a personal reflection, when I was younger I did not believe in my abilities in school. As a result, I graduated high school toward the bottom of my class and decided to pursue a career in the U.S. Marine Corps. I served four years in a variety of units and finished my service in the infantry. My time serving in the U.S. Marine Corps was a great experience for me, in part, because it is where I learned to believe in my own abilities—I simply applied that belief when I returned to school. In college, I had much greater success than in high school. My grades in college put me near the top of my graduating class, and I eventually went on to earn a PhD. My "ability" in high school and in college was the same, but my belief in my own abilities changed drastically—and thus so did my success when I entered college. The same can be true for you, if you only give yourself a chance. A belief in oneself enables one to believe in his or her own abilities and success.

This chapter in particular will reveal to you many different ways to realize and create opportunities. Believe in your pursuits; take action—in all that you do. For example, you may not ask a person out on a date because you do not believe he or she wants to "go out" with you; you may not apply for a job because you do not believe the employer will offer you the job; you may stop putting in time to study for a course because you do not believe your efforts will improve your grade. In each case, your *beliefs* largely guide your *actions*. Realize that the biggest critic of your life will most likely end up being *you*. Stop criticizing and start encouraging. Stop being pessimistic and start being optimistic. Start believing; start taking action. It can be your first step toward finding your own success.

Seven Goals for Your Sophomore and Junior Years in College

"Man is a goal seeking animal. His life only has meaning if he is reaching out and striving for his goals."

Aristotle

There are key goals you will want to pursue in your sophomore and junior years. These are the years for pursuing opportunity and building your résumé to be competitive for graduate schools. This chapter is organized by using each goal stated here as a heading. A full range of ideas, plans, and templates will be shared to help you meet and achieve each goal. In all, there are seven key goals you should have listed and be actively working toward in your sophomore and junior years:

1. Get connected (to establish professional contacts). Connect with professors. Establish *professional* contacts. Your sophomore and junior years are the time to shift from being "a student" to being "a colleague." Foster positive relationships with those who can help you achieve your goals.

2. Pursue scholarship (and apply for scholarships). Research, teaching assistant positions, internships, employment, and more can and should be pursued. Knowing where to look can be just as important as competing for these opportunities.

3. Find opportunities to present and publish (if possible). Find opportunities to present at conferences and publish in peer-reviewed journals, if possible. These types of achievements can substantially help you stand out because these achievements are often hard to find for undergraduate students, and rarely achieved.

4. Pursue activities and international studies (to show an interest in your field). Once you have a college GPA for a full year, you can typically qualify to join societies and clubs in your field of interest. Join these clubs and be actively involved in them. Pursue studies internationally, if you can afford this option, to further gain experience and demonstrate an interest in your field of study.

5. Write a résumé or curriculum vitae (and revise it as you go). Write a résumé, or curriculum vitae, as it is called in academia, as early as your sophomore year and revise it through your time in college and into your career. Use your

résumé as a template for what you need to achieve to be competitive for graduate schools. Use it to guide the opportunities you pursue.

6. Keep track of your GPA. Your GPA is important, and there are ways to improve your GPA and to maintain your GPA if it is already high.

7. Prepare to take the GRE or other standardized exams (to be taken in the summer before your senior year). It is best to take all standardized exams *before* your senior year—be proactive and prepare early.

Get Connected

"The antidote for fifty enemies is one friend."

Aristotle

By your sophomore year it is definitely time to get serious about making connections—no, not connections with your friends, but connections with professionals, such as professors, who can help you achieve your goals. How does this benefit you? Well, consider that professors likely know other professors at other universities; many were accepted to PhD programs, so they could give you advice or share insights to help you get accepted to a graduate program; they teach courses for which you could be a teaching assistant; they have research labs for which you could be a research assistant; the list of reasons why it is common sense to connect with your professors could go on and on. The takeaway message is that it benefits *you* to take time to get to know your professors.

Another very important reason to make professional connections is that you will eventually need strong letters of recommendation (LORs) to be competitive for graduate schools. A "strong" LOR is not one written by a family member or a friend; it is not one written by a professor who barely knows you; it is usually not one written by a professor who has little expertise in the area or discipline for which you are applying. A "strong" LOR is one written by someone who knows you very well in a professional capacity. As a general rule, the person writing your LOR for graduate school should know you for at least two full years. The person writing your LOR should also meet at least one of the following additional criteria:

■ He or she has expertise related to the discipline for which you are applying. For example, if you plan to apply to social psychology programs, then you will want to have a social psychologist write one of your LORs.

■ He or she has advised you in research or teaching. Scholarship is a big factor to help you get accepted into graduate school. However, it is often difficult to highlight exactly what expertise you gained while working on scholarship, so you will want one LOR to be written by a person who can speak to your accomplishments in this area.

■ He or she can speak to your "intangibles" based on shared experiences. The "intangibles" are your desirable traits and characteristics that are often hard to defend or explain with concrete examples. For example, "intangibles" such as work ethic, drive, motivation, dedication, leadership, critical thinking skills, and commitment are all desirable traits to a selection committee. However, demonstrating those traits can be difficult on paper. It will help if you have someone who has observed these "intangibles" in action—someone like a coach who can observe your leadership on the playing field, or a lab manager who can speak to your critical thinking skills demonstrated in your ability to evaluate and resolve problems in the lab.

Keep in mind that it is in your best interest to develop professional relationships with professors, and even administrators. What is important is to match your professional connections with your interests for graduate school. For example, suppose you work for a university organization, such as an orientation leader. The administrator running this program may be a good person to know and a good person to write your LOR if you apply to programs related to organizations—such as organizational psychology or organizational behavior, or even business programs. However, if you apply to programs that have little to do with organizations—a health psychology program, for example—then the orientation program administrator is not the "best" person to write your LOR; an administrator at a hospital would be better suited to write your LOR in this case. The take-home message is simple: You need to be strategic about the professional connections you make in college. You need to connect with people who know you well and who have relevant interests and expertise in the field you want to pursue in graduate school.

Graduate school selection committees know when they read an LOR written by someone who barely knew you. And it does not reflect well on you if you can't find at least three strong LORs to support your application. The impression from the selection committees is that if you cannot find at least three people who know you well enough to write an LOR for you, then you must not have been very involved in college. The simple solution is to start making connections now. The following are three tips for making professional connections with professors and administrators:

1. Take their classes; express an interest; go to their office hours. Take a page from your freshman plan in Chapter 3. Express an interest in your professor, and he or she will likely express an interest in you. If a professor's interests fit well with your goals for graduate school, then take as many classes as possible with him or her. On a few occasions, take the time to compliment his or her course or teaching, such as during his or her office hours. The purpose of doing so is to make clear that you share in the same interests as your professor. Do not leave it to your professor to "connect the dots." Make sure you attend office hours on a few occasions. This is one-on-one time with your professor; it is where you can specifically connect with your professor's interests—where you can pursue "Big Three" opportunities, as described later in this chapter.

2. Be proactive; try not to be shy. Before the semester begins, "stop by" your professor's office to say hello. If you want to get involved in academic clubs or programs, then visit the offices of the administrators who run those clubs and

programs to express an interest and ask how to get involved. Initiative is a virtue that is highly regarded—you can make strong connections with faculty and administrators by being the one who takes the initiative to meet them and get to know them.

3. Join a professional network, such as LinkedIn. It could be inappropriate to request to be added to a professor's personal social networking site, but a professional site, such as LinkedIn, would be much more appropriate. One advantage of doing this is that you can stand out among your peers because not too many students think to connect to professors in this way. Always be careful, of course, when joining even a professional networking site, to only include information about you that you are willing to share with everyone.

The strategies listed here are simple ways to start making connections. So often students go to classes, and that's all. You need to do more than this. You are less likely to connect with the people who can best help you achieve your goals by making a minimal effort. To connect with your professors often takes a little initiative. Shake their hand, say hello, go to their office hours, and express an interest in *their* interests. You have a lot of control over the opportunities you seek, and it truly takes relatively small steps, really, to create big opportunities. Doing the little things to make strong positive connections can markedly improve your chances of finding the opportunities you need to be competitive for graduate schools.

Pursue Scholarship

> *"Opportunities multiply as they are seized; they die when neglected."*
>
> John Wicker, *Into Tomorrow*

The "Big Three" are academics, scholarship, and activities. Academics are the first of the "Big Three" and also the most concrete—go to classes, study, and earn good grades. We will revisit "academics" in the final two goals. Yet, first and foremost, you will want to prioritize scholarship in your sophomore and junior years. I refer to scholarship as the TRIfecta: Teaching, Research, and Internship. Graduate schools at the master's, and especially at the doctorate, level will closely evaluate your scholarship experiences. There are many ways in which you can find and even create opportunities for scholarship, as is described in this section.

Teaching

Teaching is not literally something you will be able to do as an undergraduate. "Teaching" as an undergraduate student really refers to your on-the-job experience to prepare to be a teacher. Truthfully, teaching experience can be invaluable. In many ways, you can learn the most through "teaching" or trying to make sense of material to others who are having difficulty understating the material. It can be fun and exciting to see that your mastery of a topic is such that not only do *you* understand the material, but you can help *others* understand the material as well. There are two common opportunities that count as teaching experience (each opportunity is numbered and described in this section):

- Teaching assistant [1]
- Tutor [2]

[1] As a teaching assistant (TA), you will not teach in college as an undergraduate student, but you can be a teaching assistant for a college-level course. As a TA, you will typically hold office hours each week, possibly assist with grading, and meet with the professor of the course about once each week or every other week. In some cases, you may even be asked to teach one class. The experience is generally laid back. The grading structure for a TA position is sometimes pass/fail or can be for a letter grade. Usually, as long as you do your "job" as a TA, your grade will be an A. In most cases, the professor acts as your advisor, which can make being a TA quite a rewarding experience.

To become a TA, you really need to create this opportunity yourself. Rarely are undergraduate TA opportunities "posted" on a notice board or another public site. TA opportunities are mostly open to students who take the initiative to seek these opportunities in the first place. So, to create a TA opportunity, you can follow three basic steps:

1. Earn an A or a B+ (at worst) in a class for which you want to be a TA. Generally speaking, a professor wants a TA who can help him or her. A professor does not want a TA who has not mastered the material or who has not yet taken the course. For example, how can you hold TA office hours to help students who are struggling in a course if you, yourself, struggled in that course? You need to demonstrate a high grade in the class for which you want to be a TA. A professor is unlikely to select you as a TA for a course if your grade in that course was less than a B+ when you took the course as a student.

2. Make the request to be a TA. To be a TA, you typically have to make the request yourself. The best way to make this request is in person. Do not, however, show up to the professor's office unannounced. To be most respectful, first request a meeting with the professor or come to his or her office during scheduled office hours. You can also make this request via e-mail. A few examples of how to write requests are given in this section.

3. Follow up and be proactive. Often, registering for TA credits involves paperwork and possibly even signatures. Do not leave it to your professor to get the paperwork completed. Find out what needs to be done to get registered and take the initiative to get it done. Find the paperwork, print it, fill it out, sign it, obtain your professor's signature at a time that is convenient for him or her, and submit the paperwork on his or her behalf. The more convenient you make this process for your professor, the more positively he or she will view you—which can be especially beneficial when it comes time to request an LOR.

In your sophomore year, you should have already taken the introductory course for your major. In psychology, that would be Introduction to Psychology. If you earned a high grade in that course, then it would be a good course to TA. After your sophomore year, you should complete at least one course in your area of interest, one course in statistics, and one in research methods. You should pursue being a TA for one of those courses as well. Hence, in the area of "teaching" you should pursue being a TA for the introductory course in your major and also for one course in your area of interest, or in a statistics or research methods course. Those three additional courses will be among the most relevant and important to graduate school selection committees.

Keep in mind that outside of law school or medical school, graduate programs in the behavioral sciences will heavily weigh your grades in statistics and research methods courses because your grades in those courses are highly predictive of your potential success in graduate school. To do well in those classes is a very strong achievement—to TA those classes is rare and will substantially help you stand out among other graduate school applicants. You will want to make a concerted effort to seek TA opportunities in those classes, if possible.

TA opportunities can be very competitive, or not at all competitive. Regardless, the first step is always to ask. In some cases, a student becomes the TA for a course because he or she was the first to make the request. So be proactive here. Make a request to be a TA for the next semester immediately after you receive your grades for the course, if you can. If you choose to make the request in person, then meet with the professor at a time that is convenient for him or her and be respectful when making the request.

The basic format for a request should be to start with an introduction, then give a compliment, and then make the request. The following is an example of how a former student who successfully earned a TA position started her request when she first met with her professor:

Hello Dr. [Smith], how are you doing? Thank you for taking the time to meet with me. My name is [name of student]. As you may recall, I was a student in your [statistics] class last semester, and I scored an A. I really enjoyed the course, and I would like very much to gain applied experience as a teaching assistant for that course. Could we talk about such a possibility? I have the flexibility in my schedule to commit to being your teaching assistant, and I am very excited about this possibility.

Anywhere there is a bracket, please just change the wording to fit your name, the name of your professor, or the name of your course. The student who made the above request earned a TA position the following semester in her professor's statistics course—of course, following further dialogue between her and her professor.

Such a request can also be made via e-mail. Again, anywhere there is a bracket, please just change the wording to fit your name, the name of your professor, or the name of your course. The following is an example e-mail request made by a former student who also successfully earned a TA position for a different course:

Dear Dr. [Smith],

My name is [name of student]. As you may recall, I was a student in your [introductory psychology] class last semester, and I scored an A. I really enjoyed the course and your teaching style. I would like to talk more with you about the possibility of being your teaching assistant (TA) for your course next semester. I have the flexibility in my schedule to commit to being your TA. Please let me know if such an opportunity is possible. I would be very happy to talk in person if you would prefer before making such a decision.

Thank you for your time and consideration.

Sincerely,

[Name of student]

The examples provided here just give a general template for how these requests have been made by students who successfully earned TA positions—even for a course (in introductory psychology) that did not previously have a TA position where the professor taught. Sometimes making the request can thus open up new opportunities that did not exist before the request was made—you'll see that the same strategy can be applied to create research and internship opportunities as well. Sometimes knowing *what* question to ask can be just as important as knowing *how* to ask it.

[2] Another teaching experience is to become a tutor. To become a tutor you usually can go to the teaching and learning center at your school and ask to become a tutor for just about any course. The criteria are usually that you earned a B or higher in the course for which you are a tutor. Being a tutor can be a paid position (at minimum wage usually). Once hired, you will either be assigned hours to be in the center ready to tutor as needed or be "on call" in cases where the center sets up times for you to meet with students to tutor them (usually one-on-one). This type of experience can be readily achieved by simply asking to become a tutor—and this experience can be listed as teaching experience on your résumé or curriculum vitae.

Research

Working on research can be a valuable experience because you can engage in learning in a more experiential setting in which the outcomes and hypotheses being tested are often innovative, cutting edge, or new. It is an opportunity to see how the research process is applied and to engage others in a collaborative setting in which you must often apply critical thinking skills to address questions and hypotheses being tested by the researchers. Having experience in a collaborative setting and in settings in which you can develop critical thinking skills is highly regarded among graduate schools, and is therefore valuable experience to gain.

While many opportunities for research will be at the school you attend, the possibilities for research are seemingly limitless. To make this manageable, we can simplify research opportunities into three general categories (each category is numbered and described in this section):

- Research at your college or university [1]
- Research anywhere for which you apply to join the labs [2]
- Research anywhere for which you create the opportunity [3]

[1] The same professors who teach your courses typically conduct research at your college or university. In this light, it is important to connect with your professors who conduct research in an area that specifically relates to the types of graduate programs you plan to apply to. To create opportunities to join a research lab, follow four steps:

1. Research each of your professors—the background of most professors can be easily found on your school website. Do this research in your sophomore year at the latest. Pick out the professor or professors whose research most closely fits your interests.

2. Take a course taught by a professor whose research interests matched yours.

3. Express an interest in his or her field of study during the semester.

4. At the end of the semester, when you are close to completing the course, make a formal request to join his or her labs.

Suppose, for example, you plan to pursue social psychology programs. Here is what you do. Find the full list of psychology professors and go to their faculty page on the school website—many faculty who conduct research have their own page. Find a social psychologist on campus whose research most closely fits your interests and, for Step 2, register for one of his or her courses. This step is a simple way for you to *show* an interest in your professor's interests.

During the semester, on at least one or a few occasions, comment to your professor about how interested you are in his or her research area. You can often do this before or after class, or during office hours. This should not be "kissing butt." In fact, you will want these conversations to be genuine, and not mere flattery. In truth, you are making these comments because you *do* find your professor's research area interesting, which is why you want to join his or her lab in the first place. To show a *genuine* interest, you can use the following two strategies:

- Ask questions that apply more than memorization to show that you are thinking beyond just "what is tested." In your conversations, ask intelligent, educated questions. You can, for example, reference something from class, such as "I noticed that many studies in education do not use experimental designs. Is this due to the difficultly of using random assignment?" This question provokes critical thinking in a way that is interesting and demonstrates that you are thinking about the material and not just memorizing definitions. Your question shows an interest in your professor's research area, and it demonstrates a skill that is valued by researchers: critical thinking.

- Express interest with an example or qualifier. To be genuine, you should show or express an interest and also be able to explain why or qualify what interests you. For example, do not say, "I find this area of research interesting." Why do you find it interesting? Instead say, "I find this area of research interesting because . . . ," and then explain why you find it interesting. It is more meaningful to have a reason for your interest than to just say that you have an interest. As another example, you could qualify your intentions, such as "I am interested in pursuing this area of research in graduate school." Such a comment identifies your interest in your professor's area of research, and speaks to your potential level of commitment to studying that area of research. This can get your professor interested in having you join his or her labs—all researchers desire to have lab groups who genuinely find the research area interesting and worthwhile.

On occasion, just following through with Step 3 can result in a professor making an offer to you to join his or her labs—before the semester even ends. However, if he or she does not make an offer, then in the last week or so of the semester, make this request, which is Step 4. It is best to make the request in person, but again, e-mail is an appropriate alternative. The basic format for a request should be to start with some background, then give a compliment, and then make the request. The following is an example of how a former student who successfully earned a spot in his professor's lab stated his request when he met with his professor at the end of a semester:

Hello Dr. [Smith], how are you doing? Thank you for taking the time to meet with me. I just wanted you to know that I have really enjoyed taking your course. I want very much to continue pursing courses and research in this area of study in psychology. I realize that you have a research lab here at the university. Is there any way that I could join your labs? I have the flexibility in my schedule to commit to being your research assistant, and I will work hard to contribute to the types of studies you are conducting or plan to conduct in the coming semester. I am very much interested in doing research with you, and I am very excited about this possibility.

Such a request could easily be adapted for writing an e-mail request. This strategy is successful because when you make this request, you have already demonstrated that you are hardworking, have thought about the types of research the professor does, and have unequivocally shown a genuine interest in his or her research. This is important because working in a research lab is a unique experience that can be time consuming. For this reason, when a professor selects students for a research assistant position, he or she usually gives preference to students who are interested in his or her research—because your interest in his or her research can predict your level of commitment to it once you join your professor's labs.

In terms of finding faculty members with research labs, note that many large universities (typically those with at least 8,000 students) will often hire "faculty" who have prolific programs of research—and these faculty then do research at the school, but they are *not* required to teach. To some extent, universities hire these "faculty" to make department lists appear more prestigious to potential applicants to the university. In truth, these faculty members were hired solely to ensure that all of their research is conducted and associated with the name of the university that hired them. These types of "faculty" will not teach; they will only conduct research. The reason they are not required to teach is that they are very productive in conducting research—meaning that they are great people to work under if you plan on pursuing a research graduate program, particularly at the doctorate level. To find these researchers and request to join their labs, you can:

- Find the "faculty" member listed on the faculty list at the school and just request to work in his or her labs. The faculty list is likely to include e-mail contacts. You can make a request similar to the template provided previously.
- You can register for courses taught by a faculty member's graduate students, and use that connection to request to work in his or her labs. While the "faculty" researcher may not teach, his or her graduate students will often teach. Take one of their courses and make a request to join the labs through the graduate student.

At large universities, the graduate students teach. Thus, knowing these students can be just as beneficial as knowing the PhD faculty researcher whose labs they work in. The graduate students at large universities can create research opportunities for you—get to know them as well. Make an effort to read the full "faculty" list for a department and find the "faculty" who are not teaching. The researchers who do not teach are among the best at what they do—that's why the university does not make them teach, because they are so productive at conducting research. In these cases, you can apply the four steps to work your way into these labs by taking the courses of their graduate students—the same way you would if the faculty member taught the course.

[2] Another way to create research opportunities is to pursue research that can be conducted anywhere for which you will need to apply to join the labs. These types of opportunities are more competitive because you will often compete nationally for spots in these laboratories. In psychology, the American Psychological Association (APA) offers a prestigious Summer Science Fellowship (SSF) that can be highly competitive. You can also find on the APA's website a full list of current research internship opportunities offered by many colleges and organizations across the country. For a current list, use the following link: www.apa.org/education/undergrad/research-opps.aspx.

Opportunities for research internships can be found within psychology and across disciplines. Many of these research internships require you to complete a full application and to submit your résumé and a cover letter or letter of intent. How to complete some of these materials is described in Section III of this book. The following major groups are key places to look to find the best and most competitive research internship opportunities in the country:

- National Science Foundation (NSF; www.nsf.gov). This foundation provides many opportunities for undergraduate students to obtain funding to conduct research and earn an internship, but it is highly competitive. You will compete nationally, even internationally, for these opportunities.
- National Institutes of Health (NIH; www.nih.gov). This institute provides many opportunities for undergraduate students to obtain research funding and earn an internship. However, like NSF, research opportunities at NIH are highly competitive.
- Council on Undergraduate Research (CUR; www.cur.org). The mission of the CUR is "to support and promote high-quality undergraduate student-faculty collaborative research and scholarship." You will find internship opportunities at this council across many undergraduate majors. You can also become a member of this council as a student—for a small annual fee.

Many universities across the country offer research internships in the summer as well. If you can travel, then you should look across the country to find these internships. Finding them is as easy as doing a Google search for "summer research internships" or a similar set of key terms. You can also look near where you live. Often, the schools in your neighborhood have summer research opportunities for which you can apply. Take advantage of these opportunities to do research in at least one summer before your senior year. Most graduate school selection committees will be impressed if your research experience extends beyond the college or university where you earned your degree.

When you do your search for summer research internship opportunities, choose internships that involve research in your area of interest and try to narrow the list down to your top three or four choices. Then bring your list to your advisor or a professor you trust. Ask for feedback about the choices you made to help you make a final decision for where to apply. After getting feedback, you can confidently make your final choices for where to apply.

[3] Another way to find research opportunities is to create these opportunities on your own. Follow the adage "If you don't ask, you don't get!" It sounds ridiculous, but all too often people do not achieve their goals simply because they did not ask. For example, suppose you did apply to many research internships across the country and did not get selected to any of them. Most students would concede, "Oh, well. Maybe next year?" Do not be one of those students.

Here is a basic reality of a research lab: Money is tight, and lab assistants are overworked. Knowing this, you now have a way in: You can offer your services in a lab for free. In other words, you offer to volunteer in a research lab—any research lab. Find the most prestigious researchers on the planet and offer to volunteer to work in their labs. You would be amazed at how many will offer you the job. And the beauty of this strategy is that the "position" you are requesting in their labs is never posted. You simply, on your own initiative, decide to e-mail the researcher (or the lab manager) to offer to work for free—and in many cases, if accepted, the researcher will actually pay you anyway. You will compete against no one for this opportunity—and it can be just as "prestigious" as a research internship you compete for.

The payoff is potentially large. Yes, you won't get paid (possibly). But who cares? You can create this research opportunity anywhere. If you do not want to travel, then pick the best option of a research lab at a university near where you live. Or pick the best researchers in the country and send out a request. You may have to travel, but if you can, you should. The following are three key payoffs for volunteering to work in a research lab that is not at the college or university where you are earning your degree:

1. Graduate school selection committees will be very impressed that your research experience extends beyond the college or university where you earned your degree. You will also stand out among most other applicants who will not have this level of research experience in their applications. This will be particularly beneficial for those applying to research-intensive graduate programs.

2. If you work well in those labs, then you can receive an LOR from the researcher you worked for. If you worked for a prestigious researcher, that is a powerful LOR you just earned.

3. If you work well in those labs, the researcher may want you to stay, and the experience could give you an inside track to being accepted into his or her labs in a graduate program when it's your time to apply to graduate schools.

Let's look at two examples of students who created research opportunities in this way. The first is a student who requested work in a large social-behavioral research lab at a large university in the Northeast. She chose a university in her hometown so that she did not have to travel. In her e-mail request, she introduced who she was, expressed her shared interests in the research being conducted in the labs she wanted to join, and closed with a request to join the labs. This request led to her being offered the research position at that university in the summer of 2012. The following year, upon graduating with her BA, she applied to graduate programs and was accepted with a full scholarship and stipend to a PhD program in social psychology at a different university.

As a template for how to make this request, the following is her exact e-mail request (some information has been removed for confidentiality reasons):

Dear Dr. [Smith],

I am a junior honors psychology major at [university]. I am planning to attend graduate school in the fall of 2013, with a focus on social psychology, following my graduation in May 2013. I have a 3.83 GPA and experience in research as a Psychology Scholar award winner.

In my research lab course this fall, I had the chance to read your article "Self-Esteem and Favoritism Toward Novel In-Groups: The Self as an Evaluative Base." I really enjoyed the topic, and would like to continue conducting research related to personality variables, social projection, and in-group favoritism in the future.

I hope you don't find this e-mail to be an inconvenience, but I'm interested in inquiring whether you are accepting research students for this summer. If you are, I'd greatly appreciate having the chance to talk to you about the position. I can be reached by e-mail, or on the phone at [number]. I would also be able to arrange a visit to campus anytime over this winter recess or during a weekend this spring, as I live only about half an hour away from [university].

I know I'm writing to you at a busy time, but I look forward to hearing from you at your earliest convenience.

Thank you,

[Name of student]

The next year another student requested to join a prestigious research lab also at a large university in the Northeast. The researcher to whom he made the request was a top, elite researcher in her field. She was the author of scores of research articles and books, with substantial funding through grants. This second student arranged to stay with a friend if offered a position in her labs—and he did get offered a position in the summer of 2013, and she even chose to pay him. He offered his time for free, and ended up with a paid research internship at a leading university and research lab in the country. Upon completing his summer internship, the researcher he worked under encouraged him to apply to her graduate program and to work in her labs as a PhD graduate student. He did apply to the PhD program. The researcher he worked under even wrote him a letter of recommendation for admission into her own PhD program—an LOR does not get much stronger than that! The following year he was accepted with a full scholarship and stipend to the PhD program in the nutrition sciences at the same university and working in the same labs where he did his summer research internship—a research internship he created by simply asking to join the researcher's labs.

As a template for how to make this request, the following is his exact e-mail request (some information has again been removed for confidentiality reasons):

Dear Dr. [Smith],

I am a junior honors psychology major at [university]. I have a 3.8 GPA and experience in research through our departmental curriculum, independent study, and serving as a Psychology Scholar award winner. Following my graduation in May 2014, I am planning to attend graduate school in the fall, with a focus on behavioral health and nutrition. In particular, I am interested in testing strategies to promote healthy eating, with a specific focus on encouraging consumption of low-energy-dense foods. In reviewing some of your articles, I feel that this fits well with your research area, and I believe that I can contribute to the work you are doing now in your labs.

In my independent study research lab this spring, I had the chance to read through a number of your articles, including your 2011 article "Hidden Vegetables: An Effective Strategy to Reduce Energy Intake and Increase

Vegetable Intake in Adults." I was able to incorporate your research outcome into my own research on the influence of the proximity of low- and high-energy-dense foods on food intake in a competitive food environment. I really enjoyed the topic, and would like to continue conducting research related to this important area examining the promotion of healthy eating behaviors.

I hope you don't find this e-mail to be an inconvenience, but due to my interest in your research, I would like to ask if you are accepting volunteer student research assistants for the upcoming summer. If you are, I would greatly appreciate having the chance to talk to you about the opportunity. I can be reached by e-mail or by phone at [number]. I would also be able to arrange a visit to campus during a weekend this spring, or anytime this summer, as I live less than two hours away from [university], and I am currently making arrangements to reside in that area this summer.

I know that I'm writing to you at a busy time, but I look forward to hearing from you at your earliest convenience.

Thank you,

[Name of student]

You now have two examples of students who were selected for research positions at major universities, working under the advisement of leading researchers in their respective fields of study—and both for positions that did not even exist until those students wrote their requests. Both students subsequently were accepted with full-ride scholarships and stipends to PhD programs in their respective fields of interest. Do not wait for research opportunities. If opportunity does not come "knocking," then create an opportunity. The opportunities you create yourself can often be just as "prestigious" as the ones you have to compete for. Take initiative, and create the opportunities you need to be competitive for graduate schools.

Internships

The research you do can be thought of as one type of internship, although internships are described here as job-related experiences that relate to the type of graduate programs to which you will apply. Internships can be found just about anywhere you can be hired. You can volunteer your time or even find paid positions at hospitals, law firms, mental health clinics, schools, law enforcement, and even the headquarters of many businesses.

You will want to find internships or paid positions that offer you professional experiences. Being the cashier at a fast-food restaurant is probably not going to help you get into graduate school. However, being the assistant manager may help because it is a leadership position. Sales positions, likewise, could help, particularly if you have sales records to show your effectiveness in this role because it requires strong interpersonal skills to be successful in sales. Your internship experiences are applied experiences in real-world settings. Internships can strengthen your expertise in an area, such as working in a mental health clinic prior to applying to a mental health counseling graduate program. Moreover, internships further demonstrate your "intangibles," such as your work ethic, dependability, focus, drive, and ability to work as part of a team, or other traits by which you can be characterized.

Applying, and completing application materials, for internships can be a bit different from applying to graduate schools. For this reason, I briefly look at how to adapt a résumé and cover letter to apply for internships and jobs in Section III of this book. You can refer to Section III to help you complete these materials.

To find internships or paid positions, you need to do some research. You can look for positions near your home and near where you go to school. To search, you can use the following strategies that have worked for many other students:

- Type key words in Google or another search engine. Use *internship* as one word and add others related to the job you want. For example, suppose you have interests in criminal behavior. If you enter *FBI internship* in Google, then you will find multiple links to current and past internship opportunities for college students at the Federal Bureau of Investigation (FBI).
- Search at common job search engine sites. Job sites often list jobs available in a wide range of fields. Specifically search for positions with *assistant* in the title because those positions usually mean that you will work directly for someone in charge or high ranking. Also look for "entry-level" positions. Many "entry-level" positions can be well compensated and offer highly professional experiences. To help you get started in your search, here are 10 of the most popular websites to search for jobs:
  - Beyond: www.beyond.com
  - CareerBuilder: www.careerbuilder.com
  - Glassdoor: www.glassdoor.com
  - Indeed: www.indeed.com
  - Job: www.job.com
  - The Ladders: www.theladders.com
  - Monster: www.monster.com
  - Simply Hired: www.simplyhired.com
  - Snagajob: www.snagajob.com
  - USA jobs: www.usajobs.gov
- Go to company websites. For example, if you want to work for Nike or another specific business, then go to the company's website. Odds are you will find a link to job openings and even internships or volunteer work needed at the company. If you find positions available, then follow up by calling a secretary to confirm that the positions are still open and how to apply.
- Make "cold calls." This is a pre-Internet strategy, but can still be effective: Just blindly call someone. Find a number for a secretary or an employee and inquire about job opportunities available where he or she works.

Keep in mind that an internship is like a long job interview. You have an opportunity to impress those you work for—take advantage of this opportunity to extend your connections. Work hard, and stay in touch with the people you meet during your internship. Exchange contact information or connect with them using professional social media sites. Ask for a business card before you leave your internship, and stay in touch from time to time with those you worked under. You never know when a connection can come back to benefit you.

Find Opportunities to Present and Publish

"A wise man will make more opportunities than he finds."

Francis Bacon

Joining a research lab is a significant achievement and alone can go a long way toward getting you into graduate school. To really stand out, though, you should try to present a poster or even publish while in those labs, particularly if you plan on applying to research-intensive graduate programs. Admittedly, a lot of this may be out of your control. To really understand how to accomplish this, you first need to know what these achievements are.

In any given research lab, researchers conduct a series of studies on a particular topic or area of interest. To report their findings, researchers often go to a conference to present their research as a poster. The posters that are presented will have authors listed—and the authors typically include any students who were involved in the conduct of the study. If you are completing a research project, talk with your research advisor about presenting your work at a conference. The rejection rates for presenting a poster at a conference are generally low, and it looks very good to graduate schools that you have attended and presented research at a conference.

A second way in which researchers can share their research findings is to write a manuscript that describes their research and submit the manuscript to a peer-reviewed scientific journal for publication. This is an important achievement, even for a researcher. The rules for authorship on a peer-reviewed article are admittedly vague, but if you participated in conducting the study and reviewing the manuscript, then you should be named as an author. The rejection rates for publishing a manuscript in a peer-reviewed journal are generally high (up to 85% to 90%), which is why graduate schools will hold this achievement in high regard if you are listed as an author on a publication.

A lot of being able to present a poster or publish a manuscript will come down to simply being in the right place at the right time. But there are steps you can take to make it more likely that you will find yourself in that "right place" at that "right time." The following are strategies you can use to increase your chances of finding a research lab that can lead to an opportunity for you to present or publish:

- Read the researcher's personal webpage. Most university researchers have a faculty page or a laboratory page online. There, you are likely to find their list of publications and their conference poster presentations. If you find in your search that a researcher has few publications and conference poster presentations, then it is unlikely that you will publish or present a conference poster if you participate in his or her lab. If you want to increase your chances of being published, then find researchers with a lot of recent publications and presentations and join their labs. Their productivity could be your productivity if you get involved and join in on the research projects they are working on.

- Talk to the researcher's graduate students. Another good source of information about the productivity of a lab is to talk to the graduate students of a researcher, or other students in the lab. The students are likely to "spill the beans" on everything from the likelihood you can author a research project in the labs to whether they like being in the lab. When talking with the graduate students, just ask questions. The students will usually do the rest of the talking, and you will likely learn a lot about the lab and whether or not you want to join.

- Find the publications for a researcher, and review the lists of authors of those publications. Suppose a researcher publishes often. Now look at the names of the authors listed on his or her publications. How many authors are undergraduate students? If none, then it may be unlikely for you to publish if you join that lab, particularly if you know that many undergraduate students work in the lab, yet none are published. Also, talk with the graduate students in that lab; find out if the researcher will allow undergraduates to publish as authors for research being done in his or her labs.

- Find the posters for a researcher, and review the lists of authors of those poster presentations. While publishing a scientific paper is a rare feat for undergraduate students, presenting a poster at a conference is relatively more common. Look at the names of students listed. If many authors listed are names of undergraduate students, then joining those labs may very likely lead to an opportunity for you to be an author and present a poster. You can also talk with the graduate students in that lab; find out if the researcher will allow undergraduates to present a poster as authors for research being done in his or her labs.

- Find out if the researcher has grant money or if the department has funding. Keep in mind that it costs money to make trips to conferences where you will present the research. In many cases, if the researcher has a grant, then you can have your trip reimbursed. Sometimes grant information is given on a researcher's website, or you can ask his or her graduate students—they would know if the researcher has a grant. Also look into whether the department has funding for conferences. Many small schools will have researchers with no grants, but the department they work in will have funding to reimburse students for going to a conference.

In all, these five strategies can help you navigate the different types of labs you could join. Of course, being in a research lab is certainly a good enough experience to be competitive as an applicant to graduate schools. However, taking extra steps to find and join a lab that is well funded and highly productive can "stack the deck" in your favor to help you increase your chances of presenting or even publishing research as an author or coauthor. Doing so as an undergraduate student can help you create greater opportunities that allow you to stand out among all the applicants you will be competing against when it comes time for you to apply to graduate schools.

Pursue Activities and International Studies

> *"You are what you do, not what you say you'll do."*
>
> C. G. Jung

Activities

Showing a strong record of academics and scholarship is very important, but also being involved in other activities can make you look like an all-star. A graduate school selection committee is unlikely to base its decision solely on the activities you are involved in, but activities will be considered because they can show that you are a well-rounded student. Keep in mind that your activities do not need to take up too much of your time, and can help you stand out among other applicants who have the same level of academics and scholarship but not the activities. As described in Chapter 2, activities can be broken down into three categories: (1) clubs, (2) sports, and (3) service and more.

A readily accessible opportunity is to join a club at your school. For example, many psychology departments sponsor a psychology club. It is a department-run club that allows psychology students to join and be a part of activities in the department outside of classwork. Many clubs vote members into offices, such as having a president and secretary, and many have no GPA requirements. A psychology club can be involved in any number of activities, including renovating psychology office spaces, coordinating a speaker series to bring speakers in from other universities to talk about their research, and sponsoring graduate and job workshops for graduating seniors. Psychology clubs can also be involved in fund-raisers and other types of organizational events, depending on the size of the club and the bureaucracies of the school. At a school level, you can get involved in similar activities, such as joining your campus's student government association or an academic fraternity or sorority.

Most academic majors will have clubs for students to join. If the clubs do not exist, you can actually take an active role in establishing a club. A psychology club, for example, is actually somewhat easy to create. First, you need to find a faculty member to sponsor the club. The faculty member could be the chair of your department or any other faculty member. The sponsor's role is typically minimal because students essentially run the day-to-day activities of the club. You would mostly need your faculty sponsor when you need money! Second, recruit a few interested students to join, and that is it. While the bureaucracies of schools may make this process a little more difficult than it needs to be, most will likely be excited to help you get students more actively involved in academics outside of the classroom.

You can also join clubs at a national level, including national honor societies and other organizations. One key organization is the National Society of Leadership and Success. The organization offers talks, scholarships, awards, and many other resources and benefits to students wanting to achieve success. You must be nominated to become a member and meet additional criteria. Go to www.societyleadership .org to learn more. To join a national honor society you also need to formally apply or be nominated, and the major criterion for becoming a member is typically your college GPA. For this reason, students often must wait until their sophomore year to apply for honor society memberships. In psychology, however, there are many other influential organizations that only require you to be enrolled as a student. A list of many of the organizations that you can join as a student is given in Table 4.1. The organizations listed in Table 4.1 are among the most common in psychology. Similar organizations and national honor societies will exist for any number of majors in the behavioral sciences.

Table 4.1 Organizations That Undergraduate Students in Psychology Can Join

Organizations for Psychology	Description
Psi Chi (National Honor Society)	To learn about requirements, schools with a chapter, and how to start your own chapter, go to www.psichi .org/?page=become_member.
American Psychological Association (APA)	To enroll as an undergraduate student affiliate, go to www.apa.org/membership. There is a small fee to join.
Association for Psychological Science (APS)	To enroll as an undergraduate student affiliate, go to www.psychologicalscience.org and select the membership tab. There is a small fee to join.
Eastern Psychological Association (EPA)	To enroll as an undergraduate student affiliate, go to www.easternpsychological.org. There is a small fee to join.
Western Psychological Association (WPA)	To enroll as a student member, go to www .westernpsych.org/convention/fees.cfm. There is a small fee to join.

NOTE: Psi Chi is a national honor society and has GPA requirements to join. All others only require that you be enrolled as a student.

In addition to memberships in clubs, societies, and organizations, it can help if you show evidence of service or are an athlete. Being an athlete is a great way to demonstrate the intangibles of your character in terms of linking your experience to the three strengths of leadership, collaboration, and commitment. How to connect these three strengths to your experiences in sports and to the interests of a graduate school will be described in Section III, with many examples given of how other student athletes have related their experiences in sports to each strength. Find opportunities to also engage in at least one service project each year. You will feel good for having served people at the college or in the community, and when you apply to graduate schools, you will have four service projects to list in your application. Many ideas for types of service projects you can get involved in are given in Chapter 2.

International Studies

You can also choose to pursue international study options, which are opportunities to engage in academics or scholarship in another country. This opportunity is described here because it is a big commitment, and can be costly—so this option is not for everyone. The "study abroad" programs at your school typically offer international study opportunities. If your school participates in this program (and many do), then you can find a list of courses that participate and where you can study. You typically get to choose where in the world you want to study. While the cost for studying abroad is typically at a reduced rate, it will still likely cost a good amount of money to make the trip.

You can find international internship opportunities as well, either one created by an instructor of a specific course or one created by the study abroad program. You can also look into these types of opportunities for internships or research that fits your interests. Seeking these types of opportunities adds international experience to your résumé, which can stand out. The drawback is that this option can be quite expensive. You will want to factor cost into your decision when deciding if an international learning experience is right for you. The length of a trip, however, can save you some money. These trips can last a few days or weeks, or can last for a full semester. The shorter the trip, the less costly it will usually be.

Write a Résumé or Curriculum Vitae

"A schedule defends from chaos and whim."

Annie Dillard

As you can imagine, all of your accomplishments may be difficult to keep track of. One useful way to "keep track" is to write a draft of your résumé at the start of your sophomore year. Think of your résumé as a log. When people work out in the gym, many keep track of the exercises they completed, their "reps," and weights lifted. They do this so that over time they can see their improvements in the gym. In the same way, you can write a draft of your résumé as a "schedule" or log as you pursue opportunities in college. Also keep a copy of your résumé on you to share with people you meet. For example, if you can attend a conference, you will meet many people from many different colleges—having a résumé on hand to give them can help you make connections.

In academia, your résumé is called a *curriculum vitae*, or CV. Indeed, it is likely that you will need to write a CV when applying to graduate schools. A résumé should not be longer than one page (maybe a little more), even if you have the credentials of a CEO! Your CV, however, is basically a résumé, but it has no page limit; it can be as long as you want. For your purposes, you will likely have a two- to five-page CV by the time you start applying to graduate schools. The CV you write can have any number of headings, and the headings you use are largely up to your judgment—there is no standard template to use, which can make writing CVs stressful to students. There are many different versions of a "good" CV, and it can be hard to choose which one is best.

To resolve the concern of not having a standard template for writing your CV, here is one tip that is safe to follow: Use headings in your CV that appeal to the credentials that graduate schools are looking for anyway. Hence, use the "Big Three" as headings in your CV. To get started, let's look at some examples of headings you can use. A full chapter is devoted to showing you how to write résumés and CVs in Chapter 7—here I will focus only on the headings to help you "keep track" of your achievements.

To write your CV, include your name and contact information (typically centered) at the top. "Education" is typically the first listed heading. From there, it is anyone's preference. In your case, you will be applying to graduate schools. Graduate schools for master's and doctorate-level programs are most interested in the "TRIfecta" of your Teaching, Research, and Internships. These three should frontline your CV. Figure 4.1 shows an annotated example of the types of headings you could have in your CV (more detailed examples are given in Chapter 7). Note that many other headings can be created from these three major criteria.

In the CV, your first heading is for academics. In many cases, that is the only heading devoted to your "grades." One optional heading not included in the sample CV is to add a "Relevant Coursework" heading under the "Education" heading, where you can list key courses you have taken that relate to the graduate programs to which you apply. One caveat is that all of your courses are listed in your transcript, which will be required anyway in a graduate school application. Thus, without good reason to add this heading (such as to identify prerequisite courses you took that are specifically listed as required by a graduate school), this added heading is not needed.

In contrast, three headings can be devoted to research: "Research Experience," "Peer-Reviewed Publications," and "Presentations." Your goal is to fill in as many headings as possible. If you fail to accomplish something under a heading, then simply omit the heading when it comes time to write the final draft of your CV. For example, if you do not publish (which most undergraduate students will not), then simply remove the heading entirely. You can then list your tutoring and TA experience under the "Teaching Experience" heading and list your internship and work experience under the heading below that. Then list your honors and awards, such as scholarships or membership in honor societies. This order is likely the order you will keep because the most important criteria are listed from top to bottom of the page.

The next heading covers the last of the Big Three: activities. List all activities under an "Activities and Services" heading to include service and sports. In the final heading, "Training and Skills," you can highlight your skills that will appeal

Figure 4.1   An annotated curriculum vitae with key headings that can often be listed

Name

Address

Contact Information

EDUCATION
Degree Earned, Name of Major.......................Conferral Date: Month, Year
College Name, City, State
Overall GPA

RESEARCH EXPERIENCE
Name of Laboratory...Dates of Time in Lab
Advisor: Name, Title (e.g., PhD)
Give a brief description of your role in the lab.

PEER-REVIEWED PUBLICATIONS
Give the APA-style reference for your peer-reviewed publication. Number each
listing.

PRESENTATIONS
Give the APA-style reference for your abstract presented at a conference.
Number each listing.

TEACHING EXPERIENCE
Title (TA or Tutor), Name of Course, School Name............Dates of Teaching
Faculty Advisor: Name, Title (e.g., PhD)
Give a brief description of your responsibilities.
Pay Rate (if applicable)

INTERNSHIPS AND WORK EXPERIENCE
Job Title ....Dates of Employment
Name of Organization, City, State
Supervisor: Name, PhD (if applicable)
Give a brief description of your responsibilities.
Pay Rate (if applicable)

HONORS AND AWARDS
List all scholarships, awards, and honor society memberships and provide a
brief description of each (if applicable), Dates

ACTIVITIES AND SERVICE
List activities, sports, and service experience and provide a brief description
of each (if applicable), Dates

TRAINING AND SKILLS
List all skills valued by graduate schools and provide a brief description of
each (if applicable), Dates

NOTE: A "conferral date" is the expected date of graduation.

to graduate schools, such as proficiency using Microsoft® Office, IBM SPSS® statistical software, or laboratory instruments. Trainings can include workshops you have attended at your school or at conferences. Trainings can also include those that led to certification, such as CPR training or completion of the free NIH web-based course, "Protecting Human Research Participants." The NIH course is available for anyone to complete by registering at http://phrp.nihtraining.com/users/login.php.

In all, your CV now lists major headings that are of the greatest importance to graduate school selection committees. Use your CV as your guide as you work through your experiences in your sophomore and junior years. Try to have something listed under as many of the headings as possible and be confident that, by doing so, you are becoming more and more competitive for getting into graduate schools.

Keep Track of Your GPA

"In the best classrooms, grades are only one of many types of feedback provided to students."

Douglas Reeves

What is interesting is that almost all parents and students harp on GPAs, yet this chapter on what you need to do in your sophomore and junior years, until now, has made little mention of your GPA. Of course, maintaining a high GPA is important, but that alone is not likely to get you into graduate schools. It can, if you apply to master's programs only; but PhD and doctoral programs will want more than just a high GPA to get accepted. In terms of setting goals for maintaining a competitive GPA:

1. Always maintain a 3.0 or higher overall GPA each semester.

2. Always maintain a 3.0 or higher in-major GPA each semester.

3. To compete for master's programs, a 3.1 or higher overall GPA is competitive, although a GPA closer to 3.4 or higher is preferred.

4. To compete for doctoral programs, a 3.5 or higher overall GPA is competitive, although a GPA closer to 3.8 or higher is preferred.

To be "competitive" means that your GPA will not eliminate you from being able to apply to graduate schools, and a few graduate schools may have even lower GPA requirements. Keep in mind, though, that the higher ranked schools will likely require GPAs much closer to the preferred GPAs listed here. You need to know the GPA requirements for each graduate school you apply to—each school can have different GPA requirements. Also, while it's not always going to be possible, you can sometimes get around having a low GPA. Strategies for getting around having weak areas in your application (such as having a low GPA) are discussed in Section III.

Your GPA is important in that it can open doors of opportunity. Maintaining a high GPA ensures that you can compete for a degree program at any level when it comes time to apply to graduate schools. You can and should keep track of your GPA. If your advisor asks you what your GPA is, you should know the answer. You can likely find a GPA calculator on your student university webpage. Use it; track your GPA at the end of each semester. Play with the calculator to see what grades you need in the coming semester to keep pace with your goals.

You also need to be strategic in your course enrollments. As you know, all college courses are not the same level of difficulty—even for the same course! The following are four ways that you can strategically improve your GPA:

- Retake classes.
- Take "easier" classes.
- Take "easier" professors.
- Take summer and winter classes.

Retake Classes

Suppose you earn a C− in one class. That is a 1.67 GPA, which substantially pulls down your overall GPA. If you retake that class, the C− is erased and will be replaced with your new grade. Simply erasing that C− substantially helps you pull your GPA up. If you earn a B in that same class, you now have a 3.0 GPA for that course, and the 1.67 is gone. Retaking classes is a great way to improve your GPA. Especially consider retaking classes in your major because those grades may be most important to graduate school selection committees. Also, courses in your major count toward your overall GPA and your in-major GPA, which is another good reason to retake classes in your major if you did not do well in them on your first try.

Take "Easier" Classes (in Some Cases)

If you take a course in biochemistry or an introduction to sociology, which course do you think is "easier"? The fact is that some courses have much higher workloads and more difficult content than other courses. Be selective with the courses you take. Make sure you take "difficult" classes only if (1) they are in-major courses, (2) you will meet college requirements to graduate by taking them, or (3) you will meet prerequisite course requirements indicated by a graduate school to which you plan to apply. Otherwise, for the most part, stay away from overloading yourself with unnecessary stress and workloads that will potentially pull down your GPA. If the course you want is "difficult" but does not fit one of the three criteria given here, then do not register for the course if you feel that you will not do well in the class.

Take "Easier" Professors

One thing tends to be certain in college: You take the professor, not the class. Realize that most college professors are *not* trained teachers. The model in college is that being an "expert" in a subject area is sufficient to put you in front of a classroom—many professors are thus experts first, teachers second. Some professors make a course very difficult often because they think that the harder or more challenging the course, the better it is. Not true. If two professors teach the same course and one has a better grading system or lesser workload, then take the "easier" professor. You can use the following two steps as a student when choosing between two different professors who teach the same course:

- First, go to each class and read a copy of the syllabus for each professor. The course with fewer assignments listed in the syllabus is more preferable because it opens your time to do other work, such as lab work with researchers. Ultimately, graduate schools do not ask how "hard" your professors were, but they will ask what courses you have taken. Why voluntarily take a "harder" professor if an "easier" professor teaches the same course? In the end, you need to protect your own best interests—and a high GPA is in your best interests if you want to go to graduate school! If you don't find a course challenging enough, then do extra work on your own—you do not need to be graded on everything to get what you want out of each class you take.

- Second, ask your professor what percentage of students usually earn an A in his or her class. A fair number is anything near 10% or more, in my judgment. However, some professors will say, "Only students who 'earn' an A will get an A. If no students 'earn' an A, then no students get the A." If this is the response, then avoid this professor if you can. As a reality check, any professor can make his or her course too difficult for even the best students. A course with no students earning an A is simply a course that is too hard. The professor should curve grades in this case to allow the top students in the class to earn an A. If he or she will not, then that hurts your GPA, even if you are at the top of the class! Avoid a professor who sets a course up like this, if you can.

Take Summer or Winter Classes

Here is another reality of college: Summer and winter courses for any class are notoriously easier, because not all of the course content taught during a full semester or quarter can be taught in a summer or winter—it is simply not possible (in many cases) to teach all content in only six to eight weeks (summer) or in two weeks (winter). Many courses offered in the winter are for difficult courses, such as micro- and macroeconomics—taught in only two weeks! And these courses often have all-take-home assignments and exams. For classes that are not related to your major and for classes that you simply need to graduate but are not related to the type of field to which you plan to apply, such as language or English requirements, take these courses in the summer or winter. You can substantially boost your GPA by taking these difficult courses in the summer and winter.

Keep in mind that the suggestions here are not to imply that you should take the "easy" way through college. Rather, they are about being practical. They are about balancing how hard you are working to make sure all of your hard work pays off. Focus your time and energy on the experiences and courses that will stand out most to the graduate schools to which you will apply. Otherwise, yes, take it easy and do not overwork yourself in other areas. Just be realistic and balance your efforts and time—and your sanity! There is no need to overwork yourself in every course you take; be practical.

Prepare to Take the GRE or Other Standardized Exams

"Do what today others won't, so tomorrow, you can do what others can't."

Brian Rogers Loop

For most graduate schools, you must take a standardized exam to apply. For most behavioral and science-based master's and doctoral programs, the GRE will be required. For law school, you take the LSAT; for medical school, it is the MCAT; for business, it is the GMAT. You may need to take a subject test for the GRE as well, depending on the graduate program you apply to. Each test is described in Table 2.4 in Chapter 2. The takeaway message is that you will likely need to take a standardized exam. This is not a surprise; you need to anticipate this.

It will be to your advantage to start preparing for your standardized exams *before* your senior year. Start as early as possible. For most students in psychology and the behavioral sciences, you will take the GRE. You should begin preparing for the GRE at least four to five months prior to the summer before your senior year. You should plan to take the GRE in that summer before your senior year. The reason you want to complete the GRE in the summer before your senior year is so that you can focus more attention in your senior year on completing the graduate school applications, cover letters, résumés and CVs, and other materials required. The last thing you want is the pressure of having to prepare for and take the GRE during this process. Be prepared, think ahead, and get studying in the spring of your junior year. Schedule to take the GRE in the summer before your senior year. All information for scheduling an exam is given at the website for each test, which is given in Table 2.4 in Chapter 2.

The first time you take the exam, you may not score where you needed or desired. Keep in mind that you are allowed to retake the exam. However, you also want to keep in mind that the schools you apply to will "see" how many times you took the exam. As a general rule, do not take a given standardized exam more than three times. Schools will typically view a student who takes the exam more than three times as a student who was underprepared and too focused on only one part of the graduate school application. The more you prepare in advance for the standardized exam, the better your score should be. If you still do not like your score, then go ahead and schedule to retake the exam if you wish. But be cautious in doing so—you should limit your "tries" to three.

The advantage of preparing for the GRE (or any other standardized exam) in your junior year is, again, so that you can focus on completing your application materials in your senior year, and/or have the flexibility to retake the exam ahead of the graduate school deadlines. Many other students will not heed this advice, and you should have an advantage over them because you can dedicate more time to completing your application materials for graduate schools, while the less prepared are still studying for the GRE. It goes without saying that gaining any advantage over other applicants you will compete against is worthwhile.

Putting It All Together:
Making the Most of Your Opportunities

"Give me six hours to chop down a tree and I will spend the first four sharpening the axe."

Abraham Lincoln

The goals and suggestions provided here are numerous. However, keep in mind these goals can be pursued throughout your time in college and will help you become highly competitive for getting into many graduate schools. It can substantially benefit you to read this chapter again and again—as often as you need as you continue to pursue opportunities into your senior year. All of your work as an undergraduate student is meant to enable you to realize your ultimate goal of getting into graduate school. The more you apply the strategies and suggestions provided here, the stronger your graduate school applications will be and the more fun the outcomes can be when it comes time to receive decision letters from graduate schools.

It is also worth noting that you can always pursue the goals described in this chapter. Whether you are a sophomore reading this chapter or an upperclassman, it is never too late or too early to be using the tips and strategies described in this chapter to help you seek out and realize opportunities by which you can gain relevant experience and become increasingly competitive for graduate school admission. While this plan is outlined as a freshman- to senior-year plan, there is no timeline by which you *must* begin or stop using the ideas and strategies shared in this book. Continue to apply these tips and strategies throughout your time in college. If you are a junior transfer student or an upperclassman picking this book up for the very first time, you can start now to apply ideas and strategies shared here. The first step to being competitive is to take action. Using an analogy from the 16th president of the United States, it is never too late to begin "sharpening the axe" to prepare to "chop down a tree."

CHAPTER 5

Senior Year: Select Schools and Complete Applications

SENIOR: Steady Effort Now Is Opportunity Realized

"Only in the present can I act."

Abraham Maslow

Welcome to your senior year, when Steady Effort Now Is Opportunity Realized. In your freshman to junior years you pursued 12 goals, and you should continue to pursue these goals into your senior year. Specifically, your senior year should be a busy one in three predominant ways:

- You are preparing to graduate on time. [1]
- You are continuing to pursue opportunities. [2]
- You are completing applications for graduate schools. [3]

[1] You are preparing to graduate on time. This is really the second goal of your freshman year: Know your major requirements. You need to check that you are keeping pace with graduation requirements. Remember that you need 120 total credits to graduate (in some cases maybe a little more). You must make sure you have taken all the required courses for your major, and have completed all general education requirements. Check your student record, check with an advisor, and check with someone in a registrar's office to make sure you will graduate on time. Do not assume that you are good to go; make an effort to confirm that you will graduate on time.

Also, at many schools, you will need to submit a form indicating your intent to graduate or your intent to "walk" during the graduation ceremonies. Follow up on this to make sure that the paperwork needed to graduate is completed. Again, do not just assume you are good to go; make an effort to confirm that you will be allowed to "walk" during the graduation ceremonies and receive your degree.

[2] You are continuing to pursue opportunities. The seven goals for how to pursue and realize opportunities in your sophomore and junior years given in Chapter 4 should continue into your senior year. There are two reasons why you should continue to pursue opportunities, particularly for achieving the "Big Three" in your senior year.

First, you should continue to pursue the Big Three in your senior year to gain more experience that you will need anyway. The "Big Three" are key skills you will need to be successful in graduate school. Hence, you should continue to develop in the core areas of academics, scholarship, and activities because doing so will help prepare you for success in graduate school.

Second, you should continue to pursue the Big Three in your senior year to appeal to the interests of graduate schools. As you complete your applications for graduate school, you will find that graduate school selection committees want to know as much about what you are currently doing as they do about what you have already done. The committees want to see evidence of an ongoing pursuit of experiences that are relevant to success in graduate school. They want to see that you have been and still are engaged in research, for example. Continue in your senior year to take advantage of the opportunities that you realized in your previous years in college.

[3] You are completing applications for graduate schools. The focus of Chapter 5 is on this third predominant pursuit that makes you busy in your senior year. This is a year in which you will apply to graduate schools. Completing the application materials can be time consuming. Think of the application process as another course you will take in your senior year, and put the time in accordingly to complete the graduate school applications. Plan on at least four to six hours of work per week to complete the applications until you have submitted them all. While applications can come in many different forms, there are six basic parts to the graduate school application: the application itself, the standardized exam scores, your academic transcripts, your letter of intent, your résumé/curriculum vitae (CV), and letters of recommendation (LORs). I will take a closer look of each component of your application in this chapter.

Know that you will be busy in your senior year, which is why I represent your SENIOR year as "Steady Effort Now Is Opportunity Realized." You need to keep pace with graduating on time, including taking the courses you need to graduate. You need to continue pursuing opportunities as you did in your sophomore and junior years. And you need to be applying to graduate schools—this last part alone can be very time consuming if you put in the time you should to complete the application process.

If you follow the graduate school plan outlined in this book, then you can be confident that you will be competitive for graduate school. In your senior year, it is now mostly a matter of effectively communicating this to graduate schools. In truth, it is one thing to achieve what you need to be competitive; it is quite another thing to effectively *communicate* what you achieved. For this reason, this chapter and all of Section III are devoted to the graduate school application process. Hence, Section III is really an extension of your senior-year plan. You will receive step-by-step instructions for how to complete the graduate school application process and how to make the writing of your applications appeal to the interests of graduate schools—with a full complement of sample materials from students who have been accepted to and enrolled in graduate schools and doctorate-level programs within only the last few years.

Setting Priorities for Your Senior Year

"Action expresses priorities."

Mahatma Gandhi

In terms of the three predominant ways you will be busy in your senior year, you need to make sure you are keeping pace to graduate on time, and then you need to prioritize completing the application materials for graduate schools. To prioritize the application process, the best solution is to "clear your schedule," which you can achieve in the following ways:

- Try to set it up so that you can take a reduced course load in both semesters of your senior year. Take 12 credit hours of coursework in the fall, and if you can, also take 12 credit hours in the spring of your senior year. A 12–credit hour semester is considered a full-time load, so you will still qualify for tuition assistance and other benefits of being a full-time student. Reducing your course load can reduce your schedule to four courses (or 12 credit hours) per semester. Taking 3–credit hour courses in a previous summer or winter can offset the reduced load in your senior year. Having a reduced load in your senior year will give you more time to devote to the graduate school application process.
- Take the GRE or other standardized exams *before* your senior year—this step is listed as the last goal for your sophomore and junior years. You will want to avoid having to take a standardized exam in your senior year, if possible, so that you can focus on completing the other parts of the graduate school application process (described in the next section), and avoid being overwhelmed in your senior year.
- Start researching graduate schools in the summer *before* your senior year, and have a final list of schools to which you will apply by early in your senior year. This will allow you more time to shape your applications in line with the specific interests of each graduate school. It will also allow you to give your list of schools to your recommenders early, thereby allowing them more time to write your LORs.

By completing your standardized exams and researching graduate schools in the summer *before* your senior year, you will reduce your workload in your senior year.

Also, reducing your coursework to 12 credit hours will further reduce your workload and give you more time to devote to completing other parts of the graduate school application. The "parts" of the graduate school application are introduced in the next section.

The Six Basic "Parts" of a Graduate School Application

"Nothing is so fatiguing as the eternal hanging on of an uncompleted task."

William James

There are six basic parts to a complete graduate school application (although note that the "parts" required can differ from one school to another):

- The application itself. Most graduate schools will offer online applications. The application is just a small part of the full process. In the application, you will fill in demographic information, grades, possibly some financial information, and other details related to the graduate program requirements. It is best to submit this application only after you have completed all other materials that are required by the school or graduate program. A processing fee or other fee is typically charged for each application you submit.
- Your standardized exam scores. You usually must submit scores for your standardized exam. However, in a few cases a standardized exam score may be optional or not required at all by a school. To report your scores to a school, either you can write your exam score on the application, or in other cases, you will need to have the test scores sent by the maker of the test—it depends mostly on the type of standardized exam you took and the school to which you are applying. The GRE, LSAT, MCAT, and GMAT all have different procedures for reporting scores, and you should refer to their websites to learn more. The websites for each of these tests are given in Table 2.4 in Chapter 2.
- Your academic transcripts. Your transcripts are a certified statement of your academic record. They list your courses taken and grades earned at your school. You will need to have official transcripts sent. To send your official transcripts, go to the registrar's office at your school to complete the required paperwork. The registrar's office will then send your transcripts to the admissions offices of the schools to which you apply. You may have to pay a small fee for each official transcript that you have sent.
- Your letter of intent. A letter of intent can also be called a cover letter, a personal statement, a statement of interest, or another name. Regardless, a letter of intent is basically a cover letter that is geared toward graduate programs and colleges. As emphasized in Chapter 1, graduate schools closely

review letters of intent. How to write many versions of a letter of intent is described in greater detail in Chapter 6.

- Your résumé/CV. Your résumé or curriculum vitae (CV) is an important part of the application. Having this written should be simple because you have been writing and revising your CV since your sophomore year (it was the fifth goal in Chapter 4). How to update your résumé/CV for submission to graduate schools is described in greater detail in Chapter 7.

- The LORs. The letters of recommendation (LORs) are important, and many of the goals in this book were aimed specifically toward helping you create positive, professional relationships with the people you want to write your LORs. In most cases, you will not send the LOR; your recommender will send it out in a signed and sealed envelope or via an online recommendation system set up by a school you applied to. Strategies for requesting LORs and following up with those you asked to recommend you are described in the second goal for your senior year in this chapter.

You will certainly have a lot going on in your senior year. You will have coursework, and if you are following the plan, you may have teaching, research, internships, or activities that take up your time as well. Now, you will add applying to graduate schools to your list of things to do. It may seem like a lot, but there are many ways you can manage your time in addition to clearing your schedule. Mostly, you should be organized and plan ahead, so we can begin there.

Be Organized and Plan Ahead

"Out of clutter find simplicity."

Albert Einstein

Keep in mind that you will likely fill out applications for many different schools, while also balancing your many other academic and scholarly commitments. Staying organized and planning ahead can be crucial to keeping pace with everything you need to do. It is easy to get overwhelmed in your senior year, and you will want to avoid this. To help you plan for your senior year, you can create a calendar with dates and goals to complete different parts of the application process. One way to stay organized and plan ahead is to create a calendar. As an example (without specific dates listed), the following is a sample timeline for completing application materials:

- Summer (*before* senior year):
  - Complete all standardized exams.
  - Research graduate schools to find programs of interest.

- September (senior year):
  - Complete research of graduate programs; choose a final list of schools to which you will apply.

○ Write a final draft of your résumé/CV.
○ Request all LORs (give recommenders the list of submission deadlines for each school to which you will apply).

- October (senior year):
  ○ Write a final draft of letters of intent for each school you will apply to (use your completed résumé to help draft letters).
  ○ Put together application materials for each school (prioritize schools with earlier submission deadlines).

- November (senior year):
  ○ Check that standardized exam scores have been sent to the schools to which you will apply.
  ○ Have all transcripts sent to the schools to which you will apply (if you took courses at more than one school, then you will need transcripts sent from each school where you earned a grade in a course).
  ○ Continue to put together application materials for each school (prioritize schools with earlier submission deadlines).

- December (senior year):
  ○ Begin submitting graduate school applications for schools with December deadlines (these are likely to be the earliest submission deadlines).
  ○ Follow up with recommenders to check that LORs have been sent to the schools you applied to.
  ○ Submit all additional application materials as per the instructions for each school to which you applied.

- January and on (last semester, senior year):
  ○ Follow the December procedures for submitting applications that are due in later months.
  ○ In a best-case scenario, you will be able to have all applications submitted by the end of January, even if some deadlines are later than this.

The schedule given here is one way you could arrange your time to complete all parts of the application and give yourself enough time to do them well. You will want to begin this process in the summer before your senior year to give yourself enough time to complete or nearly complete the process by the end of that calendar year. Make sure you set aside time each day to work on application materials and balance this time with your other academic and scholarly activities.

Also, keep in mind that submitting an application early is encouraged by graduate schools; submitting an application late (after a stated deadline), however, is unacceptable and will likely result in your application being rejected outright. Following the sample calendar here can help you stay ahead of graduate school deadlines. Do not wait until the last minute to submit your graduate school applications. Give yourself enough time to be able to handle last-minute problems, such as resolving questions about the applications or checking that your LORs and transcripts have been sent to the graduate schools.

In truth, four parts of the application really will *not* require substantial amounts of your time:

- The application itself is standard and usually can be completed (often entirely online) in one or two sittings.
- The transcripts are requested and sent by the registrar's office at your school.
- Standardized exam scores are sent by the test makers or reported by you in your application.
- Your LORs are written and sent by your recommenders.

The two parts of the application that really involve substantial time from you are writing your letters of intent (Chapter 6) and writing your résumé/CV (Chapter 7). Notice that if you follow the sample calendar in this section, you will have a month to complete your résumé/CV (in September) and another full month to complete your letters of intent (in October). As long as you give yourself ample time to complete these two key parts of the application, the rest of the application should fall into place and take relatively little additional time to complete. Planning ahead and being organized can substantially help you manage your time as you complete the application process.

Seek Advisement

"Good advice costs nothing, and it's worth the price."

Allan Sherman

With all the pressure to complete applications, realize that you do not necessarily have to go through this process alone. In your freshman year, you should have started making connections, and your advisor is one of the people you should have connected with. Continue to work with an academic advisor or someone you trust who can give you advice—someone who knows about your major, who has earned graduate degrees, and who can help you select and apply to graduate schools that best fit your interests. This is one of the many advantages of having made connections early in college—so that you can get the added help from an advisor that may not have otherwise been available if you had not developed that connection.

At many schools, you are required to meet with an advisor at least once or twice each year. Even if you are not required to meet with an advisor, you should meet with an advisor more often in your senior year. If you have a close enough relationship with your advisor, then he or she may even be willing to review your application materials before you submit them to graduate schools. You can also go to a career center at your school, where many people are trained to help students find and prepare for careers. However, keep in mind that in many cases (1) a career center is better equipped to prepare you for job applications than graduate school applications, which is very different, and (2) many career center staff will not have earned a graduate degree, so they often provide little personal insight into the process of applying to graduate school.

While a career center can certainly be a valuable option, an even better option may be to work directly with an academic advisor who has achieved and can advise you toward graduate degrees in your specific area of interest. Asking for feedback from those who have earned a PhD can prove most beneficial to you because these advisors have proven that they know what it takes to get into a graduate program and succeed. Regardless of where you seek advisement, though, make sure you seek it. Doing so in your senior year can be beneficial to you in that you will have support from someone who can help you when you need it most as you pursue your senior-year goals.

Four Goals for Your Senior Year in College

"Man is a goal seeking animal. His life only has meaning if he is reaching out and striving for his goals."

Aristotle

There are four key goals to pursue in your senior year. To add perspective, keep in mind that you really have already sought the goals you needed to *prepare* for graduate school. In your senior year, your primary additional goals are to *get into* graduate school. This chapter is organized by using each goal stated here as a heading. A full range of ideas, plans, and templates will be shared to help you meet and exceed each goal. In all, there are four key goals you should have listed and be actively working toward in your senior year:

1. Search for graduate schools and be realistic. Not everyone will get into Harvard. Not only should you look for schools that interest you, but you should also find a diverse selection of many schools that are attainable. There is no such thing as a "safety" school when it comes to applying to graduate schools, but you can still be strategic when choosing schools to be more competitive.

2. Request letters of recommendation and follow up. If you keep pace with the plan in this book, then you will have your final list of schools ready by the end of the first month of your senior year. Once you have that list, you need to request LORs immediately to give your recommenders time to write the LORs and have them sent to schools before the application deadlines.

3. Complete all parts of each graduate school application. The six basic parts of a graduate school application have been identified in this chapter. Some parts may be optional, and other parts may be required that are not listed, depending on the schools to which you apply. Do not leave parts out or incomplete;

graduate school selection committees will rarely give consideration to applicants who submit an incomplete application.

4. Apply on time and communicate effectively with schools. Plan backward from application deadlines and prioritize applications with earlier deadlines. If you do not understand application instructions (it happens), then follow up with the schools to clarify your questions. Do not rush through applications. Take your time to ensure you write strong applications.

Search for Graduate Schools and Be Realistic

"We have to be realistic. If we don't win, life will continue."

Hayden Fry

In the summer before your senior year, you really need to begin searching for graduate schools. By the end of the first month of your senior year, you should have your final list of schools prepared. Of course, you should be doing all of this if, in fact, you have decided to apply to graduate schools.

Before you begin applying to graduate schools, make sure you weigh the potential costs and benefits of attending graduate school. Graduate school is a long and potentially expensive commitment. A master's degree can take two or more years to complete; a professional degree, such as medical school or law school, can take three or more years to complete; a doctorate-level degree, such as a PhD, can take four or many more years to complete. These times to complete a graduate degree are all in addition to the time you spent in undergraduate school, and can all add to your total tuition bill. For this reason, it is important that you are certain that attending graduate school is right for you. If you are fully committed to going to graduate school, or you are confident that graduate school is not right for you, then that is just fine either way. However, if you are "on the fence," then keep the following two considerations in mind:

- If you do not apply, then you will not know if graduate school was attainable. Certainly, factors like the costs of graduate school, whether the programs match your interests, and the time it takes to complete the applications will weigh into whether or not you apply. But realize that if you do not apply, then you have no chance of getting into graduate school (in that application year).
- If you apply anyway, then you can always make your decision after the graduate schools have made their decisions. For example, if college debt is a concern, then maybe apply only to PhD programs—many of those programs offer full tuition waivers and additional stipends to cover your living expenses. Or you could limit your search to lower-cost schools. Who knows? Maybe you will get accepted to one of those programs. You will never know if you do not apply.

If you decide that graduate school is the right choice for you, then start by finding schools, programs, and degrees that interest you. The degree level you seek will largely depend on your career goals and the strength of your application—make sure you seek advisement if you are uncertain about anything as you prepare applications and apply to graduate schools. The following considerations should be made when choosing *which degree level* to apply for:

- Postbaccalaureate degrees. This degree level can lead to a second bachelor's degree or even graduate-level degrees depending on the type of program offered. This degree level is common for students looking to change their career path or apply their degree to a new field, such as nursing. You also need to meet the GPA and standardized exam score requirements, and to have taken prerequisite courses stated by the schools to which you apply.

- Master's degrees. This degree level is typically appropriate for students who want to pursue a career in an applied setting, such as being a counselor in a high school or working in business. Many master's-level degrees train you for licensure or certification in that field. You also need to meet the GPA and standardized exam score requirements stated by the schools to which you apply.

- Professional degrees. This degree level includes the JD (law), the MD (medicine), and other degrees in many fields of medicine. Professional degrees can lead directly to jobs in a specific profession. Some programs may also train for licensure in a given applied field. You will also need to meet the GPA, standardized exam score, and possibly prerequisite course requirements stated by the schools to which you apply.

- PhD and other doctoral programs. "Other" doctoral programs include the PsyD (psychology) and the EdD (education). This degree level is typically best for students who want to pursue research and/or college teaching careers, such as being a professor or a scientist. Some programs also train for licensure in a given applied field, such as PhD programs in clinical psychology. You also need to meet the GPA and standardized exam score requirements stated by the schools to which you apply. These degree programs can often have prerequisite course requirements as well.

Another key consideration is the academic programs you apply to. The programs you apply to should fit your interests. The following considerations should be made when choosing *which programs* to apply to:

- Minimum requirements. First and foremost you need to check that you meet the minimum requirements to apply to the program. Many qualified applicants apply to graduate programs each year. It is therefore unlikely that a program will make an exception. Only apply if you meet minimum requirements.

- Search faculty lists. Once you find a program of interest to you, search its faculty lists. Find faculty with academic backgrounds that fit with your career interests. Also check that the program's faculty members engage in research that fits your interests, particularly if you are applying to research-based PhD programs. Many schools specifically ask you to identify the faculty advisor you wish to work under, if accepted to the program. For example, some PhD programs at both Boston University and Pennsylvania State University require this, as do many other institutions. You must be prepared to identify a specific mentor whose research or work most closely fits your interests, if asked.

- Determine the advisement model if you are applying to a PhD program. If you are assigned one faculty member to work under (a mentorship model), then you need to make your application appeal to that one faculty member—also call to check with the program to make sure that the particular professor has an opening for a PhD student. Only apply if the faculty member has an opening. This model is obvious if you see that you must identify a specific mentor in your graduate school application. On the other hand, if you are assigned to many different labs and can choose the lab that best fits your interests (a collaborative model), then you can apply to the program without needing to appeal specifically to the interests of one particular faculty member.

- Search funding options. Check with a program director or contact person to confirm what types of scholarships or funding options the school offers. This can be accomplished with a simple phone call. Some programs may have no funding; others may have substantial funding, to include full scholarships and stipends. Be aware of these options and how to apply for them.

- Be realistic in terms of where you are willing to study. One simple way to narrow your search is by location. If you live in New York, for example, be honest about how far away you are willing to move to go to school. Avoid applying to schools in Wyoming, for example, if you know you are not willing or enthusiastic about moving there.

Another key consideration is the schools you apply to. There is certainly no such thing as a "safety" school when it comes to applying to graduate schools, particularly for doctoral programs. Of course, nationally ranked programs will be most competitive. But also the size of a school—in terms of the number of students enrolled—often corresponds to the competitiveness of a program. Therefore, the following considerations should be made when choosing *which schools* to apply to:

- Small school (fewer than 4,000 students). Small schools that are not ranked tend to get overlooked—by applicants. The best students in the country apply to the best schools in the country. If the school is small and unranked, then you have a better chance of competing for acceptance against a weaker application pool compared to a ranked school or one that is highly recognized. Make sure your final list includes at least one or two small schools to which you will apply.

- Medium-sized school (about 4,000 to 8,000 students). Like small schools, medium-sized schools can also be overlooked if they are not ranked. Therefore, make sure your final list includes at least one or two medium-sized schools to which you will apply.

- Large school (more than 8,000 students). Many large schools are ranked and also have strong name recognition—many times because of the NCAA sports teams that play there. If more people know about those schools, then more people are applying to those schools, especially if they are ranked. Be ambitious and add at least one or two of the large schools to your final list of schools to which you will apply, but recognize that the application pools are likely to be filled with stronger applicants because many large schools tend to be better known, and even ranked.

In addition to the size of a school, another key factor is whether the school is a public or private school. If you apply to doctoral programs, keep in mind that acceptance rates are very low (less than 10% on average). That being said, private schools have acceptance rates that are about two times higher than those of public schools (about 12% compared to 6%, on average). You will therefore want to consider applying to some private and some public schools to improve your overall chances of being accepted to doctorate-level programs. The master's-level degree programs have much better acceptance rates of about 40% on average, so you can consider applying to some master's degree programs in addition to doctoral programs to increase your chances of gaining acceptance to a graduate school. The important lesson here is to "play your hand" based on your odds of acceptance. Don't get caught up in the name recognition of a school. Be realistic and apply to a fair sample of colleges—ranked and unranked; known and unknown; small, medium, and large; private and public. You can decide which school to attend when the decision letters arrive.

In total, you should apply to 8 to 10 (or more) graduate programs, if possible. Applying to more schools increases your chances of finding a school that will accept your application, which is the ultimate goal. Many schools will charge a fee for submitting an application. Consequently, the cost of the fees may limit the number of applications you can submit. Some schools offer waivers for application submission fees. Check with each school to see if you qualify for a waiver. In all, the suggestions provided here should help you narrow your list of graduate schools to maximize your chances of "getting in."

As a final reminder, always remember to seek advisement as you narrow your list to make sure you are applying to the schools and programs that best fit your interests. The suggestions provided here are intended to help you organize your search and choose a final list of schools that give you the best chances of finding an acceptance letter at the end of your search. In all, search for schools and be realistic. Following this advice can help you realize your goal of "getting in" to graduate school.

Request Letters of Recommendation and Follow Up

"You don't carry in your countenance a letter of recommendation."

Charles Dickens

While the number of recommendation letters requested by graduate schools can vary, the most common number of LORs requested by graduate schools is three letters. Too often, students will spend their time trying to get three recommendation letters without concern for the quality of the people they are asking. This is a big mistake because the graduate schools to which these students apply will likely read those letters and use them to heavily weigh their decision to accept or reject an applicant. In Chapter 4, I identified three characteristics of the types of people you will want to request an LOR from—as part of the suggestions given for the first goal of your sophomore and junior years: Get connected. Follow the suggestions given in that chapter.

Also, consider the type of role of the person you request a letter from. You will likely want two of your letters to be written by a professor or an advisor (such as your academic advisor or a lab/internship advisor if you made such a connection). The professor can talk about your academic rigor; the advisor can talk about your work ethic, drive, motivation, initiative, attitude, character, critical thinking skills, and other key characteristics that graduate schools are interested in. Often many schools will state directly what they want to read in your LORs. If they do, then communicate this to the people you ask to write your LORs so that they can discuss what the graduate schools want to read.

The third letter can come from a professor or an advisor, or it can come from another source, such as a coach or boss. A coach is a great recommender for an athlete because he or she can speak to the student's ability to balance a full-time academic schedule with the rigors of athletic commitments. If you apply to programs that are applied or will involve internships, then showing evidence of applied experience (in a related field) can benefit you if a boss or supervisor writes your letter. Regardless of whom you choose, be sure that your recommenders represent the interests of the graduate schools. If you apply to a research-based program, for example, then have at least one recommender who can speak to your ability to conduct research. Remember that you will write a letter of intent to shape the story you want to tell graduate schools—make sure that your recommenders tell the same type of story.

Sometimes the most stressful parts of submitting an application are the parts that you do not actually submit. One of the parts that you often do not submit yourself is the LORs. Students can often get frustrated if one of the recommenders they asked to write a letter does not submit it to the graduate schools on time. It can be frustrating because it is largely out of the students' control. However, the following are strategies you can apply to help support your recommenders to ensure that their letters are submitted on time to the graduate schools:

- Make the request at least one month ahead of the submission deadline. Based on the plan given in this chapter, you would give notice in September, which should be at least two months before any deadlines. Doing so can ensure that they have plenty of time to get the letter written.
- For online LOR submissions, give your recommenders the list of schools with an online LOR submission process. Schools with an online LOR process will contact your recommenders to complete the required LOR forms online. You need to let your recommenders know which schools will be contacting them to request an LOR. Give your recommenders this list of schools at the time you request them to write a letter for you.

- For printed or hard-copy LOR submissions, give your recommenders all materials needed to complete the LOR and fully addressed stamped envelopes. If a school requires a hard-copy LOR submission, then you likely need to print an LOR cover form provided by the graduate school that is usually signed by both the applicant and the recommender. Print that form, sign it, and hand it to your recommender. Also have addressed and stamped envelopes for each school already completed so that your recommender does not pay the postage. Have all of these materials ready to give to your recommenders at the time you request them to write a letter for you.

- On all forms, *decline* your right to have access to the materials and letter that your recommender submits. You need to trust in your recommenders. This is why you were working to make professional connections—to ensure that you had three strong recommenders whom you could trust. If you do not trust someone, then do not ask him or her for an LOR. Graduate school selection committees will often discredit an LOR if you do not decline to see it first. Declining to see an LOR before it is submitted ensures the integrity of the letter written, and the letter will carry more weight with the selection committees.

- Be organized. Do not just hand your recommender a stack of forms, particularly if you are applying to more than one school. Separate each school into a packet. Buy folders and place the forms for each school into its own folder and label the folder with the name of each school. Also, include a cover letter in each folder with the name of the school and the name of the program to which you are applying, a brief description of the program, and the submission deadline listed. Also give your recommender a copy of your résumé or CV. He or she will undoubtedly be very impressed that you are so prepared at the time you make the request.

To follow up with your recommenders, you should be patient, but also persistent. A good strategy is to make the initial request in the first month of your senior year. About one month before an application deadline, write a simple "courtesy e-mail" to your recommenders indicating the schools with an upcoming deadline and your appreciation for their time in writing the letters. About two weeks ahead of a deadline, resend a "courtesy e-mail" to each recommender who has not yet submitted his or her LOR. If with a few days to go you still have recommenders who have not yet submitted their LOR, then about 48 hours before an application deadline, send them a final "courtesy e-mail" to remind them. In most cases, your recommenders will appreciate your reminders, if they are written as a "courtesy" and are respectful.

As stated in Chapter 4, a very important reason to make professional connections is that you will eventually need strong LORs. Now is when all that hard work to build professional connections pays off. Having three strong LORs to support your application can demonstrate that you are a strong applicant in that others can confirm the strengths of your application. In all, be strategic about selecting your recommenders. Seek an advisor, if needed, for help to choose the best recommenders based on the type of degree and the type of program you will apply to. And follow the tips provided here to help ensure that your recommenders submit their LORs on time.

Complete All Parts of Each Graduate School Application

"The secret to getting things done is to act."

Dante Alighieri

To complete the applications, it is specifically important that you (1) follow the application instructions and (2) complete all parts of the application. The following are specific things to look for to make sure that your application is complete:

- The application itself. Make sure all blanks are filled in. If an item or a question does not apply to you, then you can leave it blank or state N/A for "not applicable." Double check, however, that you have filled in all information before you submit the application. The online applications will often not accept your submission if it is incomplete, which gives you the chance to complete missing items first before it is submitted.
- Your standardized exam scores. Make sure these scores are listed on your application, if requested. If scores are sent by a secondary source, then call the graduate schools to confirm that they have received your scores. If any issues or problems arise, then try to troubleshoot them earlier rather than later.
- Your academic transcripts. You can request to have your transcripts sent by the registrar's office at your school about a week or so before you officially submit your application. Be sure to follow up with the registrar's office a week later to confirm that your transcripts were sent.
- Your letter of intent. Give yourself at least a full month to write a final draft of this letter. Realize that not all schools ask for the same letters. Some schools will give special instructions, such as word limits or specific topics they want you to discuss. Follow any special instructions exactly, or else a selection committee may disregard your letter of intent. How to complete these letters is described in more detail in Chapter 6.
- Your résumé/CV. You should have a final CV draft ready within the first few weeks of your senior year, which should be easy to do if you have been writing and revising it since your sophomore year. How to update your CV for submission to graduate schools is described in more detail in Chapter 7.
- The LORs. Request LORs early and follow up until they are sent. Follow the suggestions given in this chapter to make sure your LORs are submitted before the application deadlines. Also, follow the suggestions in Chapter 4 for selecting people who can give you strong recommendation letters—i.e., letters that will impress a graduate school selection committee.

One additional part not listed is a writing sample. Relatively few schools will require this, but the chances are decent that a school may ask you to provide a writing sample. Have a writing sample prepared. The most efficient way to do this is to take a course that requires a paper—and put a lot of work into that paper. You can also get involved in research or another type of independent study in which you must write a paper or manuscript. You can then use the paper or manuscript as your writing sample. Both strategies allow you to have a writing sample ready, without needing to add this to your "list of things to do" in your senior year.

When completing the parts of the application, focus mostly on those parts that will require most of your time: namely, the letters of intent (Chapter 6) and résumé/CV (Chapter 7). Plan to complete applications at least a few weeks before a deadline to give yourself time to proofread your application, give it to a friend or advisor and have him or her proofread it, and then proofread it again yourself. Once you have completed all parts of the application, you are ready to apply to graduate school.

Apply on Time and Communicate Effectively With Schools

"Better three hours too soon than a minute too late."

William Shakespeare

While six basic parts of the graduate school application are identified here, you still need to check whether the schools you are applying to have different parts to be submitted. If you are unsure about any aspect of the application based on your search of a school's website, then call the admissions office or a program director at the graduate school to confirm what is required to be submitted. Do not make assumptions about what is required; find out if you are unsure. Do not hesitate to contact schools directly if you have questions about an application. If you are unsure how to approach a school or how to ask your question, then talk with an advisor to get clarification before contacting the graduate school. Getting it right is most important. To communicate effectively with the graduate schools, also consider the following advice:

- Use common courtesies (e.g., *please* and *thank you*). Be polite when speaking with a person on the other end of the phone or via e-mail. Treat any interactions with a graduate school as if you are being interviewed.
- Be respectful and do not lose patience, if frustrated. Sometimes graduate schools can lose application materials or not receive them at all. Do not take it out on the person you talk to on the phone. Be respectful and kind. Ask what you can do to resolve the situation. The person you speak with will appreciate your willingness to help resolve the problem or concern.
- Do not try to sell yourself impromptu. If you have a specific reason for calling or e-mailing a graduate school, then keep the conversation focused on the reason for your message. Do not go off topic by talking about how you are a good fit for the program—particularly if you have not prepared yet for such a conversation. You will have plenty of opportunity in your application to "sell" yourself. Keep any queries to graduate schools focused on your query.

Also, plan backward from application deadlines and prioritize applications with earlier deadlines. Work first on the application materials for graduate schools with earlier deadlines to make sure you get the applications submitted on time. If deadlines are early, then also let your recommenders know and be prepared to have transcripts sent earlier if needed. Avoid having too much to do at the last minute. Planning ahead and prioritizing application materials based on deadlines for submitting applications can help you avoid being overwhelmed as deadlines approach.

Once your applications are submitted, you can feel quite accomplished! Reward yourself and relax. Now, there is little you can control. Celebrate having put the work in to prepare and submit all of your applications and having put in all the work to make yourself competitive for these graduate programs. Decision letters from graduate schools will arrive in a few months. For now, enjoy the moment, celebrate, and be positive about the many possibilities for your future.

Completing the Application . . . and More

"The secret of getting started is breaking your complex overwhelming tasks into small manageable tasks, and then starting on the first one."

Mark Twain

In all, the goals for your senior year build upon those in your freshman, sophomore, and junior years. Your senior year is mostly spent managing your time and resources so that you can continue to work positively toward graduating on time, and give yourself ample time to complete the graduate school applications. This freshman-to senior-year plan is aimed at helping you to develop professional connections and be able to find and realize many opportunities available to you. From academics, to research, to internships and activities, opportunities are plentiful in college if you know how to take advantage of them—as shown in this comprehensive plan for getting into graduate school. No matter when you first started reading this book, one thing is certain: You can be competitive for admission to graduate school by taking advantage of the many opportunities that are available to you as an undergraduate student.

Importantly, not only do you need to be competitive to get into graduate schools; you also need to be able to communicate what makes you competitive in your graduate application. The two parts of a graduate school application where you must effectively communicate what makes you a competitive candidate are your letter of intent (Chapter 6) and your résumé/CV (Chapter 7). It is also essential to plan for the process that follows the applications (e.g., interviews and waiting for a response from graduate schools; Chapter 8). For this reason, Section III is included as a continuation of your senior-year plan. This section is devoted to walking you through the completion of a graduate school application and the process that follows. Borrowing from Mark Twain: It will break the complex overwhelming task of applying to graduate school into small manageable tasks, and we will start with the letter of intent in Chapter 6.

SECTION III

Completing Parts of The Graduate School Application and More

Writing a "Letter of Intent"

Writing a Letter of Intent: Gaining Perspective

"It takes one to tell, and two to misunderstand."

H. C. Payne

A letter of intent is one part of the graduate school application. It is also one of the most important parts inasmuch as selection committees will closely review your letter of intent, particularly for doctoral programs. Your letter of intent alone can push you to the top of a list of applicants, and it can all but eliminate you from consideration. You are best served by setting aside substantial time to write your letter of intent.

It can honestly be hard to write about yourself. After all, it may feel as if you are bragging about yourself as you write. It is easy to get self-conscious when you write a letter that is essentially trying to tell graduate schools how great you are. However, keep in mind that you are not writing a letter about how great you are. Instead, you are writing a letter about how well your interests and experiences fit with the aims or goals of the program to which you apply; you are writing about how you can help to serve the needs of the program and fit within the model of teaching, learning, and research at the school. You need to take the perspective of the graduate schools. Hence, if you feel that you are "just bragging" as you write your letter of intent, then you should probably start over—that is not the perspective you should take to write your letter of intent.

As you write your letter of intent, you should focus on the tone and style of your writing. Gaining the right perspective before you begin writing your letter of intent means that you appeal to the interests of the graduate schools. Your letter of intent should incorporate the tone and language used by the school to which you apply. If a school, for example, describes its program as "focused on micro and macro perspectives," then the letter you write should appeal to both micro and macro perspectives for the field to which you are applying. In this way, you can create a template for how to write your letters, but no two letters are likely to be written exactly the same way—you will adapt each letter so that you can make it appeal to the interests of each school.

To illustrate the importance of appealing to the interests of others, imagine for a moment that a football team needs a quarterback. Does the person vying for that job spend most time catching footballs and talking about tackling? No—those skills are not related to being a good quarterback. Instead, the person throws footballs and talks about calling offensive plays—skills that quarterbacks have. In the same way, imagine that a graduate school has a program with a "particular emphasis on practice-oriented instruction." Do you write a letter to that school and not at all mention your familiarity with practice-oriented instruction (such as lab or field courses)? No. If anything, you make that a theme in your writing—because the graduate program just told you that "practice-oriented instruction" is important to it. Appeal to its interests, and the graduate school will naturally be more interested in *you*.

While it is important to "sell yourself," do not oversell yourself. In other words, do not write in a way that could be thought of as bragging. Again, if you feel that you are just bragging in your writing, then start over. In truth, it is difficult to write a letter of intent that appeals to graduate schools and highlights your exceptional qualities, but at the same time is humble. The following are some suggestions for how to write a strong letter of intent by effectively matching your interests and exceptional qualities to those of a graduate school:

- Identify your familiarity with the school's program. Read its website closely before writing the letter of intent. Add information about the program in your letter to show that you have an understanding of the program.
- Use keywords from the school's website. An easy way to demonstrate your familiarity with a program is to use keywords and short phrases, *exactly* as the school does. For example, if a program describes its goal as training students to "work in mental health settings," then you should describe your experiences and goals in terms of your desire to "work in mental health settings." Say it *exactly* as the program says it to explicitly match the program's interests.
- Identify, if possible, your familiarity with the area or community of the school. Where the school is located is important. It can take only one sentence to dispel any possible misunderstanding of your interest in moving to the area.
- Follow the instructions. Never go over the stated page or word count limits. If a school lists specific information it wants you to discuss in your letter, then discuss that information. For example, if a school asks you to "describe how this program will help you to build a foundation for a career," then address this directly. In your letter, simply start a paragraph or sentence with "Your program will help me to build a foundation for a career by . . ." Make it obvious that you are addressing what the school asked you to address in your letter.
- Identify the goals and mission of the program to which you are applying, and express an interest in contributing to the goals and mission of the program.

Simply knowing the mission, let alone indicating an interest in contributing to that mission, can impress many selection committees. Be sincere.

- Provide a rationale for choosing to pursue a program and why it is important to you. Professors put a lot of time into their work and think of it as very important. To make your professors feel important, indicate that you view their work as important. Viewing their work as important makes them feel important—and we all like people who make us feel important. Do not write with insincere flattery; you must be sincere in your writing.

- Take responsibility for weaknesses in your application. If your grade in research methods is low, for example, do not justify that you "took a difficult professor." Instead, explain how you overcame the weaknesses. For example, "I scored a low grade in my research methods class. For this reason, I sought a one-year research opportunity to gain more experience and strengthen my knowledge in this subject area." Here you explain that you recognized a weakness and that you did something about it. That sounds a lot better than simply blaming someone else.

- Name-drop, selectively. If you worked in a research lab or as an assistant to a well-known, prestigious, or successful person, then add his or her name in your letter—first, ask the person you worked under for permission to use his or her name. Do not use too many names, but if one person stands out, then certainly feel free to use his or her name in your letter, particularly if his or her name will be recognized by, and even impress, a graduate school selection committee.

- Stick to the talking points: academics, scholarship, and activities. Do not go too far off topic from these central points. The most effective letters of intent stick to these talking points, which almost always makes the writing more focused, clear, and concise.

The following are common mistakes that should be avoided when writing your letter of intent:

- Avoid backstories, unless specifically requested by a school to add this. Avoid stories of your childhood or other stories that may be too revealing, not relevant, or inappropriate. Feedback from psychology graduate school committee chairs indicates that including a backstory does not impress them—unless they specifically asked for it to be included.

- Avoid altruistic claims, such as applying to a program because you "want to help people" (why?) or you "want to make a difference in the world" (how?). Making such claims can be regarded as insincere or vague. If you do make these claims, then explain yourself, such as answering the questions in parentheses for each of the examples given here.

- Avoid literary devices or attempts to be funny. You are submitting an application to a graduate school. In this light, you are expected to write professionally. Hence, your writing should be literal. For example, do not write, "My grades were off the charts." What charts? While it is a clever saying, most selection committees will not be impressed. You can write instead, "I had high academic performance," or something to that effect.

- Avoid claiming your faith, unless the school specifically asks you to speak about your faith. It is not that your faith isn't important. Of course it is! It simply goes back to sticking to the talking points. If the school did not ask you to comment on your faith, then do not comment on it in your letter.

- Avoid misspellings. Grammatical and spelling errors reflect on your competency. Fair or not, misspellings in a letter of intent, alone, can eliminate you from being considered further by a selection committee, especially if many errors are found in your letter. Proofread your letter of intent many times before submitting it to a graduate school.

- Avoid flattery, which is a compliment without context. Your letter should express an interest in the program or school to which you apply, but you must be sincere. For example, Do not write, "Your program's focus on qualitative analysis is really interesting." This has no context; it reads as insincere flattery. Give context for why it is interesting: "Your program's focus on qualitative analysis is interesting to me because I applied this level of analysis in my research-based training at the university." Here, the writer expresses an interest, then explains why. Doing so not only helps you appeal to the interests of a graduate program but also makes your writing appear more sincere.

Also, if you are applying to a PhD program with a mentorship model—a model in which you will be assigned to work under one specific faculty member—then mention that person by name in your letter of intent. As identified in Chapter 5 (page 99), you should know the type of advisement model at a graduate school program before you submit your application. For a mentorship model, it is important to name the person you wish to work under, if accepted. Doing so appeals to the interests of the faculty member you would work under, and it shows an understanding of the culture of the graduate school to which you will apply.

In all, apply common sense in your writing. Know your audience, and know the program, the school, and the culture. Know your interests and how they relate to the interests of a graduate school, and be sincere. In this chapter, I will show you how undergraduate students have used the suggestions provided here to write their letters of intent—with a particular emphasis on examples from students who have since been accepted to graduate schools within the last few years.

The Parts of a Letter of Intent

"If you can't explain it simply, you don't understand it well enough."

Albert Einstein

A *letter of intent* is any letter that expresses an intention to take or decline some action. In the case of writing such a letter to a graduate school, it is a letter indicating your intent or desire to join a graduate program. This letter can be called by many names. Alternative names for a letter of intent include *statement of interest*, *personal statement*, *cover letter*, *personal profile essay*, *applicant statement*, and more.

Although the names may vary, the purpose of the letter is almost always the same—to indicate your intent or desire to join a graduate program.

The structure of a letter of intent can vary substantially from one school to the next. Typical letters of intent are between two and three pages. However, these letters can be as short as 300 to 500 words, or as long as five or more pages. The content of a letter of intent can also vary. Some graduate schools want you to discuss why you chose their school, other schools may ask you how you plan to apply your degree upon graduation, and still others may ask you to speak about yourself without more detailed instructions. Regardless of the length and content of your letter of intent, as requested by graduate schools, it can be structured into three general parts:

- *Introduction.* An introduction can be a few sentences or a full paragraph. In an introduction, you identify your interest in, and your familiarity with, a graduate program, and identify yourself as a good "fit" for the program.
- *Main body.* The main body can differ substantially from one school to another, depending on the word count and page limits, and the instructions given for what to include in your letter. Regardless, the main body should identify your "Big Three" accomplishments, and be organized by topic (e.g., academics, scholarship, and activities) or organized by chronology (from freshman to senior year). Organizing your letter of intent by topic or chronology can make your letter easier to follow and read.
- *Closing.* A closing can be a few sentences or a full paragraph. In a closing, you reaffirm your interest in a graduate program, summarize how you are a good "fit" for admission into the graduate program, and thank the committee members for their time and consideration.

While the content and page length can vary substantially from one letter of intent to the next, the general structure described here is typical for most letters. To further support your writing, a full sample letter of intent is also given in the Appendix. The letter of intent in the Appendix was written by a student who was subsequently accepted in 2014 to the doctoral program to which he applied.

In this chapter, I will describe how to write each part of a letter of intent with examples shown, given different page lengths and word count limits. Students who were subsequently accepted to the graduate programs to which they applied wrote the example letters given in this chapter. The advice in this chapter has proven effective for many students in recent years, although different advice for how to best write these letters may likely prove effective for other students.

Introduction

> *"The presence of an introduction is held to imply that there is something of consequence and importance to be introduced."*
>
> Arthur Machen

An introduction should be a full paragraph or a few sentences, depending on length requirements by a school. It can begin with an introductory sentence that identifies the program to which you are applying. The following is an appropriate sentence to open the introductory paragraph:

"I would like to express interest in applying for the [degree level] program in [name of program] at [name of university]."

As two examples, the first is an applicant writing to a PhD program in organizational behavior; the second is an applicant writing to a program with a specific title or name (identifying the full name of the program can help you show early on that you are familiar with the program):

"I would like to express an interest in applying for the PhD program in organizational behavior at Binghamton University."

"I would like to express an interest in applying for the master's program in mental health counseling at the Margaret Warner Graduate School of Education and Human Development at the University of Rochester."

In the next sentence (or two), you identify (1) a statement of familiarity with the area of the school, if you can, and (2) a statement of familiarity with the program using keywords from the school's website. Selection committees sometimes think of "fit" in a graduate program as being more than just the coursework or research area (see the section on *geographic matching* in Chapter 1)—they also want to know if you will "fit in" with the college community. Don't leave it to a committee to answer this question. If you are familiar in any way with the area (such as having family nearby), then say so up front to dispel any misunderstandings. In the same sentence, or in a third sentence (depending on the word count limits), make a statement of familiarity with the program. Use keywords from a school's website to appeal to the interests of a committee.

As examples, here is how two students, the PhD applicant and the master's applicant, wrote their statements of familiarity: One wrote each statement in separate sentences; the other wrote both statements in one sentence (phrases taken directly from a school's website or paraphrased are given in italics so you can see where the phrases were inserted in their writing; do not use italics in your own writing):

"As a native of the Binghamton area, I am familiar with the Binghamton campus and community. In addition, I am familiar with your program's particular emphasis on *leadership in and of organizations*."

"As a student with family in the Rochester area, I am familiar with your program's particular emphasis on *practice-oriented instruction* with a focus on *preparing students for work in community agencies, clinics, and hospitals*."

If you have no connection to the area, then you can include a statement of interest to live in the area, or skip it and only include a statement of familiarity with the program. However, if you can include both statements, then do so.

To close the opening paragraph, describe in one sentence how you were drawn to the program—to personalize the letter and show that it was specifically *this* program that you were drawn to, and not just any program. In the next sentence, make a general closing statement of how you are a good "fit" for the program you are applying to—the rest of your letter will demonstrate evidence of your closing claim. If the letter has word count restrictions (such as a word limit of 300 to 500 words), then omit the last sentence. Continue to use keywords in your closing, if possible, to make your letter appeal to the school's interests when stating how you were drawn to this graduate program.

As examples, here is how two students, the PhD applicant and the master's applicant, closed their introductory paragraphs (phrases taken directly from a school's website or paraphrased are given in italics so you can see where the phrases were inserted in their writing; do not use italics in your own writing):

> "As a former captain of the [name of current school] women's Division IA soccer team, and as a laboratory manager for research facilities at [name of current university], I found myself in a leadership role and naturally became interested in the *dynamics of individual and team behavior*. In all, I feel that these experiences along with my record of academic success in the classroom make me a unique, well-prepared, motivated, and well-adjusted candidate for admission into your program."

> "As a youth care employee at [name of workplace], and as a research assistant in clinical and health research laboratories at [name of current school], I found myself in a *diagnostic and exploratory role* and naturally became interested in the *dynamics of individual health and well-being*."

The second example shown here was for a letter that had a word count limit of 500 words, so the second closing sentence was omitted to allow for the more important content (the "Big Three") to be discussed in the main body of the letter. Regardless of the word count limits of your letter, the examples shown here illustrate how you can write with intentionality. In other words, each sentence in these introductory paragraphs has a purpose, either to express a familiarity with the school and program, or to identify up front how you will "fit" in the program.

Main Body

> *"It's much easier to be convincing if you care about your topic."*
>
> Nicholas Boothman

The main body of a letter of intent is where you have the opportunity to convince the members of a graduate school selection committee that you are a good fit for their program. The main body constitutes the entire letter, except for the brief introduction and closing. It can be a few paragraphs in length, or one paragraph if the letter must be written within strict word limits. Thus, the main body can be written very differently, depending on the experiences of the student and the type of program to which the student is applying. As a general rule, the main body of a letter of intent should emphasize your most important merits—this does not mean the merits *you* find most important; it means merits that a graduate school finds most important.

Your merits are the Big Three: academics, scholarship, and activities. Keep in mind that these merits are also listed in your curriculum vitae, or CV. You can and should use your CV to help you organize your ideas when writing your letter of intent. The main body of your letter of intent, however, should not simply repeat what is already in your CV, such as simply listing your qualifications or merits. Instead, the main body of your letter of intent should expand on, highlight, or emphasize how your merits make you a good fit for the program to which you are applying. In all, make the following considerations for writing your main body:

- Make the Big Three *the* primary focus of your main body. The Big Three will appeal most to graduate schools. You want to show how your experiences with the Big Three fit well with the program to which you are applying.
- Organize the main body of your letter of intent by topics that are important to a graduate school (e.g., academics, scholarship, activities) and tell a story. You can also organize it by chronology (from freshman to senior year), although the focus of the main body should still be the Big Three. Organizing your letter of intent by topic or chronology can help you "build upon" your CV (not just repeat it), and it can make your letter easier to follow and read.
- Begin the main body with the topic you anticipate will be most important to the graduate school you are applying to. As a writer, you want to capture the interest of the reader. Think about it: If you read the first few pages of a book and are not yet interested, what will you do? Probably stop reading—so also may members of a graduate school selection committee stop reading if they are not yet interested in your letter of intent in the first few paragraphs. Lead with what will appeal most to a graduate school to increase your chances that a selection committee will read your entire letter. You need to read each school's website to find what it states is most important.
- Address weaknesses that you anticipate could otherwise hurt your application. You cannot always be a perfect student, and graduate schools do not expect you to be. If necessary, your letter of intent is a good place to address weaknesses or limitations, and explain how you have addressed them. However, identify limitations in your letter only if you can also explain how you have addressed them.

As an example of a main body that hits on each of these suggestions, the following is how the PhD applicant described her merits by beginning with a story of how she came to find an interest and apply to the graduate program (some details in the letter of intent are omitted for brevity and confidentiality; see the Appendix for a full sample letter):

"As the captain of the [name of current school] women's Division IA soccer team, I actively participated in team and coaches' meetings, and was responsible for fostering a collaborative spirit among teammates and coaches. . . . In my team meetings and interactions with teammates and coaches, I found myself asking many questions: Why do some things motivate some people, but not others? What is it about their personalities that affect their behavior? Knowing such differences, how should coaches and other team leaders effectively lead so that the team succeeds while still allowing for individual needs to be met? In essence, I realized that my true interests were in answering these kinds of questions. These interests are what I pursued in my education.

As an undergraduate, I logged in many hours of research. I was awarded as a Psych Scholar each of my four years. This is a monetary scholarship program awarded to students who work in a research capacity under the direct supervision of a PhD mentor. Although my athletic-academic scholarship precluded me from accepting the monetary award, I gladly accepted this scholarship because I was passionate about engaging in the research process. . . . As a Psych Scholar, I was able to spend copious hours one-on-one in the laboratory working with a PhD advisor who taught me how to conduct research, analyze data, and effectively communicate results.

The combination of my experiences as an undergraduate led me to pursue further education in business and a position as the manager of a lab facility. As the manager of research facilities here at [name of current school], I manage animal and human laboratory facilities, balance budgetary and funding needs, and play a role in allocating appropriate resources to researchers who work in the lab facilities. . . . I am involved in teaching as the instructor for two courses . . . at the university. . . . While working and teaching, I also earned my MBA to gain graduate-level experience and to begin channeling my experiences and interests into fields related to business and organizational behavior.

As organizational behavior has become my passion and interest, I acknowledge that my experience in this field to date is limited. . . . This has certainly not been due to a lack of interest on my part. Indeed, the reason I pursued an MBA was to gain the general knowledge in business and organizational behavior I would need to demonstrate the potential for being successful in a PhD program like yours. . . . In all, I certainly acknowledge my potential limitations, although I feel that these certainly do not preclude me from being able to achieve the goals of your program and to meet the needs of faculty in their research."

Notice that she incorporates all four parts of a main body. Her academics, scholarship, and activities are all emphasized; she organizes the letter by topic to tell a story of "how she came to discover an interest in organizational behavior"; she begins with her experiences in leadership to appeal to the graduate school; and she finishes by addressing her potential weakness of having limited experiences that are specific to the program to which she is applying. Note also that she does not simply state her limitation. Instead, she identifies her limitation, then explains how she addressed it—by seeking further education in a business-related field before applying.

A letter of intent adds context or "a story" to a list of merits in a CV. The letter helps to shape how a committee will evaluate your experiences. Adding context helps to eliminate misunderstanding by the committee, clarify the importance of your experiences, and overcome weaknesses (if any). In the sample letter given here, the applicant shaped how a committee evaluated her strengths and shortcomings by describing her experiences in the light in which she wanted the committee to view her experiences.

Also, if you have word count limits, odds are that you need to make major cuts in the main body (you can also make cuts in the introduction and closing parts, as described in this chapter). Taking out content in the main body of your letter can be difficult. Even with the word count limit, you still need to adequately convey your "fit" for the program you are applying to. It is very possible that you write a three-page letter for one school, and for another school, you only have 500 words to write the same letter.

To show how you can make major cuts in a main body and still adequately convey your "fit" for a program, the following are two letters written by the applicant for the master's program. The first letter had a two-page limit and was written in three full paragraphs, as shown here (some details in the letter of intent are omitted for brevity and confidentiality; see the Appendix for a full sample letter):

"I have spent my four years at [name of current school] deeply engaged in research. . . . As evidence of research and academic success, I was awarded the annual Psychology Scholarship in my junior and senior years; this award is given only to the top two students in each graduating class. As a research assistant, I have completed three major research projects under the advisement of a health psychologist and psychology professor. I am named as a coauthor on two projects that are now in press for publication in peer-reviewed journals, and am now completing a third project with promising and significant results. As part of my responsibilities . . . I participated in developing the hypothesis and study design for the research, obtaining IRB approval, and also conducting research, analyzing data, and writing the posters and manuscripts for each project.

I have further placed particular focus on my coursework and teaching to specifically prepare for graduate school. As a student, I have maintained a 3.68 GPA and excelled in statistics and research methods courses that led to me being a teaching assistant for the course in fall 2012. I have also served as a paid tutor for statistics and research methods courses in psychology, and further taken courses in maladaptive behavior, clinical methods, and other psychology electives that have given me relevant knowledge for my field of interest as a mental health counselor. These courses and teaching assistant/ tutor opportunities have prepared me for . . . your program.

Through these experiences, I have discovered a passion for helping others, particularly . . . in an applied setting. While in college, I have worked in a clinical setting through employment at [name of employer]. This experience provided me with . . . a foundation for working with children with mental illness. . . . In addition, I worked with an adult population that struggles with mental illness, as well as poverty. I also completed one year as a member of [name of volunteer organization], which was a total of 300 community service hours. These hours gave me an opportunity to work in many settings, including a local student-run soup kitchen, a women's shelter, an addictions center, and a youth mentoring program on campus. My volunteer experience . . . opened my eyes to the diversity and struggles that many communities and individuals face."

The actual total word count of the above letter was almost 900 words. This same letter had to be shortened to fit a word count limit of 500 or fewer total words for a second school. The following is the main body of that letter, which was reduced to two paragraphs—notice that the letter conveys the same essential information, albeit briefly:

"I have been deeply engaged in research since my sophomore year. I was awarded the annual Psychology Scholarship in my junior and senior years; this award is given only to the top two students in each graduating class. As a research assistant, I have completed three major research projects under the direction of a PhD advisor for which I am a coauthor on each project, two of which are in press for publication in peer-reviewed journals. My responsibilities for these projects included developing the hypothesis and study design for the research, obtaining IRB approval, and also conducting research, analyzing data, and writing the posters and manuscripts for each project.

As a student, I have further engaged in academics, volunteer work, and clinical internship experience at [name of employer] as a [name of job title]. I have maintained a 3.68 GPA and excelled in statistics and research methods courses that led to me being a teaching assistant for the course in fall 2012 and a paid tutor. Also, I have worked with children who have various mental health illnesses as an employee at [name of employer]. This organization provides detailed training in crisis prevention aimed at understanding and working with clinical populations. I have further volunteered in [name of volunteer organization] for 300 service hours, and volunteered at a student-run soup kitchen, women's shelter, addictions center, and youth mentoring program. In the classroom, I also took courses in maladaptive behavior and clinical methods to further prepare for the academic rigors of your program."

Just reading these two samples should give you an appreciation for how different the main body in a letter of intent can be. There is no one right way to write it. However, following the four considerations for writing your main body described here can help you organize and write your letters to effectively convey your "fit" for a program. After all, the main body is where you can best communicate your "fit" for a program, which is why so many examples have been given in this section to demonstrate how you can organize and write the main body of your letter of intent.

Closing

"It's more fun to arrive at a conclusion than to justify it."

Malcolm Forbes

A closing should be a full paragraph or a few sentences, depending on length requirements by a school. It should be concise and to the point. In a closing, you identify (1) a summary or "takeaway message" of your letter, (2) a sentence reaffirming your interest in *this* specific program, and (3) your appreciation for being considered by the graduate school. In your closing, also remember to relate the "takeaway message" to the interests of the graduate program to which you apply.

As two examples, the following is how the PhD applicant and the applicant to the master's program wrote their final closing paragraphs:

"In all, I feel that my experiences demonstrate all the pieces needed to show that I can and will be successful at the graduate level. I have experience as a leader on the soccer field where decisions are immediate, and in an academic environment where decisions are often more reflective. I have pursued research interests as a researcher and as a lab manager. In the classroom I have taught students in courses required across majors, and earned my MBA as the final piece. A career in business would be a means by which I could begin working; acceptance into your program, on the other hand, would be a means by which I could begin my *life's* work. I am certain of my goals, and I am certain that I would be committed to learning and engaging in the academic and research interests demonstrated by your faculty. Thank you for your time and consideration of my application for the PhD program in organizational behavior at [name of school]."

"In all, I have made many efforts to prepare for the rigors of graduate school and the pursuit of a career in mental health counseling. I have maintained a high GPA, while also being actively engaged in research resulting in publication, internships in mental health counseling, and additional volunteer and organizational work. All of my experiences have led me to your program. I am certain of my goals and certain that your program offers me the best opportunity to reach my goals of being a mental health counselor. I am excited for the opportunity to continue to grow and develop in the research and applied academic interests demonstrated by your faculty. Thank you sincerely for your time and consideration of my application for admission to the master's of mental health counseling program at [name of school]."

Each closing incorporates the three parts of a closing: Each closing begins with a summary, then follows with a statement reaffirming interest in the specific program that the school offers, and then thanks the committee members for their time and consideration. Often for letters with strict word count limits, you can forgo the first part (the "takeaway message" summary) to save space. For longer letters of intent, it is important to have a summary, but for shorter letters, this is typically not needed.

Also, always keep in mind that you are appealing to the interests of the graduate school, not your interests. Read the school's website to find what is most important to the program. Seek an advisor for questions or concerns about the types of programs you are applying to and to have a person who can help you review and revise your letter. Based on the senior-year plan in Chapter 5, you should spend at least a full month writing a final draft of each of your letters of intent. Take advantage of that time to read, write, and revise each letter; use more time if needed.

Writing Effectively: Voice and Tone

"There is no greater agony than bearing an untold story inside of you."

Maya Angelou

In terms of writing, one consideration is the voice and tone you use in your writing. *Voice* and *tone* are words often used interchangeably to describe one's writing. Indeed, many sources for "how to write" treat these words as having the same meaning. One reason for treating these terms the same is that strategies or changes in writing to address concerns of voice and tone are often the same or similar. For our purposes, *voice* represents the style or personality of the writer, and *tone* reflects the mood or attitude of the writer toward his or her subject—for a letter of intent, the "subject" is the graduate school selection committee.

As a general rule, your *voice* or personality should be one of a desire to develop, grow, and learn. For example, you write of your experiences as a process of growth to prepare for graduate school. Also as a general rule, your *tone* should reflect a confidence in your abilities yet also demonstrate humility and respectfulness. Do not be shy about emphasizing that your experiences have prepared you for graduate-level work. Yet also remember that your claim of having prepared for "graduate-level work" is your opinion, and not a matter of absolute fact. A simple way to show humility or respectfulness is to begin statements of opinion with phrases such as "I believe . . ." or "It seems to me . . ." Extending courtesies, as you do in the closing, for example, can also show respectfulness. These small efforts in your voice and tone can help to impress selection committees, and not "put them off" by your writing.

To think further about the voice and tone of your writing, try to answer the following four basic questions about the *purpose* of your writing (continue to think about these questions as you revise drafts of your letters of intent):

- Why are you writing the letter?
- To whom are you writing the letter?
- What are the interests of the readers?
- What do you want the readers to learn about you?

Answering each question above can help to give you the proper perspective as you begin writing. In addition, the following considerations can be made for using proper voice and tone in your writing:

- Be formal, but not too formal. Keep in mind that your readers are researchers and professors mostly with PhD degrees. They are looking to accept students who seek professional experience at a graduate level. In this light, you will want to write with a formal voice and tone to give the impression that you are now a professional. A good way to do this is to avoid literary devices or attempts to be funny, as described earlier in this chapter.
- Be consistent in your writing. The voice and tone in your writing should not change throughout the letter. If you use the subjective case *I*, for example, then do not change to *we* later in your letter. As another example, if you focus on describing your research experience in the main body of your letter, then to be consistent, the summary in your closing paragraph should reflect this focus. Using a consistent voice and tone can reflect a thoughtful, well-written letter that is easier to follow and read.
- Take the readers' point of view. When you have finished a draft of your letter, read it once through while pretending to be a selection committee member at a graduate school. Make sure you are effectively communicating what you want to communicate to the committee. You can have a faculty member read the letter and provide feedback as well. Again, you want to make sure that you are telling "the story of *you*" that you want the committee to read.

Writing Effectively:
Grammar and Sentence Structure

"Only in grammar can you be more than perfect."

William Safire

Another important consideration for your writing is grammar and sentence structure. Without proper grammar and sentence structure a letter of intent can appear as if you put little time and thought into writing it. A selection committee can choose not to select you if you have too many mistakes. It is important to proofread and review your letter many times before you submit it with your application to graduate schools. The following are six simple ways to improve your grammar and sentence structure (that have not yet been mentioned in this chapter):

- Start each paragraph with a topic sentence. The first sentence in each paragraph should indicate the topic of that paragraph. If, for example, you will discuss scholarship and research, then open with a sentence like "I have made continual progress in attaining scholarship and engaging in research."

The topic sentence lets the reader know what you will discuss, and helps to organize your writing, which makes it easier to read.

■ Vary the length of your sentences. If you have ideas or skills, then state them simply—use shorter sentences. Use longer sentences to explain, describe, or illustrate your ideas or how you have applied your skills.

■ Use active verbs with more concise tenses. Hence, use simple present (*I study*) over present perfect (*I have studied*); use simple past (*I studied*) over past perfect (*I had studied*); use future (*I will study*) over future perfect (*I will have studied*). Simple present, simple past, and future tenses are a more concise use of language and should therefore be used preferentially throughout your letter.

■ Limit the use of *I* to start consecutive sentences. First person is of course an appropriate voice. However, do not start consecutive sentences with *I*, such as in "I did this . . . I did that . . . I went here . . ." It is distracting to read sentences that start with the same pronoun, because it feels as if you are just listing off your achievements and not trying to tell a story about how those achievements have prepared you for graduate school. Mix up how you start each sentence to improve the flow of your writing from one sentence to the next.

■ Do not repeat information. If you read two sentences and find that you lose no information by deleting one sentence, then delete the repeat sentence. So keep asking, did this sentence add something new? If the answer is no, then you should consider revising. Also, cut words within each sentence that do not add anything new or do not change the meaning of a sentence.

■ Avoid repeating the same words or phrases in consecutive sentences when possible. For example, "I am largely involved in scholarship. This is largely due to my work as a research assistant." In this example, "largely" is repeated in consecutive sentences, which can be distracting and should be revised. One way to accomplish this would be to combine these sentences into a single sentence and use "largely" one time: "I am largely involved in scholarship due to my work as a research assistant." Another strategy is to use a synonym to replace the word that is repeated.

The final words of advice are possibly the most important: Proofread and use a dictionary. It is easy for even the best writers to make grammatical mistakes in writing. Do not just assume that your letter is perfect. Read your letter of intent, reread it, put it down and read it again, and then give it to a friend or professor to read. Also make sure you spell every word correctly, and use words with proper meanings, as you intended to use the words. Obviously this chapter has given you a lot to think about, but do not forget about the little things. Doing the "little things" can go a long way in helping you to write a letter that will impress a graduate school selection committee.

CHAPTER 7

Writing a Résumé and Curriculum Vitae

Résumés and the Curriculum Vitae

"It takes a lot of courage to show your dreams to someone else."

Erma Bombeck

A résumé or curriculum vitae (CV) is one part of the graduate school application. Both your résumé and your CV are descriptions of your academic and professional experiences and qualifications. In many ways, these documents are a professional way to reveal yourself to others, which can include your "dreams" or intentions for graduate school. The fundamental difference between a résumé and a CV is that a résumé should typically be limited to one page in length, regardless of whether you are at the start or at the end of your career; a CV, on the other hand, can be any page length. Otherwise, the general aim of a résumé and CV is basically the same: to describe your academic and professional experiences and qualifications for graduate school.

Graduate school selection committees will closely review your résumé or CV. The academic and professional experiences that you include and how you organize them in your résumé or CV can help you draw attention to key experiences that fit well with the goals of a graduate program, and therefore can help you to "stand out" among other applicants. Highlighting what makes you "stand out" can impress a selection committee. It is therefore important to set aside substantial time to write your résumé or CV to help you "stand out" as an applicant. Based on the senior-year plan in Chapter 5, you should spend at least a full month writing a final draft of your résumé or CV. Take advantage of that time to read, write, and revise it; use more time if needed.

Graduate schools will likely ask for your résumé or CV, or they may call it by another name, such as a "biosketch" or an "academic résumé." However, all of these terms usually refer to your CV; thus the primary focus of this chapter is on how to write a CV. Even when graduate schools ask for your résumé, they often really mean that they want your CV. If a graduate school requests your résumé, then call to check if it has "page limits" on the résumé. If no, then the graduate school is really asking for your CV. In this chapter, I describe many parts or headings you can include in your CV, then show you how to minimize the headings to fit the one-page limit of a résumé, and finish with many suggestions and tips for improving your résumé or CV.

Headings in the Curriculum Vitae

"Organizing is what you do before you do something, so that when you do it, it is not all mixed up."

A. A. Milne

A CV can have any number of headings, depending on a variety of factors, such as where you are applying and the types of experiences you have had. In your sophomore- and junior-year plan in Chapter 4, I first introduced writing a CV as a way for you to organize the types of experiences you will want to gain in college—to fill in your CV. I described a list of headings that, if filled in, could make you a top competitive candidate for many graduate schools. Since your sophomore year, you should have been completing the CV template given, which is reproduced here in Figure 7.1.

In a header, always give your contact information with your name, address, and contact number and e-mail. The following are key headings given in Figure 7.1 by which you can organize your CV (a detailed description for how to complete each part or heading is given in this chapter):

- *Education.* Your education includes your school, degree(s), major, and GPA. Your relevant coursework, honors status, and thesis work can be listed under this heading as well. If you wrote a thesis for honors work, for example, then list the title of the thesis here.
- *Research Experience.* Your research experience includes laboratory or applied research work, dates of work, responsibilities, and skills acquired. Describe your skills and responsibilities using keywords—words that a graduate school has listed as important for success in its program.
- *Peer-Reviewed Publications.* Peer-reviewed publications are work that is accepted by editors at scientific peer-reviewed journals. These are significant (and rare) experiences for an undergraduate student, so bring attention to them under this heading, which is an extension of your research experience.
- *Presentations.* Abstract presentations include any research presented at local, regional, national, or international conferences. These are also significant experiences for an undergraduate student, so bring attention to them under this heading, which is an extension of your research experience.

Figure 7.1 An annotated CV with key headings that should be listed.

Name

Address

Contact Information

EDUCATION
Degree Earned, Name of Major.........................Conferral Date: Month, Year
College Name, City, State
Overall GPA

RESEARCH EXPERIENCE
Name of Laboratory..Dates of Time in Lab
Advisor: Name, Title (e.g., PhD)
Give a brief description of your role in the lab.

PEER-REVIEWED PUBLICATIONS
Give the APA-style reference for your peer-reviewed publication. Number each
listing.

PRESENTATIONS
Give the APA-style reference for your abstract presented at a conference.
Number each listing.

TEACHING EXPERIENCE
Title (TA or Tutor), Name of Course, School Name............Dates of Teaching
Faculty Advisor: Name, Title (e.g., PhD)
Give a brief description of your responsibilities.
Pay Rate (if applicable)

INTERNSHIPS AND WORK EXPERIENCE
Job Title ....Dates of Employment
Name of Organization, City, State
Supervisor: Name, PhD (if applicable)
Give a brief description of your responsibilities.
Pay Rate (if applicable)

HONORS AND AWARDS
List all scholarships, awards, and honor society memberships and provide a
brief description of each (if applicable), Dates

ACTIVITIES AND SERVICE
List activities, sports, and service experience and provide a brief description
of each (if applicable), Dates

TRAINING AND SKILLS
List all skills valued by graduate schools and provide a brief description of
each (if applicable), Dates

NOTE: A "conferral date" is the expected date of graduation. This figure is reproduced from
Figure 4.1 in Chapter 4.

- *Teaching Experience.* Your teaching includes your work as a teaching assistant and a tutor. List your job/teaching titles, dates of work, responsibilities, and skills acquired. Describe your skills and responsibilities using keywords that a graduate school has listed as important for success in its program.
- *Internships and Work Experience.* Your internships and work experience include internships held in the field you are applying to and any relevant jobs. List dates of work, job responsibilities, and skills acquired for each position. Describe your skills and responsibilities using keywords that a graduate school has listed as important for success in its program.
- *Honors and Awards.* Academic honors, funding, and distinctions can be listed under this heading. If you were awarded an athletic or academic scholarship or other funding (such as a grant), then add it here. List the value or amount of money that was awarded too. If you graduated with distinction, list it: summa cum laude ("with highest honor"), magna cum laude ("with great honor"), or cum laude ("with honor'). If you joined an honor society, list that here as well, with the year you first joined.
- *Activities and Service.* Your activities and service include all additional activities that you have been involved in that would be relevant. These also include sports and service experience. Describe your activities using keywords that a graduate school has listed as important for success in its program.
- *Training and Skills.* Your training and skills include any skills that have not yet been listed that show preparedness for the graduate program, such as proficiency with computer software or workshops you have completed.

The following are additional headings that can be included, although they are not always needed or recommended (these headings are not included in the annotated CV in Figure 7.1):

- *Relevant Coursework.* Many times you will see relevant coursework listed under a separate heading. However, you must send your transcript as part of a graduate school application, so this information is largely redundant. Unless a graduate school asks for specific courses to be taken as prerequisites for being accepted into its program, this information is redundant and unnecessary in a CV.
- *Statement of Research Interests.* You can add a few lines about your specific interests in research. Two cautions for adding this: First, you must be careful to make a statement of interest that fits with the interests of the graduate program you are applying to. Second, you will communicate this in your letter of intent anyway, so this heading may be redundant.
- *International Experience.* You may gain experience overseas in a study abroad program, for example. This is a significant experience, but it can usually be a better fit listed under another heading, such as *Education, Research Experience,* or *Internships and Work Experience.* Unless a graduate school asks for applicants to have international experience, there is usually no need to give this experience its own heading, although you can, if you choose.

- *Quotes From Recommenders.* Adding a quote from one or more of your strongest recommenders could appeal to a selection committee. However, doing so may also come across as "overselling" yourself in that you are repeating information that is presumably in your letters of recommendation (LORs). Also, you risk giving a quote in your CV that is not present in the actual LOR that is sent by your recommender (remember, you will likely not review the LORs your recommenders send). For these reasons, it is perhaps best not to include recommender endorsements in your CV to graduate schools.

Each key recommended heading is described in this chapter using standard formatting to be consistent throughout. However, keep in mind that there are many ways to effectively format your CV. For this reason, different tips and strategies for how to format page headers, footers, borders, fonts, and more in your CV are described at the end of this chapter. Note that if you have no experience for a given heading, you should then omit the heading. Do not include a heading and list "None" under it. Instead, it is better to just omit the heading entirely than to blatantly identify your lack of experience in the area identified by a heading. Here, I begin with a heading that usually is the first listed in a CV and one that should always be included: *Education*.

Education

> *"The educated differ from the uneducated as much as the living differ from the dead."*
>
> Aristotle

Your education is anything related to classwork, grades, and degrees. While the order of headings is debatable, the *Education* heading should be the first listed because it is your education—and you are seeking more education in graduate school, which makes it a very relevant heading to graduate schools. The following key information should be included under the *Education* heading:

- School and degree information. List the names of each school you attended, location of each school (city, state), dates you graduated or anticipate graduating, and degrees earned. Refer to an anticipated graduate date as your *conferral date*. Your high school information can be included, but it is not required because by being enrolled in college, it is assumed that you have graduated from high school.
- Major, minor, and GPAs. List the name of your major. Also list your minor, if applicable. Your minor may go unnoticed if you do not highlight it in your CV. Also, give your overall GPA; optionally, you can give your major GPA (for only courses taken in your major discipline). Only list your major GPA if it is higher than your overall GPA. You can usually find your overall and major GPA on your academic records. List your GPA as GPA/Total Possible GPA (e.g., 3.4/4.0). If your GPA is below 3.0, then it may be best not to add it to

your CV. No need to bring attention to a low GPA. Instead, bring attention to the strengths in your CV that make you stand out.

- Thesis title (if applicable). If you have completed honors or graduate work, you may have completed a thesis in partial fulfillment of your degree. If you have a thesis, then give the title for that thesis under the *Education* heading; optionally, you can list the advisor of your thesis, if applicable.

To illustrate how to put each part of the *Education* heading together, the following is a sample for how to complete this heading. The sample is an excerpt taken from the CV of a student who was accepted to a doctoral program (PhD) in social psychology at a university in the Northeast that began in the fall of 2013. Notice in the excerpt shown here that all pertinent information is included. In addition, a line is added to identify the minor that the student earned and her honors thesis title. If applicable, you can add these lines under the *Education* heading as well.

EDUCATION

Bachelor of Arts, With Honors, Psychology...........Conferral Date: May 2013
St. Bonaventure University, St. Bonaventure, New York
Minor: Political Science
Overall Grade Point Average: 3.80/4.00
Honors Thesis: "Influence of Body Esteem, BMI, and Attachment Styles on Reactions to Negative Feedback From a Potential Romantic Partner"

Research, Peer-Reviewed Publications, and Presentations

"Research is formalized curiosity. It is poking and prying with a purpose."

Zora Neale Hurston

Your research experience is any lab or applied research work with a PhD advisor. This experience alone is sufficient to be competitive for graduate schools. However, presenting research at a conference or being named as an author for an article published in a peer-reviewed journal is a substantial achievement at the undergraduate level (see the sophomore- and junior-year plan in Chapter 4 for strategies you can use to find and create these types of opportunities). If you have presented or published research, give these achievements separate headings to bring attention to them in your CV. Each heading for research is described in this section.

The following key information should be included in the first heading for research experience:

- Name of lab (if the lab doesn't have a "name," then give a name that describes the gist of the type of research conducted), name of primary advisor (the researcher who runs the lab), and dates worked in the lab.
- Start and end dates for each position. If the position was held for one semester, then indicate the semester.
- A brief description of the project or projects you worked on, your responsibilities in the lab, and skills acquired. Use keywords here for skills that a graduate school identified as important to be successful in its program.

The key information included in the heading for peer-reviewed publications is a listing of all publications for which you were named an author. You will likely use the American Psychological Association (APA) referencing style if applying to a behavioral science program. If applying to medical school, then use the American Medical Association (AMA) writing style. Using APA style, for each publication you list all authors, the name of the article, the journal name, the volume number, the issue number, page numbers, and the digital object identifier (doi). For each publication, put your name in bold type to bring attention to the fact that you are an author.

If you have also presented posters or given talks at a local, regional, national, or international conference, then list these under the *Presentations* heading. Presentations at a regional, national, or international conference are the most prestigious. Listing each presentation for which you have been named an author under the *Presentation* heading will bring attention to this valued experience. For each presentation, list all authors, the title of the presentation, the name of the conference where it was presented, and the location and dates of the conference or day of the presentation. For each presentation, put your name in bold type to bring attention to the fact that you are an author.

To illustrate how to put each part of the research headings together, the following is a sample for how to complete the research headings. The sample is an excerpt taken from the CV of a student who was accepted to a doctoral (PhD) program in industrial/organizational psychology at a university in the largest city in the Midwest that began in the fall of 2012. Notice in the excerpt shown here that all pertinent information is included (some details have been left out for confidentiality and brevity).

RESEARCH EXPERIENCE

Behavioral Health Lab ....Fall 2010–Present
Advisor: [Name], PhD
Designed and conducted experiments that manipulated rate of eating as a factor related to intake among those with high dietary restraint; conducted study procedures, entered data, analyzed statistics, and wrote a poster and a manuscript that led to publication.

(Continued)

(Continued)

Organizational Psychology Lab ....Fall 2011
Advisor: [Name], PhD

Designed and conducted an experiment regarding motivations to volunteer for peer mentors; developed the hypothesis, wrote the proposal, created surveys, ran participants, coded data, analyzed statistics, and presented findings.

Social Psychology Lab ....Spring 2009
Advisor: [Name], PhD

Conducted an experiment comparing the inspiration value of the inaugural addresses of Presidents Barack Obama and Ronald Reagan; conducted study procedures, constructed surveys, entered and coded data, and wrote a summary report of findings.

PEER-REVIEWED PUBLICATIONS

1. [Author Names.] (2012). The influence of eating rate on satiety and intake among participants exhibiting high dietary restraint. *Food & Nutrition Research, 56,* 10202. doi:10.3402/fnr.v56i0.10202

PRESENTATIONS

1. [Author Names.] (2011). *Rate of eating, weight consciousness, and intake in an experimental setting.* Presented at the National Conference on Undergraduate Research (NCUR), Ithaca, NY, March 31–April 2.

2. [Author Names.] *How inspiring was President Obama's inaugural address?* Presented at the Association for Psychological Science annual conference, Washington, DC, May 25–29.

Teaching Experience

> *"To teach is to learn twice."*
>
> Joseph Joubert

Your teaching experience includes any tutoring or teaching assistant (TA) positions that you have held. These types of experiences stand out, particularly if you are a TA or tutor for courses that are particularly difficult or important to graduate programs, such as statistics or research methods courses.

Sometimes the *Teaching Experience* heading can catch students off guard because being a tutor or a TA is not literally teaching per se. However, most schools will assume that you do not literally mean that you are a "teacher" by adding it as a heading. The true reason for this heading is that it matches the types of experiences that are considered teaching experience in graduate school. For example, one way to earn a scholarship is to "teach." What that actually means is that you earn your scholarship by volunteering to be a TA for courses each semester at the graduate school you attend. In this way, showing evidence of "teaching" experience as an undergraduate student really shows preparation for the types of skills and responsibilities you will have as a graduate student.

The following key information should be included under the *Teaching Experience* heading:

- Title (TA or tutor) and name of course. State the title of your position and name the course or topic for which you were a tutor or teaching assistant. List also the school name or organization for each position. You can include an advisor's name (and degree or title), if applicable.
- Indicate the start and end dates for each position. If the position was held for one semester, then indicate the semester.
- A brief description of responsibilities, skills acquired, and pay (if applicable). Use keywords for skills that a graduate school identified as important to be successful in their program.

To illustrate how to put each part of the *Teaching Experience* heading together, the following is a sample for how to complete this heading. The sample is an excerpt taken from the same student CV used to illustrate research experience, peer-reviewed publications, and presentations. Notice in the excerpt shown here—for a student eventually accepted to a PhD program in industrial/organizational psychology—that all pertinent information is included (some details have been left out for confidentiality and brevity).

TEACHING EXPERIENCE

Tutor, Psychological Statistics and Research Methods, [School Name]......2011–Present
Faculty Advisor: [Name], PhD
Tutored students for a 200-level course in statistics and research methods.
[Pay Rate]

Tutor, Spanish, [School Name] 2010–Present
Faculty Advisor: [Name], PhD
Tutored students for 100- and 200-level courses in Spanish.
[Pay Rate]

(Continued)

(Continued)

TA, Psychological Research: Statistics and Methods II, [School Name].....Spring 2012
Faculty Advisor: [Name], PhD
Held office hours and assisted with grading and proctoring exams.
[Pay Rate]

TA, Psychological Research: Statistics and Methods I.....................Fall 2011
Faculty Advisor: [Name], PhD
Held office hours and assisted with grading and proctoring exams.
[Pay Rate]

Internships and Work Experience

"Nothing is a waste of time if you use the experience wisely."

Auguste Rodin

Your internship experience can include your job experience when given in your CV. An internship for which you are selected can be highly prestigious, such as internships with the National Institutes of Health (NIH) and the National Science Foundation (NSF), which are highly competitive. Internships can also include other types of work that are less competitive but also apply the skills and responsibilities you need to be successful in graduate school. You can find such positions anywhere that you can work, such as hospitals, mental health clinics, law firms, elementary schools, law enforcement organizations, and even the headquarters of many businesses. These positions can be voluntary or paid.

The following key information should be included in the *Internships and Work Experience* heading:

- Job title, name of organization, and job location (city, state). Start each listing with your job title to bring attention to it. Do not abbreviate unless your job title is a very common title. For example, if your title has the word *assistant* in it, then you can use the abbreviated *asst.*, but abbreviate sparingly. You can also include a supervisor's name (and degree or title), if applicable.
- Indicate the start and end dates for each position. If the position was held for one semester or over the summer, then indicate the semester or summer with year. For longer engagements, give the full range of dates employed.
- A brief description of responsibilities, skills acquired, and pay (if applicable). Use keywords for skills that a graduate school identified as important to be successful in its program.

To illustrate how to put each part of the *Internships and Work Experience* heading together, the following is a sample for how to complete this heading. The sample is an excerpt taken from the CV of a student who was accepted to a doctoral program in behavioral neuroscience at a university in the Northeast that began in the fall of 2013. Notice in the excerpt shown here that all pertinent information is included (some details have been left out for confidentiality and brevity).

INTERNSHIPS AND WORK EXPERIENCE

Technician, Department of Neurobiology .... November 2012–Present
University of Pittsburgh, Pittsburgh, Pennsylvania
Supervisor: [Name], PhD
Coordinate research projects in lab, ensuring care and supervision of laboratory animals; maintain more than 20 strains of transgenic mice; and perform polymerase chain reaction methods to establish mouse genotypes.
[Pay Rate]

Health Systems Intern, Unity Health Care............................ Summer 2010
Upper Cardozo Clinic, Washington, DC
Supervisor: [Name], PhD
Collected, entered, and analyzed data; maintained patient medical records and assisted with transition from paper to electronic medical records; provided clerical and administrative support to designated departments; and participated in professional workshops.
[Pay Rate]

Health Fair Coordinator, Unity Health Care......................... Summer 2010
Upper Cardozo Clinic, Washington, DC
Supervisor: [Name], PhD
Organized community health fair to target underserved populations in Washington, DC.
[Pay Rate]

Honors and Awards

> *"Awards mean a lot, but they don't say it all."*
>
> Ernie Banks

Honors and awards are important, particularly if you have many to list or you earned a highly prestigious award. Types of awards can include memberships in honor societies, scholarships and other types of academic or athletic recognitions, certificates, medals, plaques, and trophies you have earned. These types of awards show evidence of being actively involved in athletic or academic activities. While honors and awards are important, particularly those you earned while in college, be concise in this section and only include as much information as needed to identify the honor or award.

The following key information should be included under the *Honors and Awards* heading:

- Name of the honor or award with year earned. The name of the award should be able to capture how or why you earned the honor or award.
- A brief description of the award if there is ambiguity for how or why the honor or award was earned—that is, if it is necessary to add this detail.

To illustrate how to put each part of the *Honors and Awards* heading together, the following is a sample for how to complete this heading. The sample is an excerpt taken from the same student CV used to illustrate internship and work experience. This student was also a college athlete, so her honors and awards were for athletics and academics. Notice in the excerpt shown here—for a student eventually accepted to earn a PhD in a behavioral neuroscience program—that all pertinent information is included (some details have been left out for confidentiality and brevity).

HONORS AND AWARDS

Eastern Psychological Association Student Member, 2011–Present

Psi Chi Inductee, International Honor Society in Psychology, 2011

Presidential Scholar, the most prestigious academic award at St. Bonaventure University, [Monetary Value], 2008–2012

All-Tournament Team, Puma Big 4 and Army West Point tournament, Fall 2012

Team Captain, Women's Division IA Soccer, 2010–2012

Dean's List, while maintaining above a 3.4 GPA, 2009–2012

Honorable Mention, National Soccer Association of America Scholar All-East Region, 2011

Nominee, Psychology Scholars Program, 2011

All-Rookie Team, Atlantic 10 Conference Women's Division IA Soccer, 2008

Activities and Service

"Everybody can be great . . . because anybody can serve."

Martin Luther King, Jr.

Your activities and service experience show evidence of being actively involved in activities that are related to your academics, but "go beyond the classroom."

Active involvement in service, for example, is a strong reflection of your character. These types of experiences, then, are of interest to graduate schools. However, like honors and awards, be concise in this section and include only as much information as needed to identify the activity or service that you participated in.

The following key information should be included in the *Activities and Service* heading:

- Name of the activity or service and dates of completion or participation.
- A brief description of the activity or service. It is sometimes necessary to add detail, particularly if the activity or service is uncommon.

To illustrate how to put each part of the *Activities and Service* heading together, the following is a sample for how to complete this heading. The sample is an excerpt taken from the CV of a student who was accepted to a master's program at a university in the Northeast to earn an MS in educational psychology and a Certificate of Advanced Studies (CAS) for school psychology with preparation to take the Educational Testing Service Praxis exam to become a Nationally Certified School Psychologist—her program began in the fall of 2012. Notice in the excerpt shown here that all pertinent information is included.

ACTIVITIES AND SERVICE

Psychology Club, actively participated in organizing events to engage students in psychology, 2010–2012

Student Ambassador, gave campus tours and held special events for prospective families, 2010–2012

First-Year Experience Mentor, helped transfer students adjust to the college setting, 2010–2012

Committee Chairperson, Campus Activities Board, 2010–2012

Training and Skills

"The best contribution one can make to humanity is to improve oneself."

Frank Herbert

Your training and skills experience shows evidence of professional development. Professional development is the continued pursuit of education or experience beyond that required by a job or school alone. It is a core part of "being a professional," as you will likely be involved in professional development throughout your career. Professional development involves continued education or experiential opportunities to develop or learn to improve within a specific field or discipline, such as attending a workshop or an online seminar. Your training is also important because it reflects the skills needed in graduate school that you have acquired as an undergraduate, such as expertise with using Microsoft® Office and statistical software. Evidence of professional development and other skills reflects your preparedness for graduate school and your initiative to grow and develop in your career, which is important to graduate schools. Again, be concise in this section (as in the previous two sections); include only as much information as needed to identify your training or skills.

The following key information should be included under the *Training and Skills* heading:

- Name of the training or skill acquired and dates of completion or participation.
- A brief description of the training or skill. It is sometimes necessary to add detail, particularly if the training or skill is uncommon.

To illustrate how to put each part of the training and skills headings together, the following is a sample for how to complete this heading. The sample is an excerpt taken from the CV of a student who was accepted to a doctoral program in clinical psychology at a university on the West Coast that began in the fall of 2013. Notice in the excerpt shown here that all pertinent information is included.

TRAINING AND SKILLS

American Red Cross Foundations of Disaster Mental Health, 3.0 hours of training, St. Bonaventure University, 2012

American Red Cross Psychological First Aid, 3.0 hours of training, St. Bonaventure University, 2012

Online Counseling and Suicide Intervention Specialist, QPR (Question, Persuade, and Refer) Institute, 2012

Mandatory Reporter Training, 2.0 hours, Center for Development of Human Services, Buffalo State College, 2011

Safe Schools Against Violence in Education (SAVE) Workshop, 2.0 hours of training, Genius Genius of New York, 2011

Introduction to Grant Writing and Reporting, 5.0 hours of training, Center for Community Engagement, St. Bonaventure University, 2011

Technical Proficiency, Microsoft® Office, IBM SPSS® statistical software

Language Proficiency, English (primary), Italian (proficient), Spanish (proficient)

Notice in this chapter that there are many possible headings in a CV. For the template given in this chapter, there are nine headings, and each of the last four headings really is a combination of two headings (e.g., *Honors* and *Awards*). The headings in this chapter are not at all exhaustive of all headings you can include in a CV. For example, some graduate programs may emphasize leadership as a key desired trait, in which case you can rearrange your CV to include a *Leadership Experience* heading. If you have not presented research at conferences but have attended conferences, then you may want to replace the *Presentations* heading with a *Conferences Attended* heading. If you have both, then you may want to add both headings. If you have joined many honor societies or professional organizations, you can highlight this by adding an *Honorary and Professional Memberships* heading, then listing the name of all the organizations you have joined (instead of combining these under an *Honors and Awards* heading). In this way, the CV template given in this chapter is meant to be just that—a template. It can be used to list all your major and minor accomplishments that you will want to include in your final CV that you submit to graduate schools. However, feel free to change headings at your discretion if you feel that, by doing so, you can bring attention to certain parts of your CV that would be of particular interest to the graduate school or schools to which you apply.

Converting a Curriculum Vitae Into a Résumé

"A bird doesn't sing because it has an answer, it sings because it has a song."

Maya Angelou

As identified at the beginning of this chapter, a CV and résumé are similar, except that a CV can be any length and a résumé is usually limited to one page in length. Most graduate schools want you to send your CV. However, your résumé is often needed to apply for internships, jobs, and certain service opportunities. For this reason, it is essential to learn how to structure your résumé so that you can adequately communicate what makes you stand out as an applicant in only one page. The nine headings given in the CV template would make limiting your résumé to one page almost impossible. So we need new headings, and we need to revise existing headings from the CV template given in this chapter. The structure of your résumé can take many forms, but the following five headings can be used as a template to structure your résumé:

- *Objective.* Your objective appears under a new heading not given in the CV template. It is a single-sentence statement of your goals or your aims for submitting your résumé. It is a concise way to highlight what you want to achieve or communicate in your résumé.
- *Summary of Qualifications.* A summary of qualifications is a concise way to identify the skills you have already acquired. Try to match the skills you list with skills identified by the company or school as being essential skills for the position being offered. Your qualifications are typically listed as keywords or phrases that can be readily recognized by an employer or a school.
- *Education.* This is the same heading as that given for the CV template. One difference is that you should add any training under this heading, particularly if the training led to a certification or licensure. Also list any prestigious academic honors that stand out.

- *Employment.* Under this heading, combine your internship, work, research, and teaching experiences; include only your most substantial or important experiences. This heading is usually ordered chronologically from most to least recent experience. If you have received awards or recognitions, then you can include each one under the experience that corresponds with the award or honor. Use bold type to bring attention to significant recognitions you have earned.

- *Activities and Service.* This final heading is where you list activities and service, particularly those in the community. The strength of your application is in the first four headings, so this section should be brief.

To illustrate how to write a résumé, Figure 7.2 shows a sample for how to complete a résumé using the five headings listed here; a second sample résumé is given in the Appendix. The sample in Figure 7.2 is taken from the résumé of a psychology student who used it to apply for a paid internship at a law firm for which she was selected in the fall of 2013. Notice in the excerpt that all pertinent information is included despite having only one page to show how she stood out among other applicants (some details have been left out for confidentiality).

Figure 7.2   An example résumé

[NAME OF STUDENT]
[Street Address, City, State, Zip Code]
[Phone, Fax, E-mail]

OBJECTIVE:

To obtain an internship at a law firm that utilizes my prelaw and/or psychology education.

SUMMARY OF QUALIFICATIONS:

♦ Education in prelaw and psychology ♦ Recipient of multiple academic scholarships ♦ Excellent interpersonal skills ♦ High motivation for professional development in preparation for law school ♦ Applied dispute resolution and mock trial experience ♦ Proficient in PC and Mac, Microsoft Office programs, and social media ♦ Proficient in IBM SPSS statistical software

EDUCATION:

Bachelor of Arts, Psychology   Conferral Date: May 2015

St. Bonaventure University, St. Bonaventure, New York

Minor: Law and Society

Overall GPA: 3.39/4.00

Honors: Fr. Albert O'Brien Scholarship Recipient, Fr. R. Fleishall Scholarship Recipient, Fr. Thomas Plassman Scholarship Recipient, Merit Award Recipient, Merit Resident Award Recipient, Dean's List (2012–2013)

EMPLOYMENT:

Member, Steering Committee for the Middle States Accreditation Self-Study

St. Bonaventure University   3/2013–Present

- Participate as a student member to facilitate the university-wide evaluation and assessment of the comprehensive reporting of the accreditation standards that reflect an institution to the Middle States Commission on Higher Education to obtain reaccreditation of the university.

Office and Event Ambassador, Office of Admissions

St. Bonaventure University   8/2012–Present

- Recognized as a key representative of the university by providing guided tours of campus for prospective students and families.
- Assist in creating marketing tools for prospective students and families.

Student Circulation Desk Assistant, Friedsam Memorial Library

St. Bonaventure University   8/2012–5/2013

- Assiste students and faculty in obtaining library supplies, controlling the circulation computer system, and checking books, laptops, and cameras into and out of the library.

ACTIVITES AND SERVICE:

- ♦ **Mock Trial**, *Witness and Attorney*, 2013 ♦ **Peer Coach**, *Volunteer*, 2012–Present
- ♦ **St. Bonaventure Warming House/Soup Kitchen**, *Volunteer*, 2012–Present

NOTE: The résumé shown here is for a psychology student who was selected for a paid internship at a law firm in the fall of 2013.

In truth, you should probably have one of each: a CV and a résumé. In Figure 7.2, the student's résumé was less than one page; the CV for this student was closer to three full pages in length. The résumé is essential in business, often being required to apply for internships and jobs—something you will likely want to do while in college. In academia, however, the CV is commonly used in place of a résumé—to apply to graduate schools, for example. Hence, having a résumé and CV version of your accomplishments will be advantageous as you aim to pursue graduate schools and a career.

Creating a Résumé and Curriculum Vitae That Stand Out

"The art is in getting noticed naturally, without screaming or without tricks."

Leo Burnett

The writing of your résumé and CV is certainly a thoughtful process. You need to be considerate of where you place each heading, what you describe in each heading, and how to appeal to the interests of the graduate schools to which you apply. In this chapter, you have been shown how to structure your résumé and CV, with many examples given. In addition, you have been shown how to effectively present yourself to graduate schools. Some added suggestions for bringing attention to content and presenting your résumé and CV professionally can help you put the finishing touches on your final draft.

The following additional suggestions can help you make the *content* in your résumé or CV stand out:

- Make the link between responsibilities and outcomes. For jobs, internships, or other work, you typically list your responsibilities. Yet it is also important to show evidence of achievement. For example, notice in the CV excerpt under *Research Experience* that the student described her achievements in the research lab as "[leading] to publication." Thus, she clearly identified how she excelled in her responsibilities.

- Do not contradict in your CV information that is in other parts of your graduate application. Use language consistently and make sure that the dates and types of experiences you describe in your CV are consistent with each part of the graduate school application that you submit.

- Use *Selected* in headings if the list is not exhaustive of all of your experiences or accomplishments. Under *Honors and Awards*, for example, you may want to list your honors and awards that stand out most. If you exclude any, then you can list the heading as *Selected Honors and Awards*. Such a heading implies that you have more honors and awards than those listed in your CV.

- Use *Relevant* in headings if only the most relevant experiences are listed. For work experience, for example, list the three or four jobs that stand out most and do not include your odd jobs. If you leave out the least relevant jobs, then you can list the heading as *Relevant Internships and Work Experience*. Such a heading implies that you have more work experience than that listed in your CV.

- Use different fonts, font sizes, and/or bold type for major headings and important content. You can bring attention to your headings by changing the font size and font type, or using boldface type. Using a border below the heading can also help bring attention to each heading. Also, you can bring attention to certain content that is important in each heading, such as your name as an author in a publication or the title of your degree. Use boldface type to bring attention to specific content within each heading.

- Be consistent in your use of fonts, formatting, and page borders. If you use boldface type to bring attention to specific content in one heading, for example, then use boldface type to bring attention to similar content in all headings. If you use a lower border to separate one heading, then use it to separate all headings. It is easier to find important content in your résumé and CV if you bring attention to it using consistent fonts, formatting, and page borders.

The following additional suggestions can help you present a more *professional-looking* résumé or CV:

- Always send an electronic copy as a PDF. This advice is true for *any* documents you send electronically, such as via e-mail, to graduate schools. A PDF file should ensure that your formatting is not lost when the recipient opens it, and it gives a more professional look to your CV or résumé.
- Print your résumé or CV on high-quality paper. Do not use parchment paper, which is a bit excessive. Instead, use plain white paper that is of a high quality. Do not use colored paper, and do not use scented paper when submitting your résumé or CV to a graduate school.
- Avoid folding your résumé or CV. Send your application materials in a full-sized manila envelope instead of a letter envelope when possible. Folding your résumé or CV can smudge the ink. If you must fold it, then wait about an hour after printing before folding the document.

In all, the structure, formatting, and presentation of your résumé and CV can be substantially improved by following many of the suggestions and templates provided in this chapter. In many ways, writing your own résumé and CV can be fun because you can begin to see, on paper, how you stand out and what you have accomplished—and if you write it effectively, so also will the members of graduate school selection committees who read it.

The Parts of the Graduate School Application: A Final Thought

"I love deadlines. I love the whooshing noise they make as they go by."

Douglas Adams, *The Salmon of Doubt*

In Chapters 6 and 7, you have been shown a detailed account of how to complete two major components of your graduate school application: your letters of intent and résumé/CV. All that is left for you to do is to give yourself enough time to complete each part—so that you do not hear the "whooshing noise [that the deadlines] make as they go by." Notice that the examples given in each chapter are from actual application materials that were submitted by actual undergraduate students who were subsequently accepted to the graduate programs to which they applied. These examples, then, are based on actual work that has resulted in acceptance letters from graduate schools and doctoral programs across the United States from the West Coast to the Northeast.

Throughout both Chapters 6 and 7, you have examples of application materials from students who were accepted into master's and PhD programs, including programs in organizational behavior, mental health counseling, social psychology, industrial/organizational psychology, educational and school psychology, and clinical psychology. The programs to which these students were accepted are located across the country with schools on the West Coast, in the Midwest, and in the Northeast. In other words, the examples given in these chapters show templates that can effectively help you communicate your skills and achievements in a way that can help you appear more than just qualified to graduate schools; these templates can help you to stand out among other applicants and help you get accepted to the graduate schools to which you apply.

In the Appendix, examples of a complete letter of intent, a CV, and a résumé are given. The samples given in the Appendix were written by a psychology student accepted into a PhD program, and another who was accepted for a paid internship at a hospital. As should be evident by the types of samples given in just the last two chapters and the Appendix, applying the Big Three in psychology and the behavioral sciences can prepare you for a wide range of career and educational pursuits.

CHAPTER 8

Submitting, Interviewing, and Waiting

Submitting and Waiting

"The secret to getting things done is to act."

Dante Alighieri

Submitting your graduate school applications can feel as if you lifted a weight off your chest. It is a great feeling in that moment that you hit "Send" on your computer or send the application via mail. It is a well-deserved feeling of accomplishment that you should try to enjoy—go out, celebrate with friends and family, and just enjoy the moment. A lot of work went into preparing your strong application materials. You can rest assured that by following the plan in this book, you likely put well more time, thought, and planning into completing your applications than many other applicants, which, for now, gives you the competitive advantage over them.

For many students, the initial feeling of accomplishment turns to anxiety a few weeks later when students start wondering if and when they will hear back from the graduate schools. For job searches, it is not uncommon at all for employers to simply not respond to you unless they are interested in you. For most graduate schools, however, their policy is to send decision letters, both rejection and acceptance. So in most cases, you should expect a reply from graduate schools one way or the other. A decision from graduate schools can be sent to you in only a few weeks from when you submitted your application, or it can take many months, depending on a variety of factors that are largely out of your control.

The decision process for graduate school selection committees can take a long time because the process itself can be demanding. Full-time professors with teaching and research commitments need to set aside time to read and review the applications. Then, they need to coordinate dates and times to meet to discuss potential applicants—so they can reach a consensus on which applicants are at the "top" of their list. A few meetings are typically required to make final decisions, and it is not always as easy as you might think to find common times when university faculty can meet. One typical reason for a long wait to receive a decision is that a committee sets an initial meeting late—say, a few months after the initial deadline. This can happen, and will result in decisions being made at much later times—sometimes five or more months after the initial submission of your application to the school.

The takeaway message is that waiting a long time for a response from graduate schools is a perfectly normal part of the process. Students all too often get anxious about having "not yet" received a decision from a particular graduate school. But that anxiety is misplaced because it assumes, somehow, that one can predict exactly when decisions from graduate schools should be made. In truth, there is no way for you to know when a decision *should* be made. So stop worrying. Do not be anxious. Waiting for a decision is an established part of the application process, and your wait can be long, even when the decision ends up being to accept you into a graduate program.

Being Productive While You Wait

"It is not enough to be [busy] . . . The question is: What are we [busy] about?"

Henry David Thoreau

Take a break for a few weeks once all applications are submitted. Certainly you deserve at least that. However, also keep in mind that the next steps in the application process will likely involve actually interacting with the members of a graduate school. In the same way that your writing needed to be professional, you will also need to present yourself as a professional when interacting with committee members. Graduate school selection committees are typically not looking for a "diamond in the rough." They want students who are already "well polished," prepared, and mature enough to excel in a graduate school environment.

Hence, the application process does not end simply because you have submitted an application. Selection committees want to make sure that the students they select are the best candidates for the school. You must anticipate that the graduate schools will do their "homework" on you. You must expect that they will vet you—on paper (the application that you submitted), online (social media searches), and in person (interviews).

Of course, do not oversell yourself. Do not start calling graduate schools dozens of times, for example, to check on the status of your application. You still need to "play it cool" while you wait. But that is only one of the things you can do while you wait for decisions from graduate schools. While there are many things to do while you wait for decisions, the following are five practical things you can do to be productive while you wait for decisions:

- Be patient.
- Manage your networking and social media.

- Attend a conference; bring your curriculum vitae.
- Schedule an impromptu campus visit.
- Be prepared for interviews.

Be Patient

"I am an old man and have known a great many troubles, but most of them never happened."

Mark Twain

Being patient is admittedly difficult, particularly when you are trying to be patient about something that can substantially influence your future. Decisions from graduate schools will largely play into whether you attend graduate school, where you will attend, and what types of opportunities will be available to you. It is absolutely reasonable that you will be impatient during the time that you are waiting for the decision letters to arrive from graduate schools.

For most students, their impatience derives from their worry of being rejected by graduate schools. Of course, graduate schools can have notoriously high rejection rates, particularly doctoral programs. So it is a fair concern or worry, but it is also one that is unnecessary. Keep in mind that for all you know, you could be worrying about "troubles" that will "never happen." You need to make an effort to focus more on practical things you can do to manage your time while you wait, such as focusing on the following ways to be productive, yet patient.

- Focus on the positive: You are about to graduate from college! Think about something else, other than the thing that is worrying you. There is more you can be doing, but try also to focus on the big positive: You are about to earn a college degree. You have some control over earning your college degree, so take control by taking the necessary classes and making the arrangements needed to graduate on time. Graduating from college certainly makes this an exciting time in your life, so focus on that as you wait for graduate schools to make their final decisions.
- Make a "courtesy" call or e-mail to confirm receipt of full application materials. Surprisingly often, students will think their application was submitted when, in truth, parts of the application were not received. By the time students figure this out, it is often too late, and they learn that they were never considered for the program to which they spent so much time applying. A very good practice is to call or e-mail each school about two weeks after submitting your full application to confirm receipt. Once each school has confirmed receipt of your application, you can rest assured that you did your due diligence to make sure that you are among the applicants who will be considered by the selection committees.
- Do not check on the status of a completed application too often. If it has been many months since your application was submitted, then by all means call the

school if that will set your mind at ease. However, "setting your mind at ease" is really about all you usually accomplish. In truth, making more than one call to "check on the status of your application" can possibly annoy members of a selection committee, can make you look desperate, and still will *not* increase the speed of the decision process. Decisions will eventually be made; the schools did not forget. Be patient.

- Believe in the adage that "no news is good news." The adage or phrase "no news is good news" is commonly credited to author and playwright Ludovic Halévy. This phrase is very true for the graduate school application process. In fact, many schools send rejection letters as they eliminate candidates, so if you have not yet received a rejection letter, then you can reasonably assume that you have not yet been rejected, and are therefore still being considered by the school. No news is good news; believe that. Until you receive notice to the contrary, an opportunity for graduate school has not been lost.

In truth, being positive can potentially be the *most* productive thing you do while you patiently wait for decision letters. It is also important to be aware that the graduate school process is still going on as you wait for decision letters. This is one reason that you do not want to bombard schools with e-mail queries and phone calls. Be patient yet productive; be positive. Know that the graduate schools you applied to will eventually make their decisions and will notify you accordingly. In addition, there are many other productive things you can do to manage your time, and to get prepared for the next steps in the application process.

Manage Your Networking and Social Media

"You are what you share."

Charles Leadbeater,
We-Think: Mass Innovation, Not Mass Production

Networking using social media is an important way in which we communicate with friends, family, and colleagues. However, you need to also recognize that how you communicate with friends and family (a personal profile) is fundamentally different from how you communicate with colleagues (a professional profile). Communicating your "professional profile" is valuable; however, you do not want selection committees to have free access to your personal profile. Any information that you post on social media sites, whether it is personal or professional, can be used by selection committees to help them make their decision to accept or reject your application. Therefore, the following are two things you can do to manage your networking and social media:

- Clean up or deactivate personal social media profiles [1].
- Effectively use professional networking profiles [2].

[1] In terms of personal social media profiles, you must assume that selection committees will search your name in Google and social media sites. Do not fall into the trap of thinking that a selection committee is allowed to review only your application materials. Realize that any way of learning about you is "fair game" if it is publicly available. Therefore, you need to make sure that your online presence reflects the same person you made such a strong effort to describe in your application. You can start by searching yourself by name online to see what you can find. Whatever you can find, so can graduate schools. There are basically two ways that you can manage your personal social media profiles.

First, clean them up. The time-consuming option is to go through your entire history on your social media accounts, then delete all posts and pictures that are inappropriate, questionable, or strongly opinionated, such as identifying your political views. Realize that selection committees will look for more than just what you are saying; they will even evaluate how well you write (e.g., they will check if you have grammatical errors in your posts). Honestly, keeping your social media clean will become a daily job. You will also need to start practicing good online behavior moving forward so that you can present the same person in your social media that you presented in your application. In all, it is a lot of work to clean your social media and keep it clean. There is a simpler solution.

Second, deactivate your personal profiles. Honestly, the graduate schools may be more impressed if they cannot find your Facebook and Twitter accounts at all than if they find them and they are clean. You also largely cannot control what other people post on your sites. It will surely become a tireless job of "checking" your Facebook and Twitter accounts to make sure the accounts are still "clean." The simple solution is to deactivate your social media accounts while graduate schools are considering your applications; you can always reactivate them later. Deactivating your social media accounts is probably the safest and easiest way for you to ensure that the members of a selection committee learn about you only from what they read in the application you sent them—and that is a good thing!

[2] In terms of professional networking profiles, it is important that your online "presence" is professional. There are many options for professional networking online. Possibly the most used professional networking site for college students who are pursuing graduate school is LinkedIn, although you certainly do not need an account. You can think of a LinkedIn account as an online résumé. It is important, then, to edit and review anything you post on LinkedIn in the same way you did for your résumé and CV that you submitted to graduate schools. The following are five essential tips for creating and managing your professional networking profile with LinkedIn (the suggestions given here can often work for other professional networking sites as well):

- Complete a full profile. Make sure that the information in your résumé and CV matches with what you have listed online. It can look very unprofessional to have an incomplete profile. Complete your education, your work history, and other common headings that are also in your résumé and CV.

- Upload a photo. A professional profile does not look very "professional" without an image. Upload an image to go with your profile, but also remember to add one that is professional and formal, not casual.
- Include a professional summary. In the summary, you want to communicate keywords that would get the attention of the graduate schools to which you applied. You can review the keywords you chose to use in your letters of intent to choose keywords for your professional networking profile.
- Add professional connections. Some graduate schools may be impressed if, for example, they see that you are "connected" with many professors at the school you attend. They can view your connections as a reflection of how well you work with others in a professional environment, and being a "professional" is exactly how you want these graduate schools to see you.
- Customize your URL. LinkedIn will assign a long, meaningless URL to your profile. Change the URL to a name that is meaningful. To change the URL with LinkedIn, click on "Edit Profile," then "Edit" next to your URL. To the right, select "Customize your public profile URL" and type in a URL that actually has meaning. Having a meaningful URL can give your page a more professional appeal.

In all, the goal is to make sure that you present yourself as a professional to graduate schools. Do not allow graduate schools to see your personal interactions with friends and family—that must be personal, not public information. Clean up or deactivate your personal profiles, and further manage your professional profiles to make sure that your online presence reflects the same person that you described in the applications you submitted to graduate schools.

Attend a Conference; Bring Your Curriculum Vitae

"If opportunity doesn't knock, build a door."

Milton Berle

One of the difficult things about applying to graduate schools is that most schools will know who you are only on paper. Of course, they may ask to interview you, but even that interview occurs only *after* they liked what they read about you on paper (i.e., what you wrote in your application). It can be stressful to wait for responses knowing that you really never had a chance to *show* the committees that you will work hard and be a good fit for their program.

Sometimes, it is easier to get noticed by a committee if members of the committee have met you and can "put a face" to your application. Indeed, in one year, an advisor I worked with on a graduate school selection committee chose two students for her PhD program—both of whom had reached out to her directly *before* the selection committee met for the first time. A coincidence? Maybe. But it doesn't hurt if a committee member has met you before he or she reads your application.

One clever way to create an opportunity to meet a committee member is to attend the same conference that he or she attends in your senior year. Keep in mind that faculty are typically the "committee members" for graduate programs, particularly for doctoral programs. And these faculty members are also the people who are attending conferences every year to present their research or other work. A conference is a very likely place to find and talk to committee members who will be reviewing your application.

Your senior year can be the perfect time to go to a conference because it is close in time to when the committees will actually meet. Many major associations across many academic disciplines hold a conference each year. A few examples of conferences in psychology include the annual American Psychological Association (APA) conference in August, the annual Association for Psychological Science (APS) conference in May, and many regional conferences, such as the Eastern (in March), Western (in April), and Midwestern (in May) Psychological Association conferences. To find a conference where a potential committee member will present his or her work, you can follow the four steps described here:

1. First, go to the school website where the researcher works (presumably this is a school to which you applied). Look up the researcher on his or her faculty webpage. Usually, the researcher will list his or her publications and presentations on that page. Hence, you can find the names of conferences where the researcher presents his or her work. Many researchers like to go to the same conferences each year. So any conferences listed are likely to be conferences where they will be presenting their work in the coming year.

2. Next, you can search the conference or association websites for the conferences the researcher is likely to attend. Most associations that hold a conference will post their program online. In the program, you will find the names of all people who will be presenting, their university/school affiliation, when and where they will be presenting, and the title of their presentations. Thus, you can confirm if a researcher will be attending a conference in any given year by searching the annual program for a conference.

3. As a third (optional) step, you can e-mail the researcher directly. If you found his or her name in a conference program, then you have good reason to believe that he or she will attend the conference. Send an e-mail to confirm that you will also attend. In your e-mail, leave open the possibility of meeting with the researcher at the conference. Often, the researcher will reply with an offer to meet—but let the researcher make the offer to meet; it is not necessary to ask this directly. The following is an example for how you can construct such an e-mail:

Dear Dr. [name of researcher],

My name is [your name]. I am a [name of major] student at [name of current school] who is applying to graduate schools for the upcoming academic year, to include an application to your program. I will be attending [name of conference] this year, and I noticed that your work is being presented at the conference. I have been very interested in your research area as an undergraduate student, and I look forward to attending a presentation of your work.

If you will be at the conference, please do let me know. I would like very much to meet you if such an opportunity presents itself. Thank you for your time and best wishes for continued success in your labs.

Sincerely,

[Your Name]

4. Finally, register and attend the conference. If you are working in a research lab, then you can even submit an abstract to present a poster at the conference. If you present a poster, then feel free to invite potential committee members to come visit your poster presentation, either (1) in your e-mail or (2) in person at the conference. It is a great opportunity to meet in a more professional setting with a researcher who will likely be on the committee to select graduate students in the coming year. Also make sure that you follow the registration and poster submission guidelines (if you present a poster) usually given online by the conference or association.

You probably want to avoid skipping these steps and blindly e-mailing researchers to ask them if they plan on attending a conference. Show some initiative and find this out on your own first (Steps 1 and 2). Then you can follow up with an e-mail in Step 3. The e-mail in Step 3 is a much better strategy than a blind e-mail because the third sentence shows that you did your homework—by naming the conference where the researcher will attend. Blindly contacting researchers can be a somewhat awkward approach, especially if you have never otherwise met them. It is always best to do your homework first before contacting a researcher who could potentially influence your opportunities for graduate school.

Once you are at the conference, take advantage of the opportunity to attend many posters and speak with many students and professors. Also make sure that you visit the poster presentation times of a potential committee member. The following is a list you can follow to make a strong first impression in a conference setting:

- Read the program abstract for each poster that you want to attend. When attending any conference, read the program and find posters that interest you. It is a good way to learn about research of interest to you and to meet others who are engaged in that area of research. If you attend the conference early in your senior year, then you may even discover that a school not "on your list" has very interesting research, and you may decide to add it to your list.
- Attend a poster session for the researcher who is at the school where you applied or plan to apply. As a general rule, the first author listed on the poster is the presenter, and the presenter can be a student or faculty member. Regardless of who presents the poster, approach the student or faculty member and ask him or her to "walk you through the study" as a way to start the conversation.

- Be engaging. Comment on the poster and be respectful as the presenter describes the study. Have questions prepared, and share an engaging conversation with the presenter. Feel free to mention your interest in his or her school and program. You can also share with the presenter your research if it is related to the research presented in his or her poster, but don't dominate the conversation—make it about *the presenter's* research more than your own. If you are presenting a poster, then invite the presenter to attend your poster session.

- Leave a copy of your CV. If you arrive at the poster and the researcher you wanted to meet is not there, do not "stalk" around the poster until the researcher arrives. Just leave a copy of your CV before you go, whether or not you met him or her. Even if you did not meet the researcher, you can still make a strong first impression on his or her graduate students (in a professional setting)—students who will then say good things about you and share your CV with the researcher; your CV is a record that they met you. Therefore, you still accomplish a lot, even if you never get the chance to speak to the researcher.

- As a final (optional) step, if you did meet the researcher in person while at the conference, then follow up with an e-mail thanking the researcher for his or her time. The e-mail should be brief and to the point. The purpose of the e-mail is just to get name recognition; the purpose is not to "sell yourself." The following is an example for how you can construct such an e-mail:

Dear Dr. [name of researcher],

My name is [your name]. I attended [name of conference] and had a chance to meet and talk with you at your poster titled "[name of poster title]." As a student who [is now applying *or* has applied] to your graduate program, I found your poster most interesting and related to the work I am doing as an undergraduate student.

I gratefully thank you for your time. I very much enjoyed the opportunity to meet you at the conference, and I look forward to the possibility of working under your direction, if accepted into your program in the coming academic year.

Sincerely,

[Your Name]

Attending a conference is also a great experience overall, and can be added to your CV. The advantage of attending a conference in your senior year is to meet and talk to potential committee members who will likely be reviewing your application. Having a face-to-face meeting in a professional setting can substantially help you stand out compared to those who did not get face time with committee members. It is really a way to create an interview opportunity by attending a conference that the researcher will attend. Of course, attending a conference can never guarantee that you will be selected, but making a good impression at the conference can certainly help.

Schedule an Impromptu Campus Visit

"Don't wait for your ship to come in, swim out to it."

Cathy Hopkins

Another clever way to basically create an interview opportunity is to schedule an impromptu campus visit to get "face time" with faculty at a graduate school. If you have a favorite school, then you are allowed to call the school and ask if the faculty would allow you to visit the campus. This is a neat and simple way to get some face time with faculty who are likely to be on the selection committees at the school.

To set up an impromptu campus visit, choose one of the schools on your list that you are willing to visit, and then call the department chair or graduate coordinator at the school. In your phone call, let the person know that you (1) are a student who has applied (or will apply) to the school's graduate program, (2) happen to be in the area at a certain date/time, and (3) would like very much to see the campus and community while you are in the area. Many schools will be very happy to oblige your request. Additional tips for making this request include the following:

- Make it seem as if you will be in the area anyway. Do not tell a story about how "out of your way" this trip will be—it makes you sound desperate and can make the person on the other side of the phone "feel bad" for you. Just be casual and act as if this visit is convenient for you, even if it is not.

- Time the visit for *after* your application is submitted because you can reference that in passing as you walk through campus. Odds are pretty good that you will be able to meet with a faculty member in the department. You can mention your application in passing when you speak with the faculty member.

- Make the focus of your conversation the school, not your application. Comment on the buildings and resources on campus. Ask questions that demonstrate a general interest in the campus and community. If you meet with a faculty member, mention your application in passing, but focus mostly on talking about his or her research, teaching, and daily life in his or her labs. Don't talk too much about yourself; talk mostly about the school to make a good first impression at your visit.

- Do your homework before visiting. For example, know who the contact person is for your visit and where you will meet this person. Arrive early to make sure you find him or her; avoid looking lost. If you know the names of the faculty members you will be talking with at your visit, then learn as much as you can about their teaching and research before visiting. Being prepared can also help you make a good first impression at your visit.

- As a final (optional) step, you can send an e-mail to thank the researcher (or other person you met) for taking the time to talk with you during your visit. The e-mail should be brief and to the point, similar to the thank-you e-mail example given for attending a conference. Again, the purpose of the thank-you e-mail is for name recognition; the purpose is not to "sell yourself."

Scheduling an impromptu campus visit is a clever way to show an interest in a school and create an interview opportunity to meet and talk to committee members who will likely be reviewing your application. Having that face time in a professional campus setting can substantially help you stand out compared to those who did not get face time with committee members. Of course, making the trip can never guarantee that you will be selected, but making a good impression during your visit can certainly help.

Be Prepared for Interviews

*"The mark of a good conversationalist is not that you can talk a lot.
The mark is that you can get others to talk a lot."*

Guy Kawasaki

In many cases, schools will not make final decisions until they have interviewed their top candidates. Hence, it is very likely that your initial interaction with a selection committee will be a request for an interview. Realize that if the school requested an interview, then that means you are a top candidate. At this stage, the process is less about if you are qualified enough for the graduate school; it is more a process of determining if you are a good "fit" for the school or program.

A qualified applicant is one who meets the academic standards of the school. By being selected for an interview, the answer is that you are among the *most* qualified—that is really not a concern at this stage. The key concern for an interview is if you are a good fit for the school or program. A "good fit" is difficult to define because it depends on the school. As a general rule, "fit" can be determined in three ways:

1. How closely your interests match those of the faculty and/or program

2. Your interest or enthusiasm for joining the school/program, and for moving to the area

3. How well you get along with the graduate students and faculty

The first two parts can be determined in your application and by talking with you. The last part, however, can really be determined only if they get to meet you in person. While the structure of an interview may vary from college to college, you will typically be asked to do one of the following three types of interviews (note that the last criterion of "good fit" can be best determined using the last type of interview listed):

- Phone interview
- Skype interview
- On-campus interview

Each type of interview is described in this chapter. However, there are rules for interviewing that can apply to any type of interview. The following are 12 general rules for applying effective interview strategies:

- Do not answer your phone for numbers that you do not recognize, while you wait for decision letters from graduate schools. Think of any communication between you and a graduate committee as an interview. You do not want to be caught off guard by a graduate school calling you. If it is a school offering you an interview, the person calling will leave a message. Let all unknown numbers go to voice mail and call the number back at a convenient time for you. Try to respond within 24 hours, or by the next business day if you were called on a weekend.

- If you will be doing multiple interviews or the interview will have multiple phases, then request an itinerary. An itinerary is a schedule for an interview. Usually, this will also include the list of people with whom you will interview. It is not uncommon at all for you to interview with administrators, faculty, and graduate students, so be prepared.

- If asked to schedule an interview, pick the earliest or latest date/time. The primacy and recency effects show that people tend to recall most what happens first and last, respectively; what happens in the middle tends to be forgotten. Thus, schedule an interview first or last so that your interviewer is more likely to remember you afterward.

- Do your "homework." Basically, study for the interview the same way you would for an important exam. Know a little bit about the history of the school; know the mission of the program you are applying to. Read the research of faculty at the school, and be prepared to talk about it to appeal to the interests of faculty. The more you know about the school, program, and faculty *before* an interview, the better "fit" you will appear to be to those who are interviewing you *during* the interview.

- Review your own application materials. Your interview can be scheduled many months after submitting your application. By then, it is easy to forget what you wrote in your application. Therefore, review your own application to make sure you describe yourself in the interview the same way that you described yourself on paper (in your application).

- Be early. Arrive at least 15 minutes early. If you are uncertain where you are going, then give yourself additional "get-lost time." But always plan on being 15 minutes early, either to the campus or in front of the phone or computer (if the interview is not on campus).

- Smile and show enthusiasm. Your body language and your prosody (i.e., your tone of voice, rhythm, and pitch) during an interview can often be as important as the content of your responses. Smile at the start and end of every conversation, and feel free to laugh if an interviewer tells a funny joke. You want the selection committee to see that you are easy to get along with and enthusiastic about joining the program. Your demeanor can even come across in how you speak, so this rule applies even for phone interviews.

- Get the interviewers talking about themselves whenever possible; be a good listener. If you know with whom you are interviewing, then learn what they do, and memorize a few questions to ask or comments you can make to get a conversation going that appeals to their interests. Express an interest in the interviewer. As a general rule, the less you talk in an interview, the better the interview is probably going.

- Do not feel as if you need to be an expert. All potential mentors know that you haven't even entered graduate school, so they are not looking for you to know everything. They more want to feel as if you will learn fast, be reliable, work hard, and be committed to the program.

- Have an *elevator story* prepared. An elevator story is a 30-second (or less) reply to questions about why you applied to a program or asking you to describe yourself. Your story should be consistent with the story you described in your application. Begin with a takeaway message such as "I am passionate about research." Avoid personal stories. For example, a committee probably does not want to know how many brothers or sisters you have. Instead, give a memorable, but brief, story that relates to the interests of the school/program.

- Have questions prepared. Many interviews end with the interviewer asking if you have any questions for them. Have at least one question prepared. Table 8.1 gives some questions you could ask to appeal to the interests of the program and give a sense of your commitment to the program, if selected.

- Always send a thank-you e-mail within 24 hours of an interview. Or you can even send a signed thank-you letter instead to make it more personal. The message should be brief and to the point. Remember that the purpose of the "thank you" is for name recognition, not to "sell yourself." The following is an example for how you can construct such a message:

Dear Dr. [name of researcher],

My name is [your name]. Thank you for your time during my interview on [date of interview]. I enjoyed having the opportunity to speak with members of the selection committee [and with students (if applicable)]. I am grateful for your time, and I look forward to the possibility of learning and engaging with faculty and students in your program.

Thank you for your time and consideration of my application. I look forward to receiving your decision in due course.

Sincerely,

[Your Name]

The general rules for applying effective interview strategies described here can be applied to any type of interview. There are also additional rules that apply to the specific types of interviews. The three types of interviews you can be asked to do are described in the three headings that follow. Additional suggestions for applying effective interview strategies are also provided.

Table 8.1	Suggested Questions to Ask During an Interview to Impress a Selection Committee	

No.	Question	
1	What can I do to ensure that you get the [Researcher or Professor] of the Year award?	
2	What types of [professors or graduate students] have been successful here? Which types have not?	
3	What activities or undertakings would you like to see me accomplish?	
4	What gets you out of bed in the morning and excited about coming to work?	
5	What is the biggest change that the department has gone through in the last year or two?	
6	Is there anything that has made you successful here that is unique to this university that someone from the outside would not likely know about?	
7	What would the "perfect" [candidate or graduate student] look like? How do you assess my experience and background in comparison?	
8	I am really excited for the opportunity to work in your labs. What would my role be in your lab in my first year, if selected?	
9	How many students are in the graduate program? How many do you plan to accept this year?	
10	How do the various academic departments work together? Is there a lot of interdepartmental collaboration?	

SOURCE: The suggestions in this table are adapted, in large part, from suggestions provided by James E. Privitera, JD, SPHR (personal communication, August 10, 2013).

Phone Interviews

"You can't reread a phone call."

Liz Carpenter

A phone interview can be most stressful because it is like being blind during an interview. Without being able to see the reactions or expressions of the committee, it can be difficult to gauge how well an interview is going. At the same time, remember that the committee members cannot see you either. So you can have any resources you need right in front of you during the interview. Hence, being "blind" in a phone interview can be both a disadvantage and an advantage to you.

There are two possible scenarios for a phone interview to be prepared for. First, some schools will limit how long you have to respond to each question. In these cases, be prepared to give quick one- or two-minute responses. Second, you may interview with one committee member or multiple committee members. In the latter case, committee members will likely join using the "speaker" feature on the phone, which can make it more difficult to hear the questions. So be in a quiet place to make sure you do not spend half the interview asking committee members to repeat themselves. The following are six additional rules for applying effective phone interview strategies:

- Be at your phone early; call on time (not early). For a phone interview, you need to wait until someone is on the other end of the line. If the committee initiates the call, then be at your phone at least 15 minutes early. Do not call early if you are asked to make the call. Wait until the agreed-upon time.

- Do not make the phone call using your cell phone. Find a landline phone. A cell phone can be dropped or have a poor connection. This is less likely to happen if you call from a landline phone, such as your home phone.

- Have notes, application materials, and the school website in front of you before the interview begins. Remember, the interviewer cannot see you. So take advantage of this benefit of doing a phone interview and have all the notes and resources you need in front of you to help you answer questions and be prepared.

- Have water within arm's reach. Your throat can get dry, and water can eliminate that. Keep in mind that for a phone interview, the interviewer can hear you (not see you), so you really need to speak clearly.

- Have a pen and paper to take names and notes. The interview is likely to begin with introductions. Write down the names of all interviewers and thank them by name at the end of the interview. It will impress the committee members that you recalled their names. Also, take notes during the interview. You may not be able to "reread a phone call," but you can reread your notes.

- Feel free to ask the interviewer to repeat a question, but try to do so sparingly. For some questions you may need some time to think of a response or to find your notes to answer a question. Dead silence can be awkward while you think. A solution is to ask the interviewer to repeat a question, which can buy you extra time to think of or find your answer, if needed.

A phone interview should typically be formal. Make limited efforts at humor on a phone interview because it is difficult to use humor over the phone. Just be sincere, respectful, and direct. A phone interview can take anywhere from about 10 minutes to an hour or more. Set aside a two-hour window for the interview to be safe. And try to find an open room where you can spread your notes and papers out to make them easier to find during the interview, if you need them. A phone interview can be very successful if you know what to expect and are prepared.

Skype Interviews

"Technology offers us a unique opportunity, though rarely welcome, to practice patience."

Allan Lokos,
Patience: The Art of Peaceful Living

Skype interviews are becoming increasingly popular in business and in academia. A Skype interview is defined here as a "face-to-face" interview over the Internet. Skype is often used for this type of interview, although other technologies can be used for such an interview. The advantage of a Skype interview over a phone interview is that it allows you and the interviewer to see each other. The disadvantage is the very real possibility of losing a connection or having a bad connection during an interview. The following are six additional rules for applying effective Skype interview strategies:

- Do some "practice runs" within an hour of the interview. Connect on Skype (or another videotelephony, if applicable) with a friend to make sure the connections are good and that you are following the correct procedures to connect.
- Have notes, application materials, and the school website in front of you before the interview begins. This rule is the same as for a phone interview, except for a Skype interview, make sure your notes and materials are out of sight. Also print faculty profiles with pictures of faculty at the school so that you can recognize faces with names easier during the interview—to impress a selection committee.
- Be at your computer early; connect on time (not early). This rule is the same as for a phone interview, except for a Skype interview, you must be in front of your computer (not your phone).
- Do the interview in an office or empty room. Do not have anything inappropriate in the background or within view. Make certain that the room is "clean" and that you will be the only person in that room for at least two hours.
- Dress formally. Look professional. Go through your daily routine as if you were meeting the committee in person. Shower, shave, and dress formally. If you *feel* like a professional, then you will *behave* like a professional in the interview.
- Address technical difficulties during the interview immediately. If the problem can be readily resolved, feel free to say, "Excuse me," then proceed to resolve the problem. If problems persist, ask to stop the call and redial. It is not an ideal scenario, but taking the initiative to fix problems is courteous and could reflect positively on you—the committee may view you as a problem solver.

A Skype interview should typically be formal, like the phone interview. Make limited efforts at humor on a Skype interview because it is difficult to use humor over the Internet. Just be sincere, respectful, and direct, and set aside a two-hour window for doing the interview. A Skype interview can be successful if you know what to expect and if you are prepared.

On-Campus Interviews

"There's no art to find the mind's construction in the face."

William Shakespeare

The members of a selection committee likely learn the most about you when they can interact with you face-to-face and in person, which is the intent of an on-campus interview. On-campus interviews can take many different forms. These can last an hour or so, or take a day or more to complete. In general, there are three types of on-campus interviews you may be asked to do.

1. <u>Screening interview.</u> This is a full-day or even a two-day event. Throughout the day you will have a series of meetings with administrators, faculty, and students. You will eat meals with students and faculty, will receive a campus tour, and may even be asked to stay overnight with a current graduate student. Throughout your visit, you will be escorted from one place to the next. You will have only a few breaks, so be prepared to keep your "game face" on all day long. Assume that you are being interviewed and evaluated at all times.

2. <u>Traditional interview.</u> You are brought in to a conference or another type of room and interviewed one-on-one or by a group. You are generally asked open-ended questions, and the interview can last less than an hour.

3. <u>Case or "problem-solving" interview.</u> In many clinical or counseling programs, you may be given a "case" and asked to solve a problem on the spot. This type of interview can be one-on-one or in a group setting with other interviewees. Here, the interviewer is more looking for the method you used to solve the problem than if you were correct.

Regardless of the type of on-campus interview you are asked to do, there are some general rules you can follow to prepare for interviewing in person. The following are six additional rules for applying effective on-campus interview strategies:

- Follow directions. Be on time. Know where to go. Do not look lost. Plan out your trip and make certain that you know exactly where to go. In the general rules, I suggest you arrive at least 15 minutes early. For an on-campus interview, give yourself even more time—at least 20 to 30 minutes early.
- Present all of yourself professionally. You need to do more than just appear professional; you need to smell good too for an in-person interview. Do not smoke at all the day of an interview. For a full-day screening interview, keep a small toothbrush and toothpaste in your pocket and brush your teeth during a bathroom break. Present all of yourself professionally.
- Turn off your phone, electronic devices, and music. You may anticipate being early, so you bring an iPod to listen to music or look through your cell phone while you wait. Do not at all touch your phone or listen to music once you

arrive at the interview, even if you are early. Your focus is on "them" until the interview is over; put all electronic devices away. Allowing distractions at any point in the interview can give the committee the impression that you are just "going through the motions" or "do not care."

- Do your research. When meeting in person, you need to put your notes to memory. Prepare, prepare, prepare. Also, find faculty profiles on the school website, and memorize faces with names. Bring a pen and small pad of paper. Write down names of people you meet who are not listed on the school website. Add a little note if you have time to help you recall their names later. Recalling names will really impress a selection committee.

- Have a résumé version of your achievements that highlights what you have added to your CV since submitting your application to the program. Doing so allows the committee to see your most current credentials, and the faculty can be impressed that you have already added to your CV since applying only a few months ago. If you have no new credentials to add, then simply skip this rule.

- Give a firm handshake upon meeting each interviewer and maintain eye contact. A firm handshake exudes confidence and will usually be positively received in an interview setting. Also maintain eye contact when responding and when listening. It can sometimes feel awkward to hold eye contact continuously, so instead you can alternate between the eyes or you can scan around the eyes, which can feel more comfortable and achieves the same goal: to make eye contact.

As a general rule for graduate school interviews, the people interviewing you are more interested in *how* you think than *what* you think. Keep it simple by sticking as close as you can to a script. In other words, do not stray too far from what you know and appeal your responses to the interests of the graduate program. Focus more on your strengths and less on your weaknesses, although be prepared to talk about both if asked. Most important, relax. Remember that the school offered you the interview, which means that the selection committee already thinks of you as a "top applicant." Now just show the interviewers what you already know is true: that you are a "good fit" for their program.

Relax, Reflect, and Reward

> *"As for the future, your task is not to foresee it, but to enable it."*
>
> Antoine de Saint-Exupéry

Throughout this book, the focus of each chapter has been to provide you with every detail for how you can pursue and create opportunities to be highly competitive for applying to graduate school and doctorate-level programs. Many examples and samples of strategies and materials were included that have proven successful for students eventually accepted to graduate- and doctorate-level programs. The plan given in this book, therefore, is a proven plan. Relax at this point in the process; you have done everything you can to be competitive, and there is little more you can do. There is no guarantee of getting into graduate school, but by following this plan you have certainly taken action to enable your opportunities for "getting in."

Also reflect on all the great work you have done to transition from being a freshman in college to being a professional. You have acquired new skills, and you have developed professionally in a way that can indubitably promote your ability to succeed, beyond attending graduate school. Regardless of the decisions you receive from graduate schools, you will be a college graduate in only a few months. Earning your bachelor's degree puts you among the top third in educational attainment as of 2012, with less than a third of U.S. adults having earned a bachelor's degree. Hence, earning your college degree is a point of pride—so reward yourself and take some extra "time off." Decisions from graduate schools will come, and there is little left to do but wait. Also keep in mind that there can always be opportunity ahead, regardless of the decisions made by graduate schools. You may not be able to foresee the future, but you can certainly "enable it." You can realize opportunity no matter the decisions you receive from graduate schools, as I explain in the next chapter.

SECTION IV

The Decision Letters And Next Steps

CHAPTER 9

Acceptance and Rejection: Realizing Opportunity in Both Cases

The "Decisions" in a Decision Letter

"Our greatest glory is not in never falling but in rising every time we fall."

Confucius

Realizing that a decision letter has arrived can be one of the most anticipated moments in your life. You are excited yet nervous, and maybe even a little scared in that moment before you open it. A *decision letter* is a notification from a graduate school of its decision regarding the application you sent. What is written in the letter can either make your day, or not so much. Waiting for, receiving, and reading the decision letters you receive from graduate schools can be an emotional roller coaster. In all, a graduate school can send you one of four basic decisions:

- <u>Accepted with funding.</u> This decision often means that you have been accepted to the school, and will receive a full, partial, or restricted tuition waiver (and likely a stipend if you applied to a PhD program). Note also that full funding is common for PhD candidates, but typically less common for students seeking master's degrees.
- <u>Accepted without funding</u> (or without comment on funding). This decision means that you have been accepted to the program to which you applied, but either funding is not available or you have been declined funding. If it is not mentioned, then follow up with the school to learn about funding options, if any.

- <u>Wait-listed.</u> This decision means that you are a top candidate, but you just missed the cut for outright acceptance. Being wait-listed does not mean you were rejected. If a student who was accepted subsequently declines (in favor of another school offer, for example), then those on the waiting list are next in line to receive acceptance letters.
- <u>Declined or rejected.</u> This decision is the most heartbreaking. It means that you were rejected for admission to a graduate program. However, keep in mind that this does not mean that you were a weak applicant; it means that compared to those who applied, you were not among the best applicants.

Decision letters are likely to be sent either in an e-mail or via postal mail. The time it takes to receive a decision letter can vary from one graduate school to another, largely depending on the graduate admissions process. Many schools evaluate applications continuously, called "rolling" admissions. These schools can send decision letters within four to six weeks of receiving your application. For applications due by a specific date, or "deadline" admissions, the wait can be many months. It is not really possible to predict when a school will send you its decision. However, most decision letters are sent around mid-February to mid-April for fall admissions.

Regardless of the decisions you receive, know that graduate schools do not take this process lightly. They put serious time and consideration into reviewing the applications that they receive. If you are accepted, it is a testament to how strong your application was. If you are not accepted, then it is simply not meant to be . . . for now. In this chapter, I describe how to respond to graduate schools after you receive decision letters, how to choose among schools that accepted you, and how to create opportunity when you are not accepted to even one school. Realize that no matter what decisions you receive, there is always opportunity for you to realize your goals . . . in time.

Reasons for Committee Decisions

"Committee—a group of [people] who keep minutes and waste hours."

Milton Berle

Graduate schools make decisions based on a variety of factors, many of which do not at all reflect the strength of your application. So often students feel as if they have "failed" or are a "failure" if a graduate school rejects them. Do not feel this way; you are reading too much into this process. A decision letter almost always communicates the decision only: acceptance or rejection; the letter rarely explains why a decision was made. There is no need for you to make assumptions about *why* a decision was made. When it comes to decisions from graduate schools, the reason could literally have nothing to do with the quality of your application.

To add context to the application process, realize that acceptance rates to graduate programs can be very low or very high. A few programs accept 100% of their applicants, particularly in years when few students apply. Most other graduate programs are much more selective. Master's-level programs can have acceptance rates of about 40% on average. Doctorate-level programs are much more selective, with acceptance rates of about 6% at public schools and about 12% at private schools on average. Not only should you consider these statistics when you are applying to graduate schools, but you also need to realize, from these statistics alone, that getting accepted to graduate school is not easy.

Also realize that the reasons for a decision can be arbitrary. Most schools will receive many more applications than they can possibly accept. In some years, too many highly qualified students apply, and schools are forced to reject students who would be accepted in other years—when fewer highly qualified applicants apply. In other years, some doctoral programs you apply to may lose funding to bring in another student, and therefore may be forced to reject all applicants who apply in that year. In other words, you could be rejected literally because of bad luck—it is entirely possible for a graduate school to reject you in one year when you would otherwise be accepted in another application year to that same school.

Consider the true story of a student who applied to two schools tied for hosting the top-ranked physics PhD programs in the United States: the California Institute of Technology (Caltech) and the Massachusetts Institute of Technology (MIT). In theory, if this student was not a competitive applicant for a top-ranked PhD program, then both top-ranked schools would have rejected his application. This did not happen. Instead, one top-ranked school accepted him with a full tuition waiver and a substantial stipend to cover his living expenses; the other top-ranked school outright rejected him. If he had applied only to the top-ranked program that rejected him, he could have erroneously concluded that he was not competitive at the top level when, in fact, he was.

Schools typically do not disclose the reason for a decision, so there is no way to know certain why a graduate school rejects an application. In the case of the student who applied to the two top-ranked doctoral programs for physics, one thing is certain: The disparity in the decision letters he received had nothing at all to do with the strength of his application; he was competitive for top-ranked schools. The reason, then, for the one rejection letter is left to assumption. His interests may not have "fit" well with the type of work being done at one school, but may have "fit" well with the interests of the other school. Maybe one school could accept more applicants in that year, or maybe one school had stronger applications to consider in that year. He will not know because he did not ask. He gladly accepted the offer from the top-ranked school that accepted him, and he went on to earn his PhD in physics there.

Keep in mind that there is no reason to give up or be discouraged by rejection, particularly early on when you have yet to hear from all the schools to which you applied. There are many reasons for a decision. Being rejected by one school, for example, does not necessarily predict that all schools will reject you. Wait to receive all your decision letters before concerning yourself with worry. You did not apply to all of your schools with the honest expectation of acceptance by them all. It would be great if you were accepted to all the schools to which you applied, but remember that it takes only one acceptance letter to reach your goal of getting into graduate school—just one.

Responding to a School
After You Receive a Decision Letter

"You have the ability to choose your reactions."

Steve Maraboli, *Life, the Truth, and Being Free*

For any decision of acceptance, you must reply with *your* decision to accept the school's offer or to decline it. For any decision of rejection, you must decide if it is worth your time to reply—typically to find out why you were rejected by the school. In both cases, you need to be thoughtful with regard to how quickly you respond and in the tone of your response. The following are two key considerations for responding to graduate schools after you receive a decision letter:

- Nature of *your* response [1]
- Timing of *your* response [2]

[1] The nature of your response must be polite and thankful. Regardless of the decision you receive, you need to maintain positive interactions with graduate schools. Positive interactions are, of course, easier when responding to a school that accepted you into a program compared to one that rejected your application. Although it can certainly be frustrating to receive a rejection letter, you must be cordial with a graduate school. In all of your communications, indicate your thankfulness for the school's time and consideration in reviewing your application. Also, be polite when speaking with faculty or administrators at the school. Do not "burn a bridge" unnecessarily; an opportunity can arise from any decision outcome.

Even if you are not accepted outright to a graduate program, you still want to have a positive relationship with that graduate school. If you are wait-listed, for example, such a decision literally means that a graduate school's decision is not yet final—there is still a real chance that you will be accepted. And do not be disrespectful or bitter after rejection. Rejection does not necessarily mean that you cannot be accepted in a later year, for either the same or a lesser degree (such as acceptance into a master's program after being declined admission into a school's doctoral program).

The nature of your response can often influence the extent to which you will have opportunities at the school in the future. By applying to a graduate school, you have made it clear that you are interested in that school. Do not take for granted your opportunity to build positive relationships with graduate schools of interest to you, even graduate schools that rejected your application. You never know what kind of opportunities may arise in the future.

[2] The timing of your response is also crucial. Do not be in a rush to reply to a graduate school. On your end, you need to be considerate of a variety of factors before responding to a graduate school. You want to be well informed at the time you respond to a school. If your top choice accepts you with full funding, then go ahead and immediately confirm your intention to accept the offer. If this best-case

scenario does not happen, then you need to be considerate of the responses from other schools before responding, if possible. In other words, you need to know what your "alternatives" are so that you can make the best decision for you.

You simply need to be considerate of your options, and be patient before responding to a graduate school. Unless your top-choice school is the first to send you a letter and the school accepts you with full funding, you will want to take your time in responding to graduate schools. In a way, you need to be considerate not only in how you respond, but also in when you respond. Once you commit to a graduate school, you have an ethical and moral obligation to honor that commitment. You should not change your mind later. For this reason, you need to think about the many alternative outcomes as you wait for a decision from graduate schools. To structure how to think about this, the following is a rank order of five basic decision alternatives and how you can respond in a way that is in *your* best interest:

1. Your top-choice school accepted you with full funding (and stipend). This is, of course, your best-case scenario. Feel free to accept the offer immediately, and celebrate your great accomplishment!

2. You receive acceptance from a school that is not at the top of your list, or the acceptance is without funding. Wait for letters from other schools to arrive before making a final decision. If a school higher on your list makes the same or a better offer, then accept the offer from the higher-ranked school. If a lower-ranked school offers funding, then seriously consider taking the offer with the most funding, especially if you are responsible for paying your own student loans.

3. You are wait-listed at a school. Respond immediately. Ask where on the waiting list you are (if you are the first or second alternate, then you have a real chance of being accepted at a later time). Let the school know that you are thankful for its decision and that you look forward to hearing more in due course.

4. You are rejected by schools early on, but have not yet received all decision letters from graduate schools. You need to seriously think about whether it is worth asking *why* you received a rejection. It truth, if you are accepted to even one graduate school, then accept that offer and forget about the rejections. Wait to receive all decision letters before concerning yourself with e-mails or phone calls inquiring about why a school rejected you. Those conversations are often best avoided.

5. You are rejected by all schools to which you applied. This is, of course, your worst-case scenario. However, even if this scenario occurs, you can still pursue clever ways to create opportunities that can help you reach your goals, as described later in this chapter.

As you receive decision letters, keep track of what schools have and have not sent letters, and what decisions have been sent. You can then weigh your options using the general rank ordering of the five basic decision alternatives given here. Once a graduate school has sent a decision letter, its decision has been made. Now it is your time to make decisions that are in *your* best interest. At the beginning of this chapter, I identified the four basic decisions that a graduate school can send you. The remainder of this chapter will look closer at each basic decision and what actions you can take for each decision.

Accepted With Funding: A Best-Case Scenario

"Success is getting what you want; happiness is liking what you get."

H. Jackson Brown, Jr.

The best-case scenario is that your top-choice school sends a letter accepting you into its program and also offers a full tuition scholarship. For doctoral programs, it is very likely that if you are offered a full tuition scholarship, you will also receive a stipend to cover your living expenses. The amount of the stipend will depend on the school and on the cost of living where the school is located. In this best-case scenario, you can certainly go ahead and accept the offer. Once you have chosen your school, you can even e-mail each school that has not yet sent you a decision letter to let the selection committee know you have chosen a school; the schools will appreciate your initiative. Feel free to let them know the school you have chosen, although it is not necessary.

A great scenario, but maybe not the "best-case" scenario, is to be accepted with full funding at a school that is not your top choice. Here, you should consider one key factor: What offers have you received from other graduate schools higher on your list?

As a general rule, it is likely in your best interest to choose the graduate program that is highest on your list that accepts you and offers you a full tuition waiver (plus stipend if a doctoral program). You need to be considerate of funding because eventually you will have to pay loans back. If you have an "accepted with funding" decision from a school that is not one of your top choices, then you can wait for the higher-ranked schools to send their decision letters before making a decision to accept an offer. You will typically be allowed some time to make a final decision.

One advantage of having an offer early is that you can use it to your advantage when contacting other schools that have yet to send their decision letters. If you have been accepted with full funding to one school, but you are still waiting on another school you would prefer to attend, then let that school know about the offer you received; that is, use the acceptance letter from one school as a negotiation tool when contacting preferred schools. Let the preferred schools know of the acceptance letter you received so that they know that the "clock is ticking," so to speak, on their chance to get you to come to their school. Graduate schools are usually grateful that you let them know about your situation, and if they know you would prefer their school, if accepted, then they will sometimes accelerate their decision process to bring you to their school.

You can contact a graduate school via e-mail, or you can call the school. For master's programs, an e-mail will usually suffice. For a doctoral program, it can be best to call directly the professor with whom you wish to work, or contact the chair or head of the department at the school. In your conversation, you do not want to sound as if you are giving an ultimatum. Instead, you want to give the impression that you are letting the school know as a courtesy. The following is a sample e-mail you can send (you can use this sample to help you organize what to say in a phone conversation as well):

Dear Dr. [name of contact person]:

My name is [your name]. I am an applicant for the [degree level] program in [name of program] at [name of university]. I am writing here as a courtesy to inform you that I have been accepted with full funding at another school for a similar program. That being said, I am very much interested in your program in particular. I would therefore appreciate knowing the outcome of your decision regarding my application before committing to my current offer.

If it is possible, please let me know when a decision can be made regarding my application. I very much look forward to your response. Thank you kindly for your time and consideration of my application.

Sincerely,

[Your Name]

Think about this process as identifying your *best alternative to a negotiating agreement* (BATNA), which is a concept developed by Roger Fisher and William Ury of the Harvard Program on Negotiation. If you are accepted with full funding to a graduate school, then that offer is your BATNA. You can put pressure on other schools by sending an e-mail (or making a phone call) to inform them that you already have an offer. Who knows? You may get a better offer. If not, then your best alternative is the school you do have an acceptance letter from. The nice part of having an acceptance letter is that you now have a great BATNA—you know that no matter what the other schools decide, you have an alternative for graduate school. And if your offer is acceptance with full funding, then your BATNA is really darn good.

In terms of the funding offer itself, you also want to consider the nature of the offer. For example, maybe you received a full tuition waiver, but the tuition waiver at one school is worth more than the tuition waiver at another school because the school itself is more expensive. In other words, consider the actual value of a funding offer before choosing between two or more schools that offer funding. Two key considerations are relevant:

- Amount of funding. How much is tuition at each school? A tuition scholarship or waiver is worth more at schools with higher tuition costs. Also, check if you are being awarded a full or partial tuition scholarship or waiver. Regardless of tuition costs, a full scholarship is more valuable than a partial scholarship because you pay no tuition with a full scholarship. Also, if you are awarded a stipend, then how much funding is being offered? And maybe more important, where is the school located? For example, if the school is located in Los Angeles, California, you will need a larger stipend to cover living expenses than you would in a place that has a cheaper cost of living, such as Buffalo, New York.

- Length of funding. It is also sometimes the case that a funding offer is restricted. Most funding offers must be renewed each year. Yet, in some cases, a funding offer may be restricted to one or a few years. At some point in the program you may have to begin paying tuition and/or living expenses. Check with a graduate school to see if the funding offer will cover all years you are in graduate school, or if at some point the funding offer may expire. A funding offer that covers all years in graduate school should be preferred to one that is restricted to one or a few years.

Ultimately, it is in your best interest to wait to receive all decision letters before committing to any one school, if necessary. Reply to each school that accepts you, and express enthusiasm for the committee's decision. Yet also take your time in confirming your intent to accept an offer from a graduate school until you are certain that the school you choose is the best school for *you* to accept among all schools to which you applied.

Accepted Without Funding: Weighing Your Options

"When weighing your options, remember that some of them get heavier over time."

Susan Gale

Being accepted to a graduate program is a great accomplishment, although it does not always come with funding. Many acceptance letters will not include a funding option. The acceptance letter may not always make it clear whether or not funding is available or being awarded. The following are two alternatives of what you are likely to read in your acceptance letter:

- A statement that no funding will be awarded or no funding is available. In this case, there is no ambiguity; you have been accepted but without funding to pay for your education. You can still apply for financial aid.
- No mention of funding at all. There are two possibilities when a funding option is not stated directly in an acceptance letter: (1) There is no funding, so the school simply did not mention it in the letter, or (2) there may be funding, but the school is not yet ready to identify how much funding is available and to which students the funding will be awarded.

In most cases, you will want to take the offer (i.e., acceptance letter) from the best graduate school that also awards you funding—in terms of a scholarship and/ or a stipend. For many students, though, none of their acceptance letters will offer funding. For cases in which you are choosing among schools that accepted you but did not offer funding, you need to be considerate of many factors; ask the following questions:

- Does the school offer tuition assistance or financial aid support for graduate students? Make sure you know how you will pay for your education. The lower the tuition, of course, the less you will pay, or have to repay later.
- Is there a possibility of funding in future years in the program? It is very possible that a graduate school may have no funding for incoming students, but students can become eligible for funding in a later year. Do not hesitate to ask about the possibility of funding in the future, and if funding in the future is possible, then learn about how you can apply or become eligible for such funding.
- What are the total costs of attending the school? The costs include tuition and living expenses. If you anticipate some funding in future years, then factor those savings in. "Crunch the numbers" to estimate the total net cost of attending each graduate school that accepts you. Do not make a final decision without factoring in an estimate of net cost.

Unless you have your heart completely set on one school, or it is a top-ranked school making the offer, it is often in your best interest to choose the best school that will be the least costly to attend. Assuming that you are interested in attending all the schools you applied to, then attending the least costly school that accepts you is a good plan: You get what you want, and it will cost you the least.

Also, keep in mind your BATNA as you consider which offer of acceptance to accept. Mitigating factors other than cost may play into your decision. For example, maybe one school is your top choice, but it is more costly than another school that is lower on your list but less costly. Talk to family and professors to get feedback regarding the offers you receive. Certainly take your time and make sure the choice you make is one you feel good about. Graduate school will be many years of your life. In this light, make sure that you not only find success (get what you want), but also find happiness (like what you get).

Waited-Listed: Be Patient and Be Encouraged

"Still round the corner there may wait, a new road or a secret gate."

J. R. R. Tolkien

You can also receive a decision letter indicating that you have been placed on a waiting list at a school to which you applied. Being wait-listed can mean that you really did "make the cut" in that your application was strong enough to be accepted to the school, but not quite as strong as those of the other applicants who were offered acceptance letters. The reason you were placed on a waiting list is that the graduate school has identified you as an applicant who could be accepted to its program at a later time, usually depending on one of two factors:

- Another applicant declines acceptance. This is the most common reason for accepting an applicant on a waiting list. Often, students receive offers from multiple schools. In these cases, it is not unlikely at all that a student will decline an offer from one school. When a student declines an offer from a school, he or she is then replaced by a student on the waiting list. If your name is on a waiting list, then it could be you who is thus offered acceptance.

- More funding becomes available. In 2013, for example, I advised a student who was placed on a waiting list for a PhD program in social psychology at a school in the Northeast. She was subsequently selected to the doctoral program just one month later because additional funding became available to not only accept one more student, but also offer that student a full tuition waiver plus stipend. Hence, she not only was accepted, but also received a full tuition waiver and stipend. She went from being on a waiting list to being accepted with a "full ride" in just one month—all due to a change in available funding.

In truth, being placed on a waiting list is a compliment. To explain, suppose that 400 students applied to a doctoral program and 12 applicants were offered acceptance. Four others were then placed on a waiting list. Hence, the top 3% (the top 12) received acceptance letters. If you were placed on the waiting list, that puts you in the top 16, or in the top 4% of all applicants. Being on a waiting list for a graduate school means that you did not make the cut for the top applicants who were offered acceptance, but the school has recognized you as being among the best and strongest applicants overall. Therefore, be proud of being placed on a waiting list; by wait-listing you, the school has identified you as a strong applicant.

In fairness, realize also that only a small percentage of students who are placed on a waiting list will eventually receive an acceptance letter. The statistics are difficult to determine because not all schools report their "waiting list" statistics. From the data that are reported, the statistics suggest that the higher ranked and more prestigious the school, the larger its wait list (i.e., the more students the school places on a waiting list), and the lower the percentage of students eventually accepted—in some cases, schools rarely accept a student who is wait-listed. That being said, as a general rule, your odds can be up to about 8% to 10% that you will eventually be accepted after being wait-listed—realizing, of course, that your odds are better at lower-ranked and less prestigious schools. If you think about it, the statistics make sense: Fewer students are likely to decline acceptance from highly ranked and prestigious schools than from lesser known or unranked schools. Hence, your odds of getting off a waiting list at "better" schools can be more difficult.

To weigh your options with a school where you are wait-listed, first consider where on the list you are. In the previous example, four applicants were placed on a waiting list—having many applicants placed on a waiting list is common. The applicants on a waiting list will likely be ranked as first alternate, second alternate, and so on. If you are the first alternate on a waiting list, then you will be the first applicant contacted with an acceptance offer if a spot in the graduate program becomes available. If you are the last alternate on a waiting list, then your chances of eventually being accepted go down substantially. Call or e-mail a professor or graduate contact person at the school to find out if he or she can let you know where you are on the waiting list.

Second, you should consider how many schools have wait-listed you. The more graduate schools that wait-list you, the better your chances can be of eventually being accepted to any one graduate school. For example, suppose that you are on a waiting list at four graduate schools and two spots in each program become available. That makes eight total spots to fill at graduate schools where you are on a waiting list (instead of hoping to be chosen for one of only two spots if you were on the waiting list at only one of those schools).

Also, realize that if you are on the waiting list for many schools, it is possible that those schools gave acceptance offers to the same student or students. In other words, if you are wait-listed at two schools that make an offer to the same student, then that student will have to decline one offer. Being on the waiting list at both schools thus increases your chances that either of those schools will have to select from students on its waiting list, simply because each school may make offers to the same students. In this way, being on a waiting list at many different graduate schools can increase your chances of eventually being accepted to any one graduate school.

Once you are placed on a waiting list, you may need to think about whether you should continue to pursue the graduate school by showing continued interest, or if you should let the school know that you have accepted an offer elsewhere and wish to be taken off its waiting list. Do not tell a school that you are "no longer interested" because that phrasing can come off as being rude. As a general rule, continue to express an interest in a school until you have officially accepted another school's offer. In terms of being wait-listed by a graduate school, two general scenarios are likely to impact your decision for how to respond to a school that places you on the waiting list:

- You are wait-listed and receive an acceptance letter from at least one other graduate school. [1]
- You are wait-listed and receive no acceptance letters; hence, your wait-listed decision letters are your best outcome. [2]

[1] If you have at least one acceptance letter, think of your BATNA. If you are happy to attend the graduate school that has accepted you, then go ahead and contact the graduate school that wait-listed you and let the selection committee know of your current offer to see if there is a good chance of being selected from the waiting list. You can contact the school via e-mail, or you can call the school. For master's programs, an e-mail will usually suffice. For a doctoral program, it can be best to call directly the professor with whom you wish to work, or contact the chair or head of the department at the school. In your conversation, you do not want to sound as if you are giving an ultimatum. Instead, you want to give the impression that you are letting the school know as a courtesy.

Let the school know that you received an offer from another school for a similar program, and that you would like to know if its wait-list decision is likely to change before you commit to the current offer. If anything, the school will appreciate your letting the committee know the current status of your application. If the graduate school that wait-listed you can make an offer, it will. If not, then no problem because your BATNA is strong anyway—you already have an acceptance letter to a graduate school, which is a very good alternative no matter how the wait-list school responds.

Be careful not to hold out too long for a school that has you on its waiting list, particularly if you already have an acceptance letter from another school. Again, the odds are low that you will be accepted after an initial decision to put you on a waiting list. Follow the suggestions given in this chapter for acceptance decisions to help you decide which graduate school acceptance offer to take. Being on a waiting list is great, but it is the same as a rejection if the school does not change its decision to "accept." If you have an offer elsewhere, you should probably take it, especially if there is no indication from the wait-list school that its decision is likely to change.

[2] If the best offers you receive are a decision to place you on a waiting list, then you need to start getting creative. As stated before, being on a waiting list is great, but it is the same as a decision to reject if the school does not change its decision to accept. That being said, being on a waiting list is also an acknowledgment of the strength of your application, and this can lead to opportunities you can create.

Even if you remain on a waiting list and no graduate school changes its decision to accept you, it is still possible to work toward creating new opportunities for the next academic year. You can create opportunities by taking advantage of the knowledge that the wait-list schools value your credentials—even if those credentials were not "good enough" in the current academic year to get you accepted. The following are actions you can take to create opportunities after a decision to place you on a waiting list (assuming that you did not receive any acceptance letters):

- Offer to work in the program or lab to which you applied; volunteer. Try to gain experience related to the type of program you are applying to. Many successful faculty members hire personnel to manage their labs or other facilities at the school. If you have no other graduate school offers, then you can offer to work at a school that wait-listed you. You would join as an employee, not as a student. If you get the position, you can prove yourself on the job possibly enough to get offered a spot in the school's graduate program in the next academic year. I have seen this work firsthand for a graduate student who earned his way into a PhD program using just this strategy.
- If applying to a PhD program, ask about the possibility of joining the master's program. Many schools will make available their master's program to students who were wait-listed at a higher degree level at their school. Joining the master's program can give you added experience you can use to apply again to doctoral programs in the following year. You could also end up working your way into the school's PhD program; it is not at all uncommon for students to earn their master's and PhD degrees at the same school.
- Use your strong credentials to find employment in a related field to gain additional experience, then apply again to graduate schools. A strong student

I worked with was rejected from all graduate schools in her first try because she did not have enough experience working with animals. She then found a job working as a lab technician in a university neurobiology lab. That was enough to earn her an acceptance into a behavioral neuroscience PhD program in her second try in the following academic year. The job was not at a school that wait-listed her, but she did make the most of her time by addressing the only weakness left in her application.

The three options given here are ambitious, but they have been used with great success. There are certainly no guarantees with any action you take, but these suggestions can be and have been successful for students I have worked with. If you hold on to your goal of getting into graduate school, then the best alternative to the options here is to get a job, preferably in a field related to your degree, and apply again to schools for the next academic year. For any action you take, try to build upon your skills each year and show continued professional development in your career and in your endeavors. Doing so will impress graduate school selection committees when you apply again for admission in the following academic year.

Rejected: Realizing Opportunity Regardless

"The optimist sees the donut, the pessimist sees the hole."

Oscar Wilde

The most heartbreaking decision that a graduate school can send you is the decision to reject your application. There are many reasons why students, even good students, do not get accepted to graduate schools. Many reasons are overtly addressed in the plan for getting into graduate school outlined in this book. For example, you were told to apply to public and private schools; to schools that are small, medium, and large; and to schools that are ranked and unranked. The rationale for doing so was to ensure that you set yourself up best for an acceptance letter from a graduate school. In all likelihood, however, a rejection from any one school is probably inevitable when you consider the competitiveness of graduate school, particularly for doctorate-level programs.

An isolated rejection letter from a single school should be expected; the hope is that you have other types of decisions from the other schools you applied to. One of basically two scenarios is likely to impact your decision for how to respond to a school that rejects your application:

- You are rejected and have an acceptance offer from at least one other graduate school. In this case, you can simply accept the offer from the school that has accepted you. If multiple schools have given you offers, then you can use the suggestions given under the acceptance headings for this chapter.
- You are rejected and receive no acceptance letters; hence, this is the same scenario as [2] under the wait-list heading. In this situation, you can pursue the same options as those given for [2] in that section.

It is natural for students to want to know or understand why they were rejected by a school. In truth, though, if you have an offer and accept it at one school, then it simply does not matter why another school rejected you at this point. As stated at the beginning of this chapter, the reason could be completely arbitrary. If you have an acceptance letter, then take the acceptance offer and forget about the rejections. It is probably best to accept a committee's decision gracefully than to question its reasons.

If you only receive rejection letters, however, it is probably worth asking why the selection committees rejected you. Maybe there is something in common among all the rejection letters—something you can quickly fix or strengthen in your application and/or curriculum vitae for the next application year. The best approach is to call a member of the graduate school to inquire about the reasons for a decision. In your conversation, you do not want to sound as if you are challenging the school's decision. Instead, you want to give the impression that you are inquiring as a way to better understand how you can improve in the future. After all, if you want to improve your application for next year, it may be helpful to understand the reasons for your rejection letters.

As is evident, a decision to reject your application is a difficult decision to accept, but it is certainly not the end of the road. In many cases, it can be the beginning of a new challenge or even the beginning of a new direction for a career. Always strive to be better tomorrow than you are today; continue to work toward your goal of getting into graduate school, and you can achieve your goal . . . in time.

Choosing Your Path and Next Steps

"Knowing is not enough; we must apply. Being willing is not enough; we must do."

Leonardo da Vinci

Throughout this book, the plan has been to take action. If an internship is not available, then create one; if a research lab has no openings, then create an opening; if a lab was unproductive, then find a lab that is productive; if you are rejected or wait-listed at one or more graduate schools, then take action to build on your existing skills and show continued professional development. Throughout this book, there has been a spirit of making things happen and never giving up. More than this, I have given you concrete and proven plans for how to create opportunities and ways to take advantage of almost any situation to advance your experiences and skills to promote your ability to be competitive for getting into graduate school.

It is easy to get stuck in a mind-set that "graduate school is just not for me" or "graduate school is not something I can do." I was there. I also felt that way at one point as a college student. It can be disheartening sometimes when you are an undergraduate student aspiring to attend graduate school, but you are not among the top 1% of students in the country. You see students who compete for prestigious internships and research programs offered only to the top undergraduate students in the country, and you get the sense that it is those students who "belong"—not you. You are wrong.

The top 1% will certainly be competitive for just about any graduate school in the country; but it is actually about the top 40% who are accepted to master's programs and the top 6% to 12% who are accepted to PhD programs each year. In other words, let the 1%ers have their prestigious offers; by creating many opportunities yourself in just about any situation, you can certainly become a top 12%er, which is enough to be competitive for master's- and doctorate-level programs—thereby helping you to reach your goals, even if you cannot necessarily compete for the most prestigious opportunities. In many ways, that has been a key goal of this book: to develop a plan that just about any student can use to be competitive for getting into graduate school.

Whether or not you were among the top 1% of applicants to graduate school, many of you were still highly competitive for "getting in," even at the doctorate level. My hope is that many of you who have followed this plan were able to get accepted to a graduate school, as many other students have achieved by following this plan. The next step is to prepare for graduate school—or, in the case that you did not get into graduate school on your first try, to prepare to go through the application process again in the coming year. No matter the outcome of your applications, you can certainly benefit from reflecting on this process to prepare for the next steps in your career.

In the last chapter, I will reflect on the process of the plan in this book for getting into graduate school, and how this plan can be applied to manage just about any challenge ahead of you. I also revisit the concerns brought up in the graduate school selection committee meeting described in Chapter 1 to identify how the plan in this book will help you address them.

CHAPTER 10

Reflecting on the Process and Graduation

Planning for the Future

"The greatest risk to man is not that he aims too high and misses, but that he aims too low and hits."

Michelangelo

The plan in this book has been structured to help you get through just your years in college. Yet ideally the reason that you attended college was to create opportunities for your future—a future that hopefully includes graduate school and spans many more decades after you finish college. It is easy to think of your future as something distant in time, but now, your future in graduate school will become a reality for many of you. And, as described in Chapter 9, even if you were rejected, this plan certainly can still help you to get into graduate school in time.

In a simple way, this plan for getting into graduate school has really been a plan of action. So many students say they want to go to graduate school, but they just can't compete against all the other students who seem better prepared. The assumption of such a statement is that the individual cannot do anything on his or her own to change the situation—he or she cannot do anything to become equally prepared. This is nonsense. Just about any student can gain the necessary skills in college to prepare for graduate school and stand out among his or her peers. The plan in this book has been a plan of action, explaining not only what you need to do (the "Big Three") but also how you can achieve the things you need to do to become prepared and competitive for getting into graduate school.

Reflecting on the Process: Building Upon Skills Acquired

"The world needs dreamers and the world needs doers. But above all, the world needs dreamers who do."

Sarah Ban Breathnach

The plan for getting into graduate school outlined in this book can also be applied to other life challenges, by adapting it to whatever outcomes you wish to pursue. The basic skills you acquired using this plan are universal for achieving just about any outcome. Throughout this book, you have been shown a full plan for preparing to be competitive for just about any graduate program in psychology and the behavioral sciences. The perspective of this plan has been to focus on four basic skills:

- Believing in one's pursuits
- Goal setting (for each year of college)
- Communicating effectively (in person and in writing)
- Pursuing skills needed to realize your goals

The plan in this book is really a good place to start—a way to realize the utility of a college plan to achieve big goals. Hence, *the* plan is more than just a plan for getting into graduate school; it is a plan that can help you build necessary life skills that can promote your success in future endeavors.

Under the next four headings, I take a closer look at each of the four basic skills in *the* plan. Regardless of the career you choose, you will certainly continue to have plans and goals well beyond your years in undergraduate school; your planning does not begin and end in college. For this reason, in this chapter I highlight the four basic skills of *the* plan. Doing so can help to show you how to apply these basic skills to organize just about any plan to achieve your own goals in your pursuits—in graduate school and beyond.

Believing in One's Pursuits

"Remember, you see in any situation what you expect to see."

David J. Schwartz

To have a plan is great, but you are unlikely to reach your goals unless you believe in your pursuits. More than this, you need to believe in yourself. As stated by David J. Schwartz, "You see in any situation what you expect to see." Expectation is a consequence of belief. All people expect those things that they believe in. Intrinsically, what we *expect* of ourselves reflects what we *believe* in ourselves.

You cannot expect to achieve your goals if you do not first believe in yourself, and thus believe in your ability to achieve the goals you set out to pursue.

So many students do not even try to pursue graduate school—not because they are not competitive, but because they have convinced themselves that they are not "good enough" to get into graduate school. This type of thinking must be avoided, and part of this plan has been to break down those walls of what you believe is possible by helping you to realize that anything is possible. If you are not competitive now, you can be; if you lack experience, you can gain it; if you do not know the "right" people, you can meet them. Regardless of your pursuits, believe in them; believe in yourself.

In Chapter 4, I explained that whether or not you appreciate it, your *beliefs* largely guide your *actions*; you are likely to be the biggest critic of your own life. To believe in yourself is the first step toward taking action in your life. It can be your first step toward finding your own success. Mark Twain cleverly stated, "Thousands of geniuses live and die undiscovered—either by themselves or by others." Do not let your beliefs in yourself limit you—ever! You may live and die undiscovered, but do not let *yourself* be the reason you remain undiscovered. Believe in yourself, take action upon those things that you believe in, and find your own successes for your pursuits.

Goal Setting

"Often it isn't the mountains ahead that wear you out, it's the little pebble in your shoe."

Muhammad Ali

The second basic skill you developed from *the* plan is goal setting. Consider how you went about setting goals. You started with one big goal: to get into graduate school. However, you cannot just stop there; you still have not considered the details for how to achieve that goal. You need to identify how to achieve that goal, which typically requires the following:

1. An understanding of what you need to do to achieve your goal: the "Big Three"

2. A new set of smaller stepwise goals: the "Sweet Sixteen"

In the plan you followed, Chapter 2 fully disclosed the "Big Three": academics, scholarship, and activities. The Big Three are the details for how to be competitive for getting into just about any graduate school in psychology and the behavioral sciences. Your academics, scholarship, and activities will be the core criteria for gaining acceptance at just about any graduate school to which you apply. The aims of that early chapter were to outline an understanding of what you need to do to achieve your goals. After all, we certainly cannot begin without first understanding what it is that we are beginning.

Immediately following the second chapter was a full four-year plan in Chapters 3 to 5, with all of Section III (Chapters 6 to 8) supporting the details of your senior-year goals in Chapter 5. In this plan for getting into graduate school, I organized what you need to do by identifying smaller stepwise goals within each academic year, which I called the "Sweet Sixteen." These goals, listed in Chapter 1 (Table 1.1), are stepwise in that achieving any one goal may not make you competitive for graduate school, but achieving all 16 goals can make you highly competitive for graduate school—thereby achieving the larger goal of getting into graduate school.

For any endeavor you pursue, you can use a goal-setting model similar to the one identified here. In this plan for getting into graduate school, you set a macro goal (getting into graduate school; the "mountain"), and you set 16 micro goals (the "Sweet Sixteen"; the "pebbles in your shoe") to help you reach your macro goal. Setting smaller stepwise goals in this plan was important because, by doing so, you could more easily identify and plan for the "pebbles in your shoe" that would otherwise "wear you out" along your path toward achieving your macro goal of getting into graduate school. This same goal-setting model can be applied to almost any pursuit that is important to you. Identify macro goals, understand what you need to do to achieve your goals, and then set smaller stepwise goals that when amalgamated can help you to achieve your macro goals.

Communicating Effectively

"If I really want to improve my situation, I can work on the one thing over which I have control—myself."

Stephen R. Covey

Ultimately you can control how you communicate with others. Your actions inherently facilitate your interactions. In this book, over 100 suggestions and tips are listed for how to communicate effectively as you progress through this plan. In addition, full chapters are devoted to effective communication in writing your letters of intent (Chapter 6) and your résumé and curriculum vitae, or CV (Chapter 7). No other part of the plan is given greater attention than your ability to communicate effectively with others. The reason is simple: To achieve almost any goal, you must be able to communicate effectively. Whether you want to meet the "right" people, demonstrate how your skills make you competitive for a position, or simply write a "request" or "thank-you" e-mail, effective communication in all regards can make or break your ability to effectively pursue your own goals.

As evidence for the importance of effective communication, recall that before I even stated the five goals for your freshman year in Chapter 3, I opened that chapter with 28 suggestions for effective communication: in e-mail, in conversation, and in how you present yourself. Specifically, I identified the need for effective communication with any professors, staff, and administrators. I explained that you will make it more difficult for yourself if you do not meet or connect with people who can help you create opportunities. The same lesson can be applied in all your endeavors: Do not underestimate the value of working together with others toward shared goals.

Effective communication is important because it can quite honestly make your path or journey more enjoyable and satisfying. You do not want to be bitter, or feel as if you must "do this on your own." There is nothing enjoyable or satisfying in going about pursuing your goals despite the people around you, and it will probably just make it more difficult for you to reach your goals anyway. Effective communication is important in all your endeavors. Three vital reasons that effective communication in your endeavors is important are as follows (the three reasons given here are adapted from the great advice of Stephen R. Covey in *The 7 Habits of Highly Effective People: Powerful Lessons in Personal Change*):

- To avoid misunderstandings. Misunderstandings often arise because, as stated by Stephen R. Covey (2004), "Most people do not listen with the intent to understand; they listen with the intent to reply" (p. 239). In other words, misunderstandings are avoidable. They can lead to mistakes and even "burn bridges," which can lead to frustration and even anger. Sometimes people even interpret a misunderstanding as an intentional sabotage of a person's character or abilities. Applying the tips and suggestions given in this book for effective communication can help you facilitate mutual understandings and avoid miscommunications—thereby leading to more positive and fulfilling communication.

- To make clear your intentions. To get something, you must ask. Making clear your intentions is about creating opportunities to get what you want. As stated by Stephen R. Covey (2004), "Is it logical that two people can disagree and that both can be right? It's not logical; it's *psychological*" (p. 277). In truth, you may find many situations in which opportunities are missed because you did not make clear your intentions. Indeed, much of the plan in this book has focused on showing you how to create opportunities by simply letting your intentions be known. Seize opportunity by creating opportunity—by making clear your intentions.

- To facilitate a network of connections. Effective communication builds trust. As stated by Stephen R. Covey (2004), "When the trust account is high, communication is easy, instant, and effective" (p. 188). It is simply more enjoyable and satisfying to engage with people whom you feel you can work with, understand, and trust. Building lasting, trusting relationships—in your personal and your professional life—is a positive, enjoyable, and satisfying approach to effectively pursing your goals for your endeavors.

Beyond the three reasons given here, effective communication can foster long-term benefits that extend beyond your current goals. Your parents may have taught you that "the last person in has to close the door." However, in your professional life, try to never close a door once it is opened—you never know when you may want or even need to walk through it again. Effective communication helps you achieve success not only in reaching your goals but also in building positive professional networks that can be used to promote success in your future endeavors.

Pursuing Skills Needed to Realize Your Goals

"All our dreams can come true . . . if we have the courage to pursue them."

Walt Disney

Finally, you must take action; you must actually pursue your goals by developing the skills you need to achieve your goals. In the plan for getting into graduate school, I outline the "Sweet Sixteen," which are the 16 goals one needs to pursue as an undergraduate in order to be competitive for graduate school admission. To realize your goal of getting into graduate school, you needed to take action, and the Sweet Sixteen goals allowed you to realize the actions you must take to attain that goal—from getting acquainted in your freshman year to searching for graduate schools in your senior year.

Often the only thing separating you from your dreams is action. That is why believing in one's self is a necessary skill of this plan: Believing in one's self leads to action toward those things one believes in. Similarly, you cannot take heed of your goals unless you know how to attain them. You need to be able to identify the skills you will need to be successful and attain your goals. Just going through the motions until you have a degree is not likely to make you highly competitive for graduate schools, or even a career.

The advantage of having this plan is that it outlines what you must do to be highly competitive for getting into graduate school. Specifically, the plan is set up at three levels of organization, as follows:

1. Identify categories of skills needed. The plan begins by identifying three major categories (the "Big Three"): academics, scholarship, and activities.

2. List examples in each category. Throughout the book, examples are given for what types of activities count for each of the three major categories.

3. Plan and develop ways to achieve skills needed. This plan identifies ways to pursue opportunities in each category, and ways to create opportunities in each category, if none are otherwise available.

By organizing the plan in this way, you know what skills are needed, what types of activities help you develop those skills, and how to attain those skills. This same level of organization can be applied to just about any endeavor you wish to pursue. Any suitable plan will have a certain level of organization; the plan in this book is no exception. By clearly organizing what you must do to realize your goals, you can achieve just about anything.

Revisiting the Graduate School Selection Committee Meeting

"You can't build a reputation on what you're going to do."

Henry Ford

In Chapter 1, we took a look inside a graduate school selection committee meeting. Although no two graduate schools are identical, major themes can likely arise during a selection committee meeting, many of which I highlighted in Chapter 1. The goal in Chapter 1 was to impart a new perspective: one from the point of view of those who select students into graduate programs. It is certainly true that not every criterion identified in the meeting I described will come up in all selection committee meetings, but these criteria can, do, and likely will come up. Therefore, being able to anticipate what criteria may be discussed in a selection committee meeting and how you can preemptively address possible concerns can give you a competitive advantage over those who do not realize they should address these possible concerns.

In Chapter 1, of course, you had not yet seen the plan in this book. Now that you have completed the plan, we can revisit the committee meeting. Take note of how the plan for getting into graduate school addresses each point brought up in the meeting. The following is a summary of my experience on a committee for the selection of candidates to a PhD program in psychology (revisited from Chapter 1):

The "Cutoff" Criteria

I noted that the selection committee spent remarkably little time talking about grades. Once the submission deadline passed, the secretary received all applications, eliminated all applicants whose GPA and standardized exam scores did not meet the minimum requirements, and then passed the remaining applications on to the faculty. Grades really did not play a big role in our conversation after that, other than in occasional discussions. Instead, final decisions to reject or accept students were largely based on the other parts of the application.

Likewise, in the plan for getting into graduate school there is an emphasis on developing a strong overall application, with little focus, other than that needed, on your grades. Indeed, only two of the "Sweet Sixteen" goals specifically address your grades (Goals 3 and 11). Grades are certainly important, but it is often everything else in your application that makes you stand out as an applicant, as is addressed in the plan in this book.

The Letters of Intent

I noted also that the selection committee spent remarkably substantial time reading and discussing letters of intent. The letter of intent quickly arose as being among the most important application materials. For this reason, a full chapter was devoted to showing you how to write these letters (Chapter 6). In addition, a full chapter was devoted to showing you how to write your résumé and CV because such documents are often considered together with your letter of intent.

Scholarly Matching

The extent to which your interests fit with the interests of the faculty, particularly the faculty's research interests, was also a concern. In general, appealing to the interests of others is a common, recurring theme throughout this book. To address this concern, the plan in this book shows you how to appeal your interests to the interests of the faculty and graduate program you apply to—via e-mail, in person, in writing, and even in how you present yourself. In actuality, faculty members who oversee graduate programs usually have a program of research, or a graduate program has specific aims or goals. It is therefore imperative to match yourself with the scholarly aims of the faculty and graduate programs to which you apply, as has been addressed throughout this book in *the* plan.

Geographic Matching

A surprising criterion was whether the committee "thought" an applicant wanted to actually live in the area. This concern is addressed in the plan for getting into graduate school, just in case it comes up. For example, you are shown how to address this concern in the opening paragraph of your letter of intent in Chapter 6, and as part of the plan for how to interview effectively in Chapter 8. It may seem like an insignificant criterion, but it was a key criterion used by the committee. You are better off addressing it ahead of time than not addressing it at all.

The "Will They Come Here?" Criteria

As the selections were narrowed, the key question was whether or not an applicant, if accepted, would actually come to our school even if another school accepted him or her. Demonstrating an understanding of the mission and aims of a program is exactly how this concern was best addressed. Applicants who showed that they "did their research" before applying were most likely to be given the first offers. In this plan, full attention is given to researching graduate schools in Chapter 5 ("Sweet Sixteen" Goal 13) and throughout Section III. Indeed, how to communicate an understanding of the mission and aims of a graduate program is a vital part of your senior-year plan to help you stand out as an applicant.

The "Did They Show Excitement?" Criteria

Often, graduate school selection committees will contact a potential candidate directly. A key area of our evaluation of each applicant was the extent to which he or she was enthusiastic during the interaction, either on the phone or in person.

On the phone, the committee members were most interested in the applicant's tone of voice, and in person, they evaluated the applicant's body language. By the time you get to an interview stage, you are already a top candidate, so the evaluation becomes less about "qualifications" and more about "fit." This criterion is addressed in the graduate school plan in Chapter 8, which includes a full section on how to effectively interview: by phone, by Skype, and in person.

The "Did They Get Along?" Criteria

For students invited to on-campus interviews, a key evaluation during an in-person interview is the extent to which applicants get along with graduate students and faculty at the school. After all, applicants selected to a graduate program will need to be able to work together within the program. This criterion is specifically addressed in Chapter 8 by identifying the three most common types of on-campus interviews, and by offering specific tips for how to effectively interview in each type of interview setting.

Of course, the plan in this book builds far more than the criteria identified here into a full plan for getting into graduate school. What is most striking about the criteria described in the selection committee meeting is how much of the selection process was qualitative. The reason that the criteria identified in this section were emphasized is that many of the criteria can be difficult to anticipate and can be difficult to address. Getting into graduate school can take a lot more than just grades. "Getting in" is often about telling the story you want graduate schools to read—and this book has shared the detailed steps you can take to tell that story and to be competitive at any graduate level.

The Summer Following Graduation

"To exist is to change, to change is to mature, to mature is to go on creating oneself endlessly."

Henri Bergson

Your next steps are now to graduate and, if everything goes according to plan, to get ready for graduate school. No matter the outcome of the graduate school application process, be proud of the many achievements you have earned along your path toward graduation. You are about to earn a four-year college degree. Although graduation data can vary from year to year, the data show that about 28% of Americans who are 25 years or older have earned a four-year college degree. While that may sound like a lot, it still puts you among the 28% most educated adults in the United States. If you are going to graduate school, then you will be among more elite company in the next few years. The point here is that you should always take pride in education—no one can take your education away from you; take pride in earning your degree.

Following graduation, you will likely have the summer to enjoy being a college graduate. Take the time to relax. You have spent many hours in classes and in pursuing scholarship and activities. If you "got in," then the summer before graduate school begins can be an important time for relaxing and preparing. It is the perfect time to take a break and also make sure your transition to graduate school goes smoothly. Essential tips for how to spend the summer before graduate school include the following:

- Buy a nice frame and hang your degree. Bring your degree with you wherever you go next. Hang it on a wall, and from time to time look at it and just appreciate what you have achieved. It can be somewhat therapeutic to look at your degree, particularly when times feel overwhelming.
- Relax for most of your summer. Try not to think about school. Read a novel or travel. Catch up with friends you have not seen in a while and spend time with family. You will likely be busy once the summer ends, so enjoy the downtime and make an effort to just relax for the summer.
- Get a summer job to save spending money for when you arrive on campus. It is probably best to have some spending money when you arrive at graduate school. Getting a summer job is a great way to save money so that you can be prepared for those unexpected expenses when you arrive on campus.
- Settle your tuition bill and get enrolled for classes. Once you pay your tuition bill, or once you settle your scholarship (if you earned a tuition scholarship), enroll in classes immediately. Talk to an advisor and ask for recommended classes to take in your first year. The sooner you have your schedule completed, the sooner you can start preparing for your upcoming semester.
- Plan and prepare to move, if applicable. If you were accepted to a school in your hometown, then moving really is not a concern. However, if you were accepted to a school away from home, then plan your move. Get maps of the school. Plan out where good places will be to eat and to relax on and off campus. It can be exciting to think about campus and college life at graduate school, even if, of course, it will be more hard work.
- Contact the graduate school a few weeks before you arrive. If you are in a PhD program, contact your advisor directly. Let the program know your expected date of arrival and your address before you make the move. It is always a good idea to make sure the school has updated records, including where you live, your contact numbers, and other essential information.
- Move a few weeks early if you can to make the transition easier. It can be easier if you have about a week or two to just explore the college campus, hang out, meet people, and get comfortable with your new surroundings. If you can arrange it, getting settled in will be easier with some extra time.

If you did not "get in," then follow the first two tips on this list. Then revisit the senior-year plan in Chapter 5 and in Section III, and revisit the suggestions in Chapter 9 for how to create opportunities if you were rejected from all graduate schools on your first try. Many students are able to adjust and get acceptance letters on their second try. Just enjoy the summer, and be encouraged by knowing that on your second try, you will likely have more experience preparing for and applying to graduate schools than those you are competing against. The opportunities for graduate schools are certainly still within reach.

Above all, embrace change. As stated by Henri Bergson, "To exist is to change, to change is to mature, to mature is to go on creating oneself endlessly." You are changing, you are maturing, and you are creating yourself. "Life is a journey, not a destination," as Ralph Waldo Emerson would say. Therefore, embrace the change in your life, and enjoy the journey as you experience change.

Endeavors in Education and the Path Ahead

"Education is the most powerful weapon which you can use to change the world."

Nelson Mandela

Success is really not something that can be easily measured; it is an outcome that is inherent in the dreams and expectations within our mind. What we imagine in our mind as being successful is our own success—no one else can define success for you, except you. In many ways, success can be thought of as a feeling we express in our emotions. We *feel* a sense of accomplishment; we *feel* a sense of pride, elation, strength, inspiration, joy, and even disbelief. To achieve something that makes us *feel* successful means that we have achieved something that has truly brought us success.

How you *feel* about earning your education tells a lot about whether or not your education has brought you success. Although I certainly encourage you throughout this book to feel accomplishment in your endeavors, this book was not necessarily written to make you successful—the extent to which this journey has made you *feel* successful is up to you. Instead, this book has been written under the assumption that an "education is the most powerful weapon which you can use to change the world." No one can know how wealthy you will become or the fame you will find. What I do know is that an education has inherent value. An education facilitates the development and growth of your mind. To develop your mind through education is to literally change the world within you and how you perceive the world around you. To become educated, then, is to become extraordinary.

"Becoming extraordinary" is a mission that is served at the university where I advise and teach. In my efforts, I explain to my students that becoming extraordinary is not about achieving those things you thought possible; becoming extraordinary is about achieving those things you *never* thought possible. If this book can somehow help you to realize the "most powerful weapon which you can use to change the world," then I am humbled and grateful to have shared it with you. My hope is that in reading this book, you will discover your extraordinary journey, and find the greatest of success in your endeavors.

Appendix

Sample Parts of the Graduate School Application

Throughout Section III of this book, you were guided through the graduate school application process. In Chapter 6, you were given detailed examples of how to write a letter of intent, and in Chapter 7, you were shown how to complete your résumé and curriculum vitae (CV). In this brief appendix, I include a full example of each type of document. To give some context to each example, allow me to explain each sample in the appendix. I hope you will find these samples a helpful guide as you work to complete your own letters and other documents in preparation for applying to internships and graduate schools.

Sample Letter of Intent and Curriculum Vitae

The first is a sample letter of intent and CV sent by a student who applied to a PhD program at a major university in the Northeast. The letter is the actual letter of intent he sent to the university. The CV is the actual CV he sent to that same university. Using these application materials, he was accepted to the PhD program at the university, which began in the 2014–2015 academic year. Some information has been removed or replaced in these documents to maintain anonymity.

Sample Résumé

Also included in this appendix is an example of a résumé sent by a student interested in pursing graduate school in industrial/organizational psychology. She applied for a paid internship as a human resources professional at a large hospital in Chicago. The résumé is the actual résumé she sent to the hospital. Using this résumé, she was selected for an interview and was hired for the internship position, which began in the summer of 2012. Some information has again been removed or replaced to maintain anonymity.

SAMPLE LETTER OF INTENT

My name is [student name], and I am a senior Honors Program student majoring in psychology at St. Bonaventure University. I would like to express my interest in pursuing admission into [name of program] at [name of school/university]. As an undergraduate student, I have developed an interest in the psychology of eating behaviors, and I have worked toward gaining the specific experience and education needed to prepare me for graduate school research in this discipline. My educational objectives are threefold: to pursue a graduate education and research in the field of ingestive behaviors, to work toward career opportunities in academic research settings, and to promote this area of research by further training and developing future scientists as an advisor of doctorate-level research. My educational objectives originate from my background and the interests that I had before even entering college. For this reason, I would like to expand on these early experiences before elaborating on my educational objectives.

Even as a young child, education and food were a central part of my life. This was due largely in part to my mother and father coming from two very different backgrounds. My father grew up in a small rural village in Jordan and was the first in his family to earn a college degree, while my mother comes from a highly educated Canadian American family. Despite their diverse backgrounds, they have many commonalities, one of which is that they both are now tenured faculty members at [name of university]. As a youth, I spent a lot of time on college campuses, leading me to a great deal of exposure to the daily routines and life of a faculty member on campus—in an administrative setting, and in more of a research/academic setting. Hence, I found an interest and passion to work in an academic setting early on, and have continued to pursue such opportunities in college.

My early family experiences also contributed to my continued interest in the psychology of eating behavior. Both of my parents shared a common interest in the promotion of health and healthy eating, and both experienced the health detriments of poor eating habits. As a faculty member in the field of nursing, my father saw the detrimental effects of poor eating habits in medical settings, while my mother experienced this firsthand in her immediate family, which has a history of obesity, diabetes, and cardiac disease. From a very young age, my parents encouraged me to pursue an education and to have a desire for knowledge. Just as passionately, they encouraged me to make healthy eating choices and to understand how my eating can affect my health. In many ways, I believe this sustained emphasis on healthy living contributed to my passion for and pursuit of athletics, which ultimately led to my serving as a scholarship student-athlete in NCAA Division IA college soccer, for which I was a three-year player and am now a student assistant coach. Also, this blend of emphasis on education and healthy eating naturally brought me to pursue educational objectives in the psychology of eating behaviors when I entered college.

I was admitted to college as a BS-DPT Accelerated Dual Admission Program student, with a major in biology, but quickly shifted my interests to food and appetite upon taking courses in psychology, instructed by a professor in the department whose research focus was on these topics. My passion for research quickly arose from my interest and success in the one-year sequence statistics and research methods course offered to majors in the psychology department. I earned an A in both semesters of the course, which is taught by [name of professor], a professor who is also the author of the textbooks and study guides for both courses in the one-year sequence: *Statistics for the Behavioral Sciences* and *Research Methods for the Behavioral Sciences*. My success in that class led to my being selected to hold the position of teaching assistant (TA) for the course in my junior year. Due to the positive response that I garnered as TA, I was invited to serve as Supplemental Instruction (SI) leader, a position that I currently hold. As an SI leader for the course, I work closely with [name of professor] to develop, review, and teach lessons for students each week in order to help students achieve success in the class. My enjoyment and effectiveness at this work has further encouraged me to pursue a career that will allow me the opportunity to teach.

Fortunately enough, my professor for statistics and research methods also happened to be the lead researcher for a laboratory on campus that studies the psychology of eating. Specifically, he studies how to enhance liking for healthier foods, how to promote healthier food choices, and factors that can influence food intake. Upon completing his course in statistics and research methods, I applied for and was selected to be a research assistant in his research labs on the psychology of eating. Through my work under his advisement, I have gained expertise in this area of research and have found a passion to specifically pursue graduate work in the field of ingestive behaviors. I also pursued additional research experience in personality and social-sports psychology labs, both of which allowed me to further pursue my interest in promotion of health—although the most impactful work has been my work in the psychology of eating labs, in which I have now worked for over a year and a half. My continued interest and participation in research led to the psychology department awarding me the *Psych Scholar* scholarship, which I have received since my junior year.

As an Honors student, I have enjoyed working at a rigorous academic level. As part of this program, I am required to take Honors-level courses and to complete a yearlong senior Honors research project. My experience in the psychology of eating labs led me to pursue this line of research for my one-year senior Honors thesis. In my research project, I examined the effects of altering proximity of high- and low-energy-density foods, in a competitive food environment, on intake. In my role, I contributed to developing the hypothesis tested, the research design, obtaining IRB approval, running all participants, collecting and analyzing all data, and writing the manuscript, now submitted to the peer-reviewed journal *Appetite*. This project will be presented at a conference at a University of Pittsburgh campus later this year and will be submitted for presentation at the 2014 annual Society for the Study of Ingestive Behavior (SSIB) conference in Seattle, Washington, in addition to being presented to the St. Bonaventure University faculty for a defense of my senior Honors thesis in the spring of 2014.

To expand my research experience, I sought out opportunities to work under the direction of a leading researcher in the related field of ingestive behaviors. Through my meetings with [name of professor], it quickly became apparent that my research interests matched most closely with those of Dr. [name of researcher] at [name of university]. For this reason, I sent a request to work in her labs as a research assistant over the summer. To my excitement, she accepted my request, and it turned out to be one of the most important experiences in shaping my goals for the future. In working under the advisement of Dr. [name of researcher], I became more aware of many exciting opportunities in the field of nutritional sciences and, specifically, ingestive behaviors. Through her mentorship, I knew that [name of university] was my best option for pursuing graduate study in the nutritional sciences. As a research assistant in her labs, I was exposed to a new research environment—one that was on a much larger scale than my previous experience in terms of the number of projects being run, the number of students and research collaborators involved, and the size and quality of the facilities. I had the opportunity to take part in three different projects that are currently in progress. For these studies, some of my work included preparing meals in the Henderson kitchen for the subjects, organizing blood work in the Noll lab, and performing basic data collection and entry. Most impactful on me was my being allowed to participate in the research meetings held

(Continued)

(Continued)

by Dr. [name of researcher]. In these, I was exposed to many research factors that I had not previously experienced, such as grant writing, clinical trials, and graduate student research meetings. My experiences have only increased my excitement for conducting research and engaging with researchers in a collaborative and academic setting.

As a senior, I can now reflect on the experiences described in this letter as leading me to my three main educational objectives. My first educational objective is to pursue a graduate education and research in the field of food behavior. From childhood to college, my experiences have led me to be more confident than ever that my interests fit most closely with those of Dr. [name of researcher], a leading researcher in the field whose mentorship and advisement would be instrumental in my development as a researcher in the nutritional sciences. My second and third objectives are to pursue career opportunities in academic research settings, and to promote this area of research by training and developing future scientists as an advisor of doctorate-level research. Both of these aims originate from my experiences as a child in academic settings with my parents, and have been strengthened by my experiences in the classroom and in research laboratories at two universities. The mentorship I have received has strongly impacted my career pursuits. I hope to share the same level of mentorship, and the best place to achieve this is in a university or academic research setting.

I am certain of my career aspiration to become a researcher in the nutritional sciences, and that I am committed to learning and engaging in the academic and research interests demonstrated by your faculty. Thank you kindly for your time and consideration of my application for admission to [name of program] at [name of school/university].

SAMPLE CURRICULUM VITAE

[Name]

[Address]

[Contact Information]

Education

Bachelor of Arts, With Honors, Psychology   Conferral Date: May 2014

St. Bonaventure University, St. Bonaventure, New York

- Emphasis: Behavioral Health, Food Psychology
- Overall Grade Point Average: 3.86
- Major Grade Point Average: 4.00
- Honors Thesis: "Proximity of Foods in a Competitive Food Environment Influences Consumption of a Low-Calorie and a High-Calorie Food"

Research Experience

Independent Study in Behavioral Health   Fall 2012–Present

Advisor: [Name], PhD

- Designed and conducted an experiment that manipulated the proximity of foods in a competitive, kitchenscape environment and determined what effect that variation had on consumption; conducted study procedures, gathered data, contributed in writing manuscript.

Psychology Scholar Research in Behavioral and Personality Psychology   Spring 2013–Present

Advisor: [Name], PhD

- Helped to design and conduct a study examining the relationship between personality traits, major, level of academic entitlement, attribution style, and course/professor selection in college students.

Behavior and Personality Lab   Fall 2012

Advisor: [Name], PhD

- Designed and conducted a study that examined the relationship between personality factors and intelligence; developed hypothesis, created design, ran participants, collected and entered data, analyzed statistics, and wrote a poster and manuscript for the study.

Independent Study in Sports Psychology   Spring 2013

Advisor: [Name], PhD

- Took part in conducting an experiment that investigated the effects of visual primers on gym goers' selection of workout equipment; collected data, helped with design of follow-up study.

(Continued)

(Continued)

Peer-Reviewed Publications

1. [Author Names.] (submitted). Proximity of foods in a competitive food environment influences consumption of a low-calorie and a high-calorie food. *Appetite*.

Presentations (Regional Conference)

1. [Author Names.] (2013). *Proximity of foods in a competitive food environment influences consumption of a low-calorie and a high-calorie food.* To be presented at Penn-York Undergraduate Research Association annual conference, University of Pittsburgh at Bradford, Bradford, PA, November 9.

Presentations (National Conferences)

1. [Author Names.] (2014). *Proximity of foods in a competitive food environment influences consumption of a low-calorie and a high-calorie food.* To be submitted for presentation at the Society for the Study of Ingestive Behavior annual meeting, Seattle, WA, July 29–August 2.

   - This poster will also be submitted for presentation at the American Psychological Association annual conference, Washington, DC, August 7–10, 2014.

Teaching Experience

TA for Psychological Research: Statistics and Methods II   Spring 2013
Faculty Advisor: [Name], PhD

- Maintained regular office hours.
- Worked with students individually and in small groups to help them with assignments.
- Graded student homework and proctored exams.

Supplemental Instruction (SI) Leader   Fall 2013–Present
Faculty Advisor: [Name], PhD

- Actively attended and participated in all lectures.
- Conducted SI sessions twice a week:
  o Retaught portions of lecture.
  o Designed learning activities for students and helped foster good study habits.
  o Answered questions, reviewed homework and test questions.

Work Experience

Undergraduate Research Assistant   Summer 2013
Henderson Lab for Ingestive Behaviors, Penn State University, University Park, PA

- Measured, prepared, and served food to subjects (as a means of data collection).
- Collected data from participants.
- Organized participant profiles for *LEAPS* trial.
- Collected, centrifuged, and organized blood work for *LEAPS* trial.
- Performed data entry (paper to electronic).
- Shared input on study design and data analysis.

Advising and Orientation Assistant   Summer 2010, 2011

Indiana University of Pennsylvania (IUP), Indiana, PA

- Knew curriculums; evaluated and indicated needed changes in student schedules.
- Organized and updated student orientation folders and student advising folders.
- Greeted and directed incoming students.

Team Coach, IUP Women's Soccer Team Camp   July 2011, 2012

Indiana University of Pennsylvania (IUP), Indiana, PA

- Organized and carried out training sessions for team.
- Managed games and practices.

Honors and Awards

American Psychological Association Student Member, 2013–Present

Psi Chi Inductee, International Honor Society in Psychology, Spring 2012

Presidential Scholar, the most prestigious academic award at St. Bonaventure University [Monetary Value], 2010–2014

Phi Eta Sigma Honor Society Inductee, Spring 2011

Psychology Department Scholarship and Mentorship (Psych Scholar) Recipient, 2012–Present

Atlantic 10 Commissioner's List Member, Div. I Atlantic 10 Conference Student, for athletes who achieve a 3.5 GPA or higher in a given semester, 2010–Present

St. Bonaventure University Dean's List Member, 3.3 GPA or higher in a semester, 2010–Present

Activities and Service

Psi Chi, 2010–Present

- President, 2013–present: held weekly meetings, created agenda, organized events and fund-raisers, took part in community service activities, managed budget and website.
- Member, 2011–2012: participated in meetings, community service, volunteer work, and events.

Model UN Conference, March 25, 2013

- Co-chair for the International Atomic Energy Agency: oversaw debates, ensured delegate decorum and debate protocols were followed, enforced rules of conduct.

Volunteer Coach for Southern Tier Youth Soccer Teams, 2012–Present

March of Dimes, St. Bonaventure University/Allegany/Olean, 2012

Intercollegiate Athletics

Men's (Division I) Soccer, St. Bonaventure University, 2010–Present

- Player, 2010–2012
- Student Assistant Coach, 2013–2014

(Continued)

(Continued)

Skills and Training

Technical Proficiency, Microsoft Word, Microsoft PowerPoint, Microsoft Excel, IBM SPSS-X, Mac, Windows

NIH Certification, St. Bonaventure University, Fall 2010

Child Abuse Training Certification, Penn State University, Summer 2013

Human Participant Research (IRB) Training, 4.0 hours, Penn State University, Summer 2013

Relevant Coursework (listed in order of perceived relevance)

PHED 309—Nutrition (3 cr.), St. Bonaventure University, Fall 2013 (in progress)

CHEM 101/102—General Chemistry I & II (3 cr. each), St. Bonaventure University, Fall 2010/Spring 2011

CHEML 101/102—General Chemistry I & II Lab (1 cr. each), St. Bonaventure University, Fall 2010/Spring 2011

BIO 211/2510—Anatomy and Physiology I (3 cr.), JCC (joint agreement with SBU), Spring 2014 (registered)

PSYC 330—Health Psychology (3 cr.), St. Bonaventure University, Fall 2013 (in progress)

BIO 105/106—Biological Sciences I & II (4 cr. each + lab), St. Bonaventure University, Fall 2010/Spring 2011

PSYC 359—Sensation & Perception (4 cr. + lab), Indiana University of Pennsylvania, Summer 2012

Sample Résumé

[NAME OF STUDENT]

[Street Address, City, State, Zip Code]

[Phone, Fax, E-mail]

OBJECTIVE:

To obtain an internship at a regional hospital that utilizes and expands my skills in human resource practices.

SUMMARY OF QUALIFICATIONS:

♦ Strong work ethic ♦ Applied experience in recruitment efforts, staffing, interviewing, and diversity practices ♦ Recipient of multiple academic scholarships and awards ♦ Excellent interpersonal skills ♦ High motivation for professional development ♦ Proficient in PC and Mac, Microsoft Office programs, and social media ♦ Proficient in IBM SPSS statistical software

EDUCATION:

Bachelor of Arts, Psychology   May 2012

St. Bonaventure University, St. Bonaventure, New York

Overall GPA: 3.8/4.0

Honors: Psychology Scholarship Recipient, Merit Award
Recipient, Dean's List

RELEVANT EMPLOYMENT:

Coordinator, Freshman Orientation Program

St. Bonaventure University   8/2009–8/2011

- Interviewed and hired a team of 12 diverse individuals to work as orientation leaders.
- Helped to develop and implement a training program for employees.
- Facilitated the development of a cohesively functioning team; coordinated meetings and training workshops; helped with performance appraisal and the rehiring processes.

Supplemental Instruction Leader, Behavioral Statistics

St. Bonaventure University   8/2011–5/2012

- Led instruction of statistical methods for students in an introductory statistics course aimed at applying statistics to make decisions in behavioral and applied settings.

ACTIVITES AND SERVICE:

♦ **Psi Chi Honors,** *member*, 2010–present ♦ **Peer Coach,** *Volunteer*, 2010–2012 ♦ **Vice President,** *St. Bonaventure A Capella Group*, 2009–2012 ♦ **Club Field Hockey,** *team member*, 2008–2012 ♦ **Paid Tutor,** *Spanish and statistics courses*, 2010–2012 ♦ **Published Author,** *named second author on a scientific peer-reviewed paper and conference presentation*, 2011–2012

References

Adams, D. (2002). *The salmon of doubt*. New York, NY: Pocket Books.

American Psychological Association. (2013a). *The don'ts of grad school applications*. Retrieved from http://www.apa.org/gradpsych/2006/01/applicati.aspx

American Psychological Association. (2013b). *Psychology clubs*. Retrieved from http://www .apa.org/education/k12/psych-club.aspx

American Psychological Association. (2013c). *Undergraduate research opportunities & internships*. Retrieved from http://www.apa.org/education/undergrad/research-opps .aspx

Baum, S., Ma, J., & Payea, K. (2013). *Education pays 2013: The benefits of higher education for individuals and society* (pp. 1–48). New York, NY: College Board, Trends in Higher Education Series.

Beeny, E. (2010). *Snowing fireflies*. Rocklin, CA: Folded Word.

Brainy Quote. (2013). *Famous quotes*. Retrieved from http://www.brainyquote.com

Burleson Consulting. (2012). *Increased earning income from bachelors, masters, and doctoral (PhD) degrees*. Retrieved from http://www.dba-oracle.com/t_increased_earnings_ income_bachelors_masters_doctorate.htm

Career Development Center. (2011). *Presenting yourself professionally* (pp. 1–4). Binghamton, NY: Binghamton University.

Council on Undergraduate Research. (2013). *Fact sheet*. Retrieved from http://www.cur.org/ about_cur/fact_sheet/

Covey, S. R. (2004). *The 7 habits of highly effective people: Powerful lessons in personal change*. New York, NY: Simon & Schuster.

Fisher, R., & Ury, W. L. (1981). *Getting to YES: Negotiating agreement without giving in*. London, England: Penguin Group.

Francis Bacon's essays. (n.d.). Retrieved from http://www.westegg.com/bacon/index.essays .html

Goodreads. (2013). *Popular quotes*. Retrieved from http://www.goodreads.com/quotes/

Institute for Learning Styles Research. (2013). *Overview of the seven perceptual learning styles*. Retrieved from http://www.learningstyles.org/styles/index.html

International Monetary Fund. (2013). *Data and statistics*. Retrieved from http://www.imf .org/external/data.htm

Julian, T. (2012). Work-life earnings by field of degree and occupation for people with a bachelor's degree: 2011. *American Community Survey*, pp. 1–4.

Leadbeater, C. (2008). *We-think: Mass innovation, not mass production*. London, England: Profile Books.

Lokos, A. (2012). *Patience: The art of peacefully living*. New York, NY: Penguin Group.

Maraboli, S. (2009). *Life, the truth, and being free*. New York, NY: A Better Today Publishing.

Moskowitz, H. (2011). *Invincible summer*. New York, NY: Simon Pulse.

National Center for Education Statistics. (2013). *Fast facts*. Retrieved from http://nces.ed .gov/fastfacts/display.asp?id=76

National Institutes of Health. (2013). *Grants & funding*. Retrieved from http://grants.nih .gov/grants/oer.htm

National Science Foundation. (2013a). *About awards*. Retrieved from http://www.nsf.gov/ awards/about.jsp

National Science Foundation. (2013b). *Find funding*. Retrieved from http://www.nsf.gov/ funding/

OnMoneyMaking. (2008). *Millionaire principles—True or false?* Retrieved from http://www .onmoneymaking.com/347.html

Privitera, G. J. (2013). *Incorporating technology and practice to facilitate classroom instruction, support student learning, and prepare students for careers*. Oral presentation given at the faculty development workshop at ITT Technical Institute, Mount Prospect, IL, May.

Privitera, G. J. (2012a). *Preparing students to be lab ready*. Oral presentation given at the annual meeting for the Northeastern Conference for Teachers of Psychology (NECTOP), Worcester, MA, October.

Privitera, G. J. (2012b). *Preparing students to use statistics in behavioral research by combining technology with interpretation*. Oral presentation given at the annual meeting for the National Institute on the Teaching of Psychology (NITOP), St. Pete Beach, FL, January.

Psychology Major. (2011). *Acceptance rates for graduate school*. Retrieved from http:// psychologymajor.org/grad-school/acceptance-rates-for-graduate-school/

Ryan, C. (2012). Field of degree and earnings by selected employment characteristics: 2011. *American Community Survey Briefs*, pp. 1–6.

Skinner, B. F. (1964). *New Scientist*, May 21.

Stanley, T. J., & Danko, W. D. (1998). *The millionaire next door*. New York, NY: Simon & Schuster.

U.S. Census Bureau. (2012). *Current Population Survey data on educational attainment*. Retrieved from http://www.census.gov/hhes/socdemo/education/data/cps/

Wicker, J. (1946). *Into tomorrow*. New York, NY: Broadman Press.

Index

⬤SAGE research**methods**

The essential online tool for researchers from the world's leading methods publisher

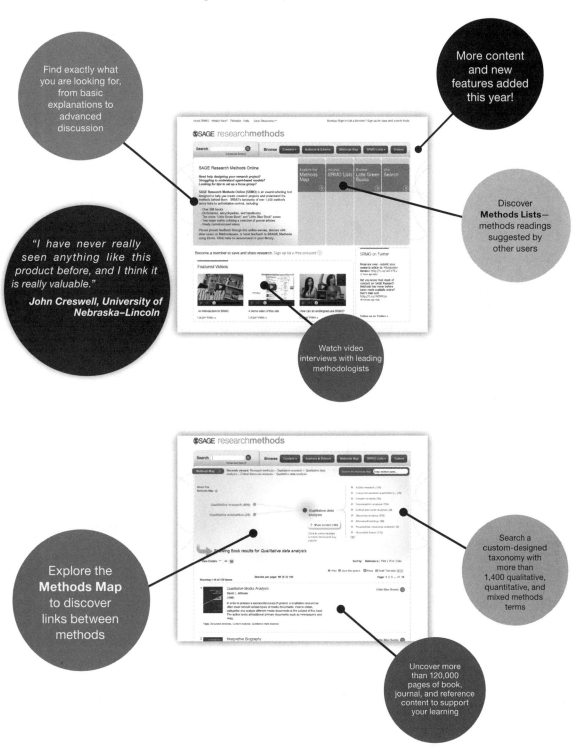

Find exactly what you are looking for, from basic explanations to advanced discussion

More content and new features added this year!

"I have never really seen anything like this product before, and I think it is really valuable."
John Creswell, University of Nebraska–Lincoln

Discover **Methods Lists**— methods readings suggested by other users

Watch video interviews with leading methodologists

Explore the **Methods Map** to discover links between methods

Search a custom-designed taxonomy with more than 1,400 qualitative, quantitative, and mixed methods terms

Uncover more than 120,000 pages of book, journal, and reference content to support your learning

Find out more at
www.sageresearchmethods.com